# *The* COLORS OF MY SUNSET

BY

JOSHUA HODGE

# The
# COLORS OF MY
# SUNSET

*My adventures and reflections in the National Parks and beautiful wild*

BY  JOSHUA HODGE

# Contents

Afterword

"Field and forest, vale and mountain,"

Flow'ry meadow, flashing sea,

Singing bird and flowing fountain

Call us to rejoice in Thee."

# INTRODUCTION

*There is no way I'm writing this book,* I told myself. *It's too personal with parts just unpleasant. It's the end of telling my adventures in the National Parks and beautiful wild,* I decided. It's curious how with time things change and how we gain new perspective, for you are holding that very book I was never going to write.

If you have read one of my books before, you probably have some expectations, and I believe those expectations will be met. If you are new here, welcome. With you as the reader and I as the writer, we will be going on an adventure together! This time the adventure starts with the scorching Mojave Desert, from remote sand dunes and places of great solitude, with the brutal beating sun and scurrying lizards. It will take us to lofty snow laden peaks of Glacier National Park in the company of mountain goats and grizzly bears. During the in-between, we will venture through the mystical Redwood Forest among banana slugs, surrounded by ferns, and we will feel diminished in size by these giants of nature. Then we will eventually find ourselves on the misty cold grey sand beaches of the Olympic peninsula. Among these marvels, we will see many other things.

Even if you may be used to my tales of adventure and reflection, what you might not expect to read are moments of my own shortcomings, my own frustrations, and a very personal look at my own grappling with reemerging physical illness. *I could just leave those parts out,* I thought. Later I responded to myself, *absolutely not!*

When I first began to take my writing seriously as a teenager, I was into writing many fictional plots and had created many characters. Then, with time, I realized my own true-life experiences could oftentimes be even more interesting than what I could make up. I began telling my own stories, and in doing so, I became the main character. We know, when it comes to the main character, everyone roots for that character to also be the hero. We paint our main characters in glorious light. I came to realize that, although I may be the main character of this book, I am not the hero. There is someone far greater at work here.

I also came to terms that we can learn from each other's mistakes and each other's experiences, and who I am in one season of life can be very much different than who I am in another, as I continue to grow and develop as a character. I also came to realize that, as much as I'm inclined to say this is my story, it's really not all mine. It's a part of something much greater.

Therefore, in traditional fashion, I hold nothing back, for it's really not up to me to decide what to share and what not to share. It's all a part of the story. So all I do, and all I think, is right here uninhibited and surrendered before you. I also must do this to keep loyal to my readers and true to my character. So, come along, travel beside me great distances. Hike with me on the trails. Explore with me dark caves. Jump with me into Crater Lake. I think you've already decided you are along for the journey.

First, I think it's fitting you know a little bit more about this so-called "main character." Maybe you know me personally, but perhaps I am a stranger. Where to begin? Well, this is my third installment in my series of books of my adventures in the National Parks. I have a rather informal lofty goal to visit every U.S. National Park and write about all the experiences in a series of books. In this book I'm twenty-eight, and don't have much holding me down except my teaching job during the school year, but in the summer I am as free as a bird and truly take advantage of that. This book is the tale of one big summer adventure all over the American West but most prominently the Pacific Northwest in the summer of 2018. I relied on journal entries, photos, itineraries, and maps to aid my memory in piecing everything together as I reflected back upon it.

My love for writing began when I was very young, and the skill was very much fostered by my mother as I was homeschooled. There has elapsed quite a bit of time between writing *Canyonlands: My adventures in the National Parks and the beautiful wild; Still, Calm, and Quiet: More adventures in the National Parks and beautiful wild;* and this book. This has been because, in the meantime, I was afforded some valuable and unique opportunities as a writer that took up a great deal of my creative time. My passion for studying Theodore Roosevelt led me to publishing several books with him as the topic. These involved a great deal of research. In return, this led me to becoming the latest coordinator of the annual *Gathering of Teddy Roosevelts: Badlands Chautauqua* just outside Theodore Roosevelt National Park. Also, another unique writing endeavor was becoming a "Dollywood Insider," writing behind the scenes content and insider tips on the official blog for Dolly Parton's theme park in East Tennessee. I am so thankful for both of these avenues for my writing, and these are experiences I truly cherish. They did, however, put my telling of my adventures in the National Parks on the backburner temporarily. I suppose I also had to come to terms with my story. I had a lot to process, and I had to arrive at the point where I decided I needed to share this. Here I am.

Though I can write about Theodore Roosevelt and Dollywood Theme Park, and delightfully so, I am most passionate about sharing my own stories of my adventures in nature. So in writing this book, I feel as a writer, I am coming back home, after having been gone a long while on some grand excursion. I have come back more passionate, thoughtful, and perhaps at times more fiery, than I ever was before. I am now very excited and filled with enthusiasm to share with you this great summer's adventure.

Thinking about this further and deeper, I suppose I also am more inclined to write about my adventures in nature because it is in the real natural world I find the most meaning. I truly believe God has left messages all over in His creation to point us back to Him. Every sight of beauty, and every oddity and marvel of nature, has a message— a truth to impart. If we silence ourselves and listen, we find these. *Beauty is never wasted.* That is a statement I am often speaking to myself. When I am faced with something astoundingly beautiful and out of the ordinary, my reaction has come to question it: *What does it mean?* Beauty is often mistaken for just a spectacle, but it also always has a message. I have been so blessed to find many of these messages in nature. They speak to my soul and help me through hard times. My deepest hope is that through my writing, and bringing you along on this adventure, I can help open your eyes to see these messages and see that there is more than just a spectacle and more than just an experience to be had. There is a message to be heard and a Creator to know.

So, onward! Let's go! There's much to see, much to hear, much to learn! As for your main character, you'll get to know me better with time.

# ALL MY FRIENDS

I had this dream in which I was at a summer camp. I found myself in my assigned cabin full of bunks. I never went to summer camp as a child, so this was something new. I got out of my bunk bed and looked in a mirror. I was definitely myself. That's good, but I looked different, younger. I had been gifted back some years in life.

I left the cabin and went to the dining hall. Somehow I knew everyone would be here. It was time for dinner. I walked over the well-worn path between the various cabins and buildings in the wooded camp. When I arrived at the dining hall, I found it to be very much like a school cafeteria, except of a more rustic nature, in tune with its natural surroundings. As I scanned the hall, considering which table I might sit down at, I noticed something strikingly surreal and exciting. The characters from my first novel and series of short stories were there: Dan, Linzy, and Sarah!

At this point I realized I was in a dream, and thus I was excited I would get to personally meet the characters I had invented, materialized in this dream. They came over to me with looks of accusation and immediately they made their concerns known.

Linzy, the red headed, usually bubbly, outspoken teenager, pointed her finger at me, "Why didn't you finish our story?" Her friends spilled out similar concerns. I knew what she was referring to. My first novel, *Wild Christmas,* ends rather suddenly. Some readers have said that the book should have had a more well-rounded conclusion. The trio of high school friends were in the midst of assisting Santa in completing his Christmas Eve present run, but the reader is never brought to see the completion of that.

I did not know how to respond to Linzy's concern. It is true I wrote her story, and it was intentional that I ended the story that way. I had nothing else to say in the matter. I had entertained a sequel for a while but never pursued it in writing.

As I looked away from the trio to collect my thoughts, I noticed another familiar character. His name was Mark, a lifeguard from a series of comic strips I wrote and drew when I was much younger. In his story, extraterrestrials invade his beach and throw the touristy beach town into chaos. Mark's lifeguarding duties greatly expand as he has to save the townspeople from not only extreme high tide but the destructive aliens. The problem was I never finished that story. I left the townspeople dangling in chaos and danger and Mark in utter distress. When my eyes made contact with Mark's, I could tell he was upset with me. He came over.

"How could you leave me abandoned with the alien invasion?" he both accused and questioned.

"I don't kn—" Before I could finish my sentence, I was silenced as I was struck with the realization that this dining hall was filled with characters of unfinished stories I had written over many years. They were all here, just as I had described them in writing. I looked out and I knew the backstories of everyone. These were all my friends, but they were all upset with me, coming over with complaints of how I didn't finish their stories.

Most profoundly of all, I noticed one of my most developed and personally explored characters, Dakota, from my novel, *Dakota Broken*. He sat alone at a table. I took my tray of food and sat next to him. His head hung low, his black hair drooping down nearly covering his eyes. With no introduction or acknowledgement, he simply asked, "What happened?" In the novel, Dakota was taken away from his abusive parents and was about to be adopted by a new family, but the novel doesn't take us to meet the new family. "I was ripped from my parents and was going to be adopted? What are they like? Do I ever get to meet them? Will I ever overcome my insecurities?"

I was left speechless. Then characters from all over the cafeteria began to crowd around me with angry accusations. I've left many a story unfinished and others have conclusions that may not answer all the questions the reader has. I've wanted the reader to speculate and think, and so I have just said, "like in life, we never have all the answers."

This definitely did not sit well with all my characters crowding around me. I couldn't distinguish one accusation from another. Too much was coming at me, blending into chaos.

Over the commotion I defended myself, "Listen, I don't write your stories anymore. You live your own lives."

"But you're the author!" One voice broke out above the others.

And I awoke.

*What a peculiar dream,* I thought. *It must mean something.* I sat with this dream for a while, and as I was driving through the desert on my way to Mojave National Preserve, I thought deeply about it. The words, "But you're the author," really stuck out to me. Here lies the deepest meaning. Before we unpack that statement, let's peer into some fundamental beliefs I have about life.

I believe we are gifted life by God. Life is not a happenstance nor an independent state. Life is dependent on God. He is the creator and giver of it. A component of life is free will, which is also a gift from God. This is the ability to make our own choices and not be controlled. Thus, as humans, we make good and bad decisions. The ability to make choices, to have freewill, is in essence to have the pen in hand to author the story of your own life. You can write for yourself misery by poor choices. You can write for yourself a tale of adventure through travel. You can pursue romance or enterprise, family, or solitude. Modern philosophy teaches that society is the author of your life; that society holds the pen and determines the projection of your life; that as an individual you have no choice but to be the outcome of societal factors. To think otherwise is to be the spoiled product of privilege. Society sure has influence, but society is not the author. YOU are the author! You have been given life and handed a pen by the almighty God. You are writing YOUR story.

Christians, and people of faith, strive to have God guide that pen, just as a young child learning to write, we desire God to help move the pen and show us the way. Thus God intervenes and guides our pen, becoming a coauthor and authority in our lives. As humans, we are made in the image of God, and a part of that image is having that ability to be able to have influence and write into the stories of others as well. Life is a book, or story being written, and we intentionally or not write in the stories of everyone we come in contact with. Think about it. When you compliment or insult someone, you are grabbing the pen and writing or scribbling into the story of another. Your words have an impact on the lives of others. When you are generous with your resources, time, and wisdom, you are writing influence upon the life of another. When you teach people, hurt people, fight people, love people, care for people, you are writing into the story of another person. You are a coauthor of many stories.

So when the characters in my dream cried out, "But you are the author," what a challenging reminder that was. You hold a pen, and you can open the book of another at any time and write into his or her story. What will that look like? Will you write in encouragement, experience, wisdom, love?

Reflect upon your life. If you are a parent, think about the influence you have had on writing the life story of your children's lives. If you are a teacher, in its many forms, your influence is so broad and expansive. If you have been a good friend, a loyal companion, a good listener, an encourager, you may never know until eternity the extent to which you have helped author the stories of others. On the contrary, have you been a complainer? Selfish? One who seeks power, or a seeker of revenge? Have you stepped on, trampled on, the lives of others in authoring your own story? Have you intentionally scribbled into the story of another, creating the ugliest of pages in his or her life?

This is quite challenging, and although as beneficial as it may be to look backward and reflect, think about each day as it comes. You begin each day with a pen in hand. There are books all around you. You have been given the power to write into their lives.

One day when I was out jogging, thinking about such matters, Dolly Parton's song, *Dear God,* came to mind. I had been listening to it in the car. Crying out to God, she sings, "The freewill you have given we have made a mockery of." That really stuck with me. I was thinking of all the selfish and immoral choices made with our freewill, and I was thinking about how freewill is not simply gifted out of love, but it has been gifted out of love with purpose, which is the part often overlooked. We are not to simply be thankful for our freewill, but we are to use it, as well, for intended purposes: to live a life pleasing to God by serving others and writing into their lives goodness, hope, and love.

At this point you may be wondering, *What has happened? Let's talk more about National Parks and the great outdoors. Why has Joshua become so preachy?* Maybe before I cared too much about what others thought of my writing. I wanted it to appeal to a broad audience. I have always been very introspective in my writing, relating matters to faith, but this time it may seem just a little bit more in your face. I don't apologize. There are things we need to talk about.

I have debated and struggled over sharing this adventure, not over matters of faith and inspiration, but in another regard. This adventure, which I am just beginning to share, very much involves other people and not just the introspection which is mine. There are some moments here when I could have authored good things into others' lives, but rather I surrendered those opportunities to neglect. I have thought, *Do I only want to share those good moments of inspiration and leave out that which bears shame? Do I do so out of courtesy to others?* I've concluded, no. Nothing grows without rain, healing does not come without pain, and learning does not come without failure. So, in my typical fashion, I lay it all out before you, so that you can learn from my life that's lived. It is intentional that I follow the noun "life" with the past participle "lived," for a life that's not lived does not have hardship. To truly live your life, you must face the hardships and let the hardships produce beauty.

I know that when my life is said and done, and my own sun sets, I don't want my sunset to be dull and boring, or covered up by the clouds. A life that's lived is the one that also produces color. I want what I've stood for, what I've accomplished, what I've lived, to be bright and vibrant – an orange on fire, a luminous pink, a deep reflective blue. May these be the Colors of My Sunset and may they touch upon the lives of others.

# The Booming Sands of the Mojave

With each elongated step of sliding down the enormous sand dune, a reverberating booming sound escaped the sands from beneath me. This was remarkable! I had never experienced such a phenomenon before. I felt as though I was the one instigating such a feat, thus giving me feelings of a supernatural essence.

I was at Mojave National Preserve in Southern California. This preserve was the first noted point of interest on my fourth great National Park adventure. The park features the largest Joshua tree forest in the world, canyons, mesas, volcanoes, abandoned homesteads, military outposts, and "singing sand dunes." During the entirety of my visit to the Kelso Dunes section of the park, I was the only one there. It was early morning, and the desert sun was just starting to become quite fiery. I was excited to take on the sand dunes. As I looked out upon them, I determined, then and there, I had to make it to the top of the tallest dune. Learning from my mistakes in the past, and after having burnt my feet at the Great Sand Dunes National Park in Colorado, I made sure my footwear was solid. I filled up a water bottle, threw a Clif Bar in my backpack, lathered up and worked in my sunscreen, and took off running into the dunes.

My fourth great National Park adventure was really starting to take off! I had embarked on such trips the past three summers, in which I'd camp and travel from National Park to National Park for the large majority of my summer break, hiking and exploring the great outdoors. This was my

second day in the Mojave National Preserve but the first
one waking up in it. Already the park had impressed me. My
expectations for it were quite low. I had been to other parks
in the Mojave Desert before, such as Death Valley and Joshua Tree. *How different could this be?* And it was a "preserve".
Such a title to me suggested less opportunity for recreation.
However, I was surprised. This place was, by far, underrated
in the National Park Service and filled with many hidden
gems. I was in the midst of discovering one of said gems at
this moment: the Kelso Dunes. They gave justice to the
term "sand dunes." But perhaps would be more justified by
the term "sand mountains." Enormous mounds of sand
rose above the rest of the desert. On the lower sides of the
dunes, desert grasses poked up sparsely from the wind
combed sand, and Mojave fringe-toed lizards scurried about.
The creatures were quite nervous and incredibly fast.
Stealthily, as if sneaking up upon my prey, I was able to approach one to capture a quite satisfying photograph. I also
had to capture photos of myself in such an area. The shock
value of such a contrasting landscape, from that which I was
accustomed to in Kentucky, was striking to me.

As I looked at that enormous sand dune in the distance, the one I resolved to climb to the top of, doubt began
to creep in. It was hard to gauge exactly how tall the sand
dune was. I wanted to be done in an hour or two, for although as exciting as this was, I also had other places to see
and other things to do. Looking at the dune, I could not determine if this would fit nicely into my plans or would require a full day expedition, and if it was the latter, I was not

prepared and rather ill-equipped, but I was determined to press forward. If it proved too much I could always turn around. Then, not only was I considering the time factor, but I started to wonder if it was physically possible, for the rising of the sand looked quite steep. *Would I be able to pull myself up that?* There was no designated trail. This was a free-for-all, and quite obviously no one had been out here this morning, and perhaps not for a while, for the traces of any footprints in the sand had been well swept away by the wind. The place looked untouched. It was just me and the desert. Graciously enough, this peak in the sand dune expanse, did not present any false summits, however dips and dives in the sandscape did surprise.

I didn't try to dig my feet in the sand, but as I started to ascend the steepest stretch, my feet naturally sunk into the sand and pressed further in when I tried to establish footing to push myself upwards. I paused to look around. The landscape was just so enormous. To my one side was the wall of sand, but out below me to the right, so immensely, sprawled the Mojave Desert. The light-colored sand expanse spilled for just a mile or so into the desert, before the long stretches of valley filled with cactus and shrub took over. The bright morning sun cast shadows, which were not noticeable individually, but collectively, gave a dark brown hue to the landscape. Then as the mountains in the distance bordering the immense valley rose up, the higher they climbed, the bluer the tone they assumed, until at their darkest summits, a crescendo of the breaking sky burst into a glorious white, only to quickly transition to a spotless blue which covered the rest of the desert sky.

I continued on, elated, feeling as though I had really arrived upon adventure's doorstep. Then, I reached the top.

Standing bold and accomplished, I looked over the other side of the dune and saw the same immensity of desert and mountain mimicked. Here at the pointed spine of the sand dune, on the eastern side, the sand was finely combed into delicate ripples by the wind. On the western slope, the sand had been blown into one smooth harmonious sheet of sand. The spine snaked up to a higher pinnacle. I crushed the delicate spine as I trampled my way to this final viewpoint, and there I stood in awe. I could assume a great number of people, especially back East, couldn't even imagine such a robust desert landscape existed in our country. I felt I was in such an exotic place, a place from fiction, as though I was the Prince of Persia.

I sat down, drank some water, ate my Clif Bar, and sucked on a few electrolyte gummies. I reveled in the comforting and consuming sun. I took off my boots and sunk my feet into the soft sand. Here, from this pedestal, I looked down upon the Earth. It was one of those mountain-top experiences which puts life into perspective. The immensity of the view before me, and the diminutive nature of everything from such heights, evoked the feeling: The canvas is much bigger than the small concerns we often get caught up in below.

When I was done taking it all in, I began my descent, and the gravity of the Earth pulled me downward, and thus a single step slid well into the sloping sand before me, carrying me quite a distance. It was nothing more than a controlled falling glide into the sand, but it gave quite the superhuman sensation— a similar sensation one might get while walking upon those automated conveyor-belt walkways at

the airport. One stride takes you much farther than hu-
manly possible alone, as the very ground beneath you
moves in conjunction. Thus I was descending nothing
short of a mountain in mere easily countable strides. The
effort was minimal, so I held my head up and looked out
upon the other more solid mountains parallel and at times
below me. I felt as though I was descending upon the
Earth in majestic style. And to top it all off, the sand beneath me boomed! That's right, the sand beneath me sen-
sationally responded to each of my steps! There's a scientific explanation behind this. It has to do with the warm
layers of sand meeting the cold layers beneath and sound
waves getting trapped within the layers, but to me, I imagined as if it was I causing the sound, or as if the Earth was
shuddering to each of my steps, as if I was Zeus or some
Greek god descending from the sky upon Olympus.

As supernatural musings took hold of my
thoughts, I began to think of Heaven. *How will man interact
with the landscapes there? Will such enormous, satisfying, efficient
strides be more commonplace?* Distance and strenuity have a
hold of man's interaction with wild landscapes, but what if
there they will be more easily traversed and enjoyed?

I had a dream, just months prior, that I was in
Heaven. I recently had read a book by David Murray ti-
tled, "Happy Christian: Ten Ways to Be a Joyful Believer
in a Gloomy World." In it, the author talks about how
work is not a result of sin, but how work, as we know it
on Earth, has been corrupted by sin. The author discusses
how Adam and Eve, before the fall of man, worked in the

Garden, attending to it and naming the animals. They were designed, in part, for work. Eve was even created to help with said work. Thus work existed before sin, and so the author proposes that work will also exist in Heaven— that we will all have our own duties, but it will be joyous and fulfilling. I think this portion of the book was responsible for my dream, for in my dream I was at work in Heaven. I was a harvester, or scavenger, in the forests and jungles of Heaven. We went collecting exotic Heavenly fruits to bring back to the people in the Kingdom. And it was thrilling! Our feet were always bare, but they were never worn nor scratched. We would jump from mountain peak to mountain peak. We'd race through all the undergrowth of the forest, unscathed. We'd fall with the waterfalls in excitement to take us from one place to another. We were a team, such great camaraderie, and we were harmonious with the land. Toil was not there. The land never caused us harm. The way we interacted with it served our purpose. There was no strenuity, danger, or fatigue. Such things were absent. Nature had no temperament. It agreed with us. Maybe we even had authority over it.

It was just a dream, fun to entertain, but at the end of the day, a creation of my imagination. But here on the sand dunes in Mojave National Preserve, I felt a fragment of what I felt in that dream. The desert had no hold on me. I had power over it. It gave a shuttering boom with every step, and I could traverse it with ease. Thus, I became flooded with the thoughts and awe of eternity.

I didn't know it then, but I know it now, eternity

would become a major theme of the summer. I would end up facing questions about life, death, and eternity here after. This would become a heavy but blessed summer. As I descended those sand dunes, along with the weight of gravity came the weightier questions of life: *What is my purpose here in life? How do I relate to others in the time I'm given? Would I leave a legacy when I'm gone? Does that even matter?* As the sand spilled down the dune, so these questions tumbled down upon me. The timing was orchestrated and perfect, although it wouldn't be easy. I had traversed the Canyonlands, learned to be Still, Calm, and Quiet, and now it was time to face the prospect of sunset.

# MONOLITHS AND STARS: WONDER OF THE MOJAVE

I thought I had seen it all, that there was no type of landscape which I had not become accustomed to throughout my travels. It was quite a disheartening feeling to consider, *what could possibly be left?* The good news, though, was I had not been completely spoiled. I was far from it. Only ignorance had pervaded my thoughts, for I stood before something entirely new– a landscape previously uncataloged in my mind– a monolithic wonder in the Mojave National Preserve. The very thought in my mind was, *I couldn't have imagined something like this.*

This moment was near the end of my day. I had started about 295 miles away in Phoenix, Arizona, where the first night of my trip had been spent at the home of my cousin Matthew and his wife Robin. By the time I traveled across the remainder of Arizona and into California to the Mojave National Preserve, it was late evening. My plan had been to visit the Kelso Dunes and hike a short three miles to a mountain peak, but this would have to wait until the following day.

Although sandwiched between interstate 40 and Interstate 15, and a mere sixty miles from Las Vegas, this park has yet preserved its remote feel. When I turned to enter the park, I was greeted with the official National Park Service sign. Visitors had tatted up the corners of the sign with stickers and a few bullet holes punctured the middle, telling me that this area was not as well supervised as some of the other parks. I entered from the south on my way to the Hole-in-the-Wall campground. It was first-come-first-served, and I wasn't concerned about finding a site, for I read that visitation was low in the summer. The Mojave Desert is just not a place most people want to be in the summer, with the sweltering temperatures, but my only concern

was the drive, for a number of roads in the park were marked unpaved, including the one to this campground. Before I hit the dusty sand roads, I was cruising along the pavement among grand stretches of desert. Dry shrubs nearly covered the terrain, and every once in a while a cactus, yucca, or Joshua tree would stick up. Around me I saw crumbly mountains and mesas in the distance. I hadn't expected the expanse of this area to be so enormous.

When I reached the bumpy dirt road, before me crawled an animal I had never seen before. Its fur was dark, and its appearance was prominent. Although not particularly large in the grand scheme of things, it was larger than anything I was expecting to see. I got out my cell phone and texted my friend Zeke, in Kentucky, who would be joining me on the adventure in a few days. "I just saw a wolverine,"

I typed. I was wrong, so embarrassingly wrong. I did not know. Wolverines do not live in the American Southwest. They are mammals of the far North. We can file this next to the instance on my first adventure, when I thought I saw a wolf, but it was really just a coyote. What I had just experienced was my first sighting of a badger. When I neared the campground, I witnessed a pair of black-tailed jack rabbits situated in the middle of the drive, jumping further down the road and then off into the shrubbery as I neared.

Finding a campsite was not hard. I was alone, except for one other occupied site. I quickly pitched my tent at a site far from the others, on the opposite side of the campground. I was distracted at times by a nosy little desert

cottontail I pursued to capture in a photo, who surprisingly let me get closer than I expected. Back to work, I got my tent set up swiftly, as I was planning to get at least one hike in before the day's end. Once I had everything set up, I drove over to the Hole-in-the-Wall Information Center. It was an old Western style wooden ranch building with a wrap-around porch. There was a clear place for a sign to identify the ranch, but it had been removed, and the flag pole out front was also bare— a sure sign that this was definitely off

season. It would have been the perfect time for a tumble-
weed to tumble on by or a vulture to sound off in the distance, for I was very much alone and very much in the desert. I checked around the perimeter of the abandoned visitor center for any maps or trail guides, but nothing. I was on
my own.

However, I did find my trail head next to the visitor
center. I then geared up. First off, I was certain to have water in my CamelBak backpack. I brought a light hoodie, expecting that soon the temperature would drop, and I
brought my headlamp, for I knew sunset was not far off. I
made sure I had my car key securely in my backpack. I was
not going to face the panic of last summer when I locked
my key in the car at Chiricahua. To help avoid repeating that
situation, I bought a short lanyard keychain at a gas station
earlier in the day.

Then, all ready to go, I hit the trail. It began with a
stroll among the shrubbery and quiet meandering around
some teddy bear cholla cacti. Then the path slithered between some boulders, and up to some rocks adorned with
Native American petroglyphs. At this point, the sun was just
resting above the horizon, casting dark long shadows behind
every protrusion in the desert, but laying gold upon anything
its light touched. The path then led around some big rocks
to a picturesque Southwest view. There were two large mesas, one laying in front of the other, and the top of a mountain peeking up behind them. The air was warm and incredibly still. All around me was silence. I climbed up a rock, not
any taller than myself, and stood upon it, gazing out into the

distant stretches of evening desert. I closed my eyes and quietly reveled in the moment, in my being, in the presence of God, in my arrival to a new adventure. I felt as if I had come back to an old friend. The desert, *I know you. We have been separated for a while, by time and space. So much has happened. So much has changed, but yet you are the same, quiet and reserved, a library of adventures past, calling me to be grateful of the years gone by.* The desert knows years gone by. It has been through them. The desert is well weathered by the ages, but yet it's calm and knows its place.

As I pondered the desert, I thought about how, in the desert, you don't have to be up high, or in any particular overlook, to look out among the immensity of the land. In the desert there are no tall trees nor overgrowth hindering your view. Here it's all laid open. One stands above and can see the great immensity of the land. And the desert here, in the Mojave, is not a barren plain. It does have features: mesas, rocks, and distant mountains. The view just stretches on seemingly forever. It derives a similar feeling of a mountain top experience, when your life is sort of put into perspective, as you observe the immensity of that which is around you and are surrendered to a humbling comfort. Your problems seem diminished and are put in their place.

The warmth of the desert also has a comforting feel to me, especially in the evening, when the sun isn't harsh, but a dry warmth still blankets and comforts. If the sun were to set, if I were to be lost for the night, I would be fine. The desert may cool some, but won't freeze. The air is still. Bugs are absent. Any perils of the night are gone. Yes, some may find the desert to be harsh and uninviting during the day, but at night I find it very welcoming and suitable for the lone traveler.

When I jumped down from the rock I was observing from, I turned around to a giant monolith in the desert: a massive rock feature just protruding solo and drastically from the desert floor. The trail wound around into a wide slot canyon that was somewhat narrow but then opened up in the middle of the monolith to a canyon wonder. Here I paused. *Wow, I could have never imagined something like this.* I was taken away by the uniqueness of the scene. This was a new terrain, a new landscape I hadn't experienced before. Here giant groupings of hoodoo-esque spires huddled together, right up against each other. They were together, yet individual, like you could pull or peel them apart. They stood as if flaunting their curvatures. And all of them were missing circular chunks, as if shot by enormous canyons,

mimicking swiss cheese, or as if they had sunken eyes looking out at me. I had never seen any rock formations quite like this. It was unexpected. The desert just outside this canyon was not drastically different from what I'd seen before, but this short walk into the slot canyon displayed a whole hidden world, so unique. It was nearly enclosed too, like its own hidden fortress. I paused and just looked around in amazement. It completely wiped away from me the thought that nothing I could see would be terribly new. This affirmed there was much more to see, and things can, and would, exceed what I could imagine.

This was only the first of two surprises on this short hike. The canyon grew narrower with each step, until there was no canyon left at all, and it seemed I had been walled in, but upon observation I found a passageway of sorts. There were cracks in the jumbles of rock, just enough space to fit a body through, and they were steep, only presenting a passage that went vertical. Affixed to the sides of the rocks were a series of steel rings. This was called the Rings Trail and I had read about it, but seeing it, I was well surprised. The rings portioned looked more challenging and more extensive than what I had imagined. This would be fun. Like a puzzle to solve, I had to figure out where to establish footing on the rock wall, and which rings to grab onto, as to establish a grip conducive to pulling myself upward. The passage grew narrower then curved. I was really immersed in this rock world all around me and the task at hand.

I appreciate a trail that presents a challenge,

unique skill, or problem solving. There is one trail back home in the Big South Fork that requires one to rappel him or herself down a boulder's face. In the Rocky Mountains I've hiked up a waterfall. Even a mere swinging bridge can add some fun and variety. This Rings Trail presented something new, and it was definitely one of a kind.

When I finished making my way through the narrow rock passageways, I found the rock terrain to open up. I found myself not completely out of the canyon, for walls still surrounded me, but I was well above the portion I had just traversed. Now I was at an established viewpoint where I could look back down in the rock world beneath me. Up around me I noticed the curvatures of the rocks. They were not jagged nor harsh points, but rather the rocks seemed to flow and lump, as though melting chocolate. The rocks were plain gray, although lumped into the mix were orange colored rocks as well. If I was handed five stars, I would rate this trail 5 out of 5.

"Unique" is the most justifiable term to use to describe it.

When I made it back to my campsite, a mere maybe quarter mile away, the sun was setting. I was walking around the campground, tracing its perimeters, trying to see if there were any trailheads from the campground. I had the intention of going on a nighttime hike. I would rest in my tent, and, when it got much darker and the stars came out, I would go for a night hike by flashlight.

When I did get to resting in my tent, I was out. I slept long and deeply. At one point I did wake up, as a different aspect of nature was calling. Inside my tent it was very dark, as I reached for the side of the tent to unzip my way out. When I pulled the flap of my tent backward, I unwrapped the most beautiful night sky. Millions of stars decorated a huge desert sky! The Milky Way ran prominently and astonishingly through the middle of the expanse above. I was amazed. This was all visible with simply my glasses on, which don't give me a real clear view. Right here, right now, in the middle of the night, well…after answering nature's call, I put on my contacts so I could really see and take in the beauty above me.

Looking out upon the desert alone is enough to make one feel small and shift one's life into perspective. But take, in addition to the desert, the profundity and awesomeness of the night sky, and then one is really put into place. One of my favorite song writers, Matthew Parker, in his song *Shadowlands,* writes, "The moon and stars are the only light to tell us that we're lost in the endless darkness of night." This moment illustrated it perfectly. Observing the stars in such a glorious display in a remote area, does initially evoke a feeling of lostness. The universe becomes so immense. You seem so small. What you witness is so immense that you feel but nothing, lost in the great immensity of what is. But Matthew Parker, as well as myself, know that we don't remain lost. What's most reassuring and comforting is, amidst feeling lost in the great order of things which exist in the universe, we are found! We have been sought out. We are accounted for by the great Almighty God and Creator of the immensity before us.

It is no wonder early peoples and cultures, whether it be Native Americans or any group of people across the sea on this Earth, spent such a great amount of time pondering the sky and trying to derive meaning from it. It is just so astounding when it is untouched by the light of civilization. It is no wonder early people and societies were so spiritual. I would find it a challenge to the human psyche to observe such wonder and not believe in a spiritual realm or a creator. Can you imagine living out in the desert and this being your view every night, or living out on the Great Plains and this being a constant entertainment for the mind? Think of the men out at sea with nothing but the ocean and these great heavens above them.

Sadly, most of human society has lost reverence for the night sky. If you live in a city, you can't see its wonders at all. It becomes easy to be consumed by you, yourself, and your own immediate surroundings. You fault the opportunity to put yourself into perspective. And you lack the beauty which calls you back to the Creator. Even those who live rurally may miss out on the powerful impact of the full night sky. Instead, people find themselves inside in front of their television sets, seeking entertainment, when really the night sky is the more noble form of entertainment, for it engages not only the senses, but the mind, and the spirit.

But you know people are afraid of the dark. I don't say this because of what we playfully think: of monsters, and bears, and things that go bump in the night. No, people are scared primarily of their own thoughts, the condition of their own souls, and the night sky is a reminder of the greatness and eternity we are all a part of.

Get outside! Don't be scared of the dark. Face your thoughts, face the eternity before you, and find your place in the order of things.

This was night one of my camping road trip. Tomorrow I'd explore more of the Mojave National Preserve and return to my favorite National Park: Death Valley!

# She Tried to Kill Me: Death Valley's Claim on My Life

*Hold on Josh. Hold on. You've got to or you're going to die.* I could feel myself beginning to slip from consciousness. I was in a desert canyon in Death Valley National Park in Southern California. It was 122 degrees outside this summer day, without a single cloud in the sky. The sun beat down harshly. I was out for a hike, not a long one, just a few miles, but I was competing with nature. I thought it wasn't going to be a challenging match, but Death Valley was winning. I began to experience lightheadedness. My hearing began to sound muffled. Then there was the dreaded fading of colors. *Hold on. Don't let yourself go.* If I were to pass out, it would only be a matter of minutes before Death Valley would dry me out and bake me in its inferno. I was hiking uphill, on a jagged triangular rock and badland formations on the Badlands Loops Trail, trying to make it out of the canyon alive. Normally this would be easy, for I'm fit and capable, and this wasn't even very steep, but here in the harshness of the desert, with the oppressive heat, my body was giving up. *Am I dehydrated? Or am I lacking salt? Or is it heat stroke? The body could be overheated, no longer having the ability to cool down to a life sustaining temperature.* Maybe my body just could not keep up with the extreme heat of Death Valley.

My heart began to race rapidly. *Oh no, I know how this goes. Soon it could beat out of control, bringing me to the ground.* I've fainted before, at Big Bend National Park, but luckily I was inside a store around other people. Here I was completely alone, except for with her, Death Valley. We had met before. She caught me in a sand storm a summer before.

There was a little bit of shade just up against the short canyon wall. There were fragments of broken rock down by my feet, which seemed, in my present state, so far away and unreachable, but there was one big enough for me to sit upon. I lowered myself slowly and cautiously. Any

quick movements, any exertion whatsoever, could cause me to black out. I crossed my legs, the most comfortable position to keep myself up from complete collapse. My vision went blurry for a moment, but I still had a grasp on it. I focused on breathing slow, deep breaths.

I had water, but I wasn't sure if that's what I needed. If I was salt deprived, this would worsen my symptoms. However, it could be life-saving as well. I took a sip of my water which had turned hot from the all-consuming heat. I poured the rest on my head. Although hot, it was not as hot as the air around me. It could cool me off just a bit. And if salt was what I needed, there was one thing I could do. Sweat contains salt. I began to lick my arms. It's not that I was particularly sweaty, for one doesn't sweat in Death Valley, as sweat immediately evaporates in the extremely dry climate. But even this being the case, there should still be leftover salt deposits on the skin, I thought.

I had overestimated my strength in the desert. It didn't help that I did this hike shirtless. I like the feeling of the desert sun on my skin, and I thought that in the heat the less clothes the better, but actually if I had worn something to cover my torso it could have provided shade for the body and maybe I wouldn't have overheated as quickly.

I had not yet cried for help. I was only about a mile from Zabriskie Point, a popular lookout point, where people would be present, marveling over nature's artistic display of giant jagged rock formations, but I was so far down in a canyon, with a sea of rock formations before me, that I could not hear any of them, and I don't think they would hear me.

If I were to exert my voice loudly, this might take too much energy and cause me to lose my consciousness. I could not make a phone call. My phone was in the car. I left it there, for there was no service out here anyway. It was just me and her, Death Valley. I've always said she is my favorite park. She is so different and unique from all the others. Her views are so astounding, Her mountains are so tall. Her valley is so wide. She is rich in history of gold, silver, and borax mining. She's the keeper of abandoned mines and ghost towns. She's so strong and so dramatic, and this was one of the many features I liked about her, but she was also ruthless. She lures people in with beauty and mystique, as in the past she tempted with her riches of gold and silver. She's a masterful artist, skillful at manipulation, luring man in to choke and turning him back to the very sand from which he was formed.

She caught me. She had me right where she wanted me. Though a lover turned hostile, I had done her no wrong, but mercilessly she pursued me. I focused on breathing and said a prayer. After a few minutes my heart returned to a normal pace, colors in my vision returned, and my hearing was sharp. I was okay. I had to get up and continue. Time was of the essence. I needed to get back to the car. I stood up slowly, and I walked carefully. A peace had brushed over me, despite concern still guiding me. I was able to be calm yet knowing the urgency. I made progress, slowly, calmly, not letting my heart rate spike.

The trail wound up and down and around wavy rocks and canyon walls until I could see up ahead the sharp

pointed rocks of Zambriski Point. I could see people on the rim taking pictures, and it was a sign of relief. Slowly and methodically, I made it back to the lookout point among the other tourists. They were nonchalantly posing for photos in front of the jagged points spiking up from the canyon. I then was assumed to be another one of them, but no one knew what I had just experienced. I got back to the car and turned the air conditioning on high. I had some hot Gatorade, and dry snacks. They seemed to help. I longed for something cold and refreshing, but nothing here would be cold. It was all hot.

*I'm done with hikes for the day,* I concluded. After resting in my car for a few minutes, I was ready to check out the Furnace Creek Inn, one of the two accommodations in Death Valley National Park. I wasn't going to stay. I just wanted to see it. I had learned about this historic inn from a documentary about National Park lodges. It was built in 1927 by the Pacific Coast Borax Company before the area was declared a National Monument and later a National Park. This inn was once a desert oasis for Hollywood elites, and, to this day, states on its website that it "still pampers every guest." I had to see it for myself.

It's a structure that very much fits in with the landscape. Its foundation and lower level walls are constructed with rocks from the very desert. Its building blocks were formed from the very sand of Death Valley. After I parked my car I walked up the drive. On one side there was a lawn with a tall fountain. Yes, there was a lawn in Death Valley! I could scarcely believe my eyes. On the other side of me was a wall, skillfully crafted out of rocks, and above it was a patio for guests. Up above stood the main level of the establishment. To ascend, there was a rounded tunnel that cut through the rock wall and seemingly went back to a staircase. Lights were affixed in the tunnel. *How unique of an entryway,* I thought. It seemed sort of like I was approaching some passageway in a medieval castle, but as soon as I entered the tunnel, a large aggressive wasp darted towards my face. I abruptly moved my head, evading its assault. It buzzed around me loudly and invasively. I ran back out of the tunnel to the drive. I had thought I was alone, but then I saw a lady walking her way around the front of the inn. I must have looked ridiculous, running away erratically from a wasp. I immediately regained composure, stood upright, and walked moderately. I smiled and nodded my head politely. "Hello," I said, as if nothing unusual had just happened.

I walked around the rock wall to another staircase that led up to the main lobby of the inn. Inside, I was quite impressed. I beheld a beautiful lobby of simple elegance. Intricate tile work spread through the lobby and into the halls. Big rounded windows looked out into palms and the desert mountains in the distance. Oriental rugs sprawled out beneath wingback chairs and floor lamps. I did feel out of place, however, and began to wonder if this was alright, that I, a mere vagabond of the desert, was welcome in such an establishment. If I knew it was so nice, I would have dressed a bit differently from my gym shorts, cut-off, and hiking boots. But I decided to ignore my attire and just walk about the place as if I belonged. No one had to know I was a foolish young man who nearly died in the desert, who really is not sure where he is spending the night, and could no way afford this place. I could pretend and carry myself as if I knew exactly where I was and what I was doing. Some National Park lodges encourage visitors and are quite welcoming. This seemed just a little bit pretentious and more intimate, like a private club. I pretended like I belonged the best I could, given the circumstances. I wanted to appreciate its architecture, elegance, air conditioning….and pool?!

I walked out into the oasis garden behind the inn. I was so completely surprised that such a place existed in Death Valley. Here was a forest of palm trees on a hillside blanketed in green grass. Small winding stone pathways and stairs meandered around it and over a bubbling brook and

rippling pond. Little stone walls held up the hillsides of tasteful landscaping. This place looked so cared for and so astounding to exist in such a barren place as Death Valley. Between the palms, in the distance, I could see the large expanse of the desert and its mountains standing tall. What a contrast! More immediately before me, I was faced with a large natural spring fed swimming pool. Its poolside was encased by beautiful stone architecture with arches resting on cornerstones, and it was all in the shade. After being so exhausted in the desert, and now strolling, still in the op- pressive heat, the thought of being engulfed beneath the water of a swimming pool seemed so perfect and just what I most wanted. I had been successful thus far in pretending as if I belonged at the inn, walking around the lobby and garden oasis. What if I just took it one step further and helped myself to a little swim? I was very close to letting myself walk through the gate and into the pool, but I first noted that it would be quite obvious if anyone was watching, for no one else was at the pool. Then my moral conscience kicked in. This was not for me. It was desirable. It would be so nice, but it was not mine.

Back at my car, I noted cell service here by the inn and sent a text to my mom, telling her about the 122 degree temperature. She responded, "You are not going to camp in that!" She knew that was my plan, and it still was my plan.

I drove thirty minutes to the Stovepipe Wells Village. I remembered the general store from my previous visit. I bought a Death Valley Black Cherry soda in a long-neck glass bottle here, back during my first National Park adventure. Inside I was greeted by a self-serve soda fountain. I got myself the mega jumbo cup, nearly filled it with small nuggets of ice from the dispenser, then poured over it cold refreshing blue Powerade. When I left the store and took the first sip through the straw, it was the most heavenly experience. My body was crying for so badly– the sugar, the sodium, the electrolytes, and most welcome of all, the cold. I couldn't take it in fast enough. I may not have made it into the pool at Furnace Creek, but this ice-filled cup of Powerade drowning me was the most perfect thing at the moment. Death Valley had tried to take me. I survived. I was still weary and war torn but now just powered up. It was going to be a good night.

Next order of business: finding a site and setting up camp. There were a number of first-come-first-serve

campgrounds in Death Valley. In accordance with my itinerary, I was on my way to the Emigrant Campground when
I discovered, along the way, a large sandy lot where others
had parked and pitched tents. It sat a little bit elevated on a
plain that sloped down into the valley. It displayed a beautiful open expansive view. The sun was setting, and I pre-
ferred not to set up camp in the dark. I figured this area
would be fine. There were no numbered sites, no bathroom,
but I could do without. I pitched my tent and then went for
a walk.

I passed by a ranger station, or some park service
building in the middle of the road, that looked closed for
the summer. Just past it I paused. I deviated from the road
and stood up upon a rock, looking out. The sun had set.
The mountains were a rich dark blue, and the sky a vibrant
pink. This beauty was enough to give a shiver with goose
bumps, even in the extreme heat. Out in the valley there
appeared to be a lake, but I knew it was just the giant salt
flats contrasting the surroundings. Everything was so giant,
so huge– the mountains, the expanse of the valley, the salt
flats. Everything seemed to flow smoothly from the Artist's
brush. Even with such an incredibly huge view, the desert
was so still, calm, and quiet. This confirmed all the more
that Death Valley remained my favorite National Park. She
has a unique overwhelming effect on my soul. I love her,
despite the fact she tried to kill me.

With a calmness of the late evening desert sweeping
through my being, I walked slowly back to my tent and relaxed after shedding a few tears in response to such beauty.

This was also my first stop of my very first grand National Park adventure back in 2015. I was coming back to where it all started, my falling in love with the Parks– where excitement and wonder were so fresh and new. The desert reminded me of all I had seen and experienced since, and I felt extremely grateful.

Back at my car, I brushed my teeth and didn't bother changing clothes for the night. It would all be coming off in this heat. I checked the temperature from the car before I locked it up for the night. It displayed an even hundred degrees. I noticed I had cell service and decided to respond to my mom's text over her concern about me camping in the heat. I informed her it was 122 degrees earlier. I followed up: "No worries. It has cooled off…It's only a 100 degrees now."

I crawled into my tent. Death Valley had spared me and now was as beautiful and captivating as ever.

# Meeting Susan: A kindred spirit

*I know this lady,* I said to myself but my mind needed a moment to place her. "Is it you?" I questioned.

"Is it you?" she returned the question with a rather stunned expression.

"Susan?" At this point I knew it was her, and I was utterly surprised. I knew there was purpose in coming here for breakfast after all. Waking up in my tent, I was debating whether to just hit the road or seek breakfast here at Red Meadow, the small village in the Inyo National Forest, adjoining Devil's Postpile National Monument. After much back and forth, I decided to take the short drive from my campground to the Mule House Cafe. Here in the village, I noticed a little general store, cabins, showers, a lot of backpackers from the Pacific Crest Trail, and the Cafe.

I opened the door to the small cabin of a restaurant, and immediately I was greeted with this familiar face, but it was only familiar from the internet. In real life, face-to-face, it was all new. Susan was one of my most devoted social media followers. She, whether she knew it or not, had been a great encouragement to me as a writer.

In the Spring of 2017, I decided to start sharing my adventures in the National Parks and the beautiful wild in a blog online. I took matters quite seriously and strategically at the time. I created blog entries regularly. The earliest of ambitions was to post every day. I shared my writing, not only on my pages, but I joined the largest National Park and hiking fan groups online. I considered these my networks that "aired" my "episodes." My posts would always need to be approved by administrators of the groups, and they always were, up until winter 2020, when the administrator of the largest group of hiking enthusiasts banned me from their group. It had to be something in my writing that the administrator took issue with. In recollections from on the trails, I do veer from the physical to discuss the spiritual. It was also very popular at the time, and remains quite common today, for people of certain ideologies, who assume power, to silence opposing viewpoints and completely reject and attempt to isolate those who differ.

Despite the unfortunate event of being banned from this group, it is here I came in contact with Susan who was a fellow group member. She would always read and comment on things I posted, and not just on the group page, but on the other snippets of thought I shared on my own personal pages. We were very different, yet at the same time so much alike. For starters, I am young enough to be Susan's son. A substantial age gap lies between us. We grew up in different times and different places. She has experienced a lot more out of life than I. Although I had not yet met her until this moment, I had such high esteem for her and there seemed to be a distinct connection between us that would take some time and study to understand fully.

Susan was my waitress in this little Mule House Cafe in the Red Meadow village. We shared our pleasantries and surprise and she led me over to the counter on the far end of the small cafe. The term "far" is gracious for it was quite a little place. There I sat on one of the brown leather backed stools that swiveled, and I rested my elbows up on the shiny faux wooden counter. Before me stood a wood paneled wall with a shelf of cups, a clock, a few framed photographs of mountain vistas, and taxidermied heads of a buck and black bear.

It was such a surprise to meet Susan here for more than one reason. I knew she was living in rural middle Nevada, so I was by no means even considering she would be here in California. Despite that, she had also been on my mind recently, for as I was planning my trip I was thinking that if I ever were to drive across Nevada again, I would want to stop and meet her.

Why did such a gal, whom one would perceive so different than I, command so much thought from me? The simple answer is that it was Susan's authenticity, but let me explain further. We had messaged a bit back and forth and found we shared some great things in common: our faith in God, our belief in the power of prayer, our sense of adventure, and our eye for natural beauty. Radio talk show host and author Dennis Prager on his *Happiness Hour* has talked quite a bit about the value in finding "kindred spirits." He describes them as people that share the same values as you in life. He claims it's kindred spirits that bring mental well-being and contribute greatly to happiness in our lives. I knew, quite early on, that Susan was a kindred spirit of mine. That was a way to describe our connection.

I ordered my breakfast of pancakes, eggs, and sausage, along with a coffee. Every once in a while, as Susan checked up on me, or had a moment, she stopped by the counter to tell me more about herself and feed my inquisitive nature. I thought she was born and raised in Nevada but learned she was originally from North Carolina and had spent most of her life out West in some of the states where only the strong and well-suited survive, such as Alaska and Montana. She worked among hearty, productive, and laborious jobs in mining, lumbering, and construction, even helping with the building of the enormous Libby Dam in Montana. She worked secretarial jobs and drove haul trucks. She worked for the National Forest Service and worked seven years as deputy of a jail. As I learned the whereabouts and general overview of her life, she said something that in the moment both broke and resonated with my heart. On the topic of family, she said, "I got married forever. He just forgot to tell me he didn't."

I could see such strength but also sadness in her eyes. Although I never have been married, what Susan said resonated so deeply with me, in regard to relationships with others, largely in terms of friendship. I, by nature, tend to be a very private and reserved person in public, but when I befriend someone, it's quite a meaningful thing for me. I only let people in my life, into my inner circle, whom I plan to keep forever. My sense of loyalty is strong, and I can be quite particular with whom I invest my own life. Sadly many of those I have considered friends have blown away with the wind. I have been lost, forgotten, or abandoned. It leaves a lasting ache upon my heart, and an ever haunting question of, *Is it a fault within my own character that is the cause of this?*

We would not get deep into conversation, for Susan was working, and this was our first meeting in person. I would go on to meet up with her one summer a few years later in Montana. I was there working at Glacier National Park, and she had moved back to her old stomping grounds of Libby, Montana, so we met up for a meal. In the meantime we had shared more, sending messages back and forth online. She asked for prayer as she struggled with her vision and eye problems. I did the same as I became quite sick with ulcerative colitis. There was a simplicity to Susan's life that seemed refreshing. She faced many hardships, but always found a way through with God's grace. Susan also is quite portable, meaning she moves quite frequently and can make for herself a home and a place to rest her head in whatever situation life throws at her. There is always a way forward in every situation for Susan. I could sense in some regard that Susan was a lover of life but also a loner such as myself. She wrote to me about loneliness, about how both of her parents were deceased, how some of her remaining family had been mistreating her. In all this I believe Susan's independent nature was forged even stronger. I too possessed that independent spirit. I too had learned to get by alone in life. Yes, it can build character, but it's overall not a desired thing. It was simply a card we were both dealt, and we had both learned to adapt to it.

C.S. Lewis in his book, *The Four Loves,* writes "Friendship arises out of mere companionship where two or more of the companions discover that they have in common some insight or interest or even taste which the others do not share and which, till that moment, each believed to be his own unique treasure (or burden)." This resonates with me in the way I relate to Susan. Though so different, we are friends because we share common interests with our love for the outdoor recreation and God, yet we also share burdens, our solitude and our health struggles. Lewis explains how true friends, whether intended or not, find themselves on the other side of the barrier from the "herd," for they have found common interests that distinguish themselves from the herd. So many people try to "fit in" and be like the rest in the herd, but by compromising their own unique individuality, these people miss out on finding true friendship. By being her true self, Susan found a friend in me. We may not see each other but for a few times, given the great physical distance between us, and our communication may be inconsistent at times, but I know she is a kindred spirit and friend, and in that there is comfort and blessing.

Before I left the cafe, I told Susan of my great adventure plans and how my next big stops would be at the ghost town in Bodie State Historic Site and Lake Tahoe in California. Before we left I asked if we could take a picture together. We found someone to snap one for us. I was delighted and filled with joy for having met Susan, and I was so excited to tell my friend Zeke, who would be joining me in a few days, about how I met the one and only Susan. I had once told him that she was my biggest fan!

A young Susan with her camper

# The Colors of My Sunset

My spirit sighed in relief, accomplishment, and comfort. It had been a full day of adventuring, and now I was done for the day. I finished setting up camp, getting my car reorganized, equipping my tent with what I needed for the night, and putting on sweatpants and loose comfortable layers for the evening. Everything that needed to be done was done, and now I could soak in the beauty around me. My feet rejoiced as I forced off my hiking boots and slid my feet into my warm soft sandals which had been baking all day in the heat of the car. It was time to quiet my soul and be wholly present in the natural beauty around me, relinquishing action for the comforting silence of creation.

I sat on top of the picnic table at my campsite to look out upon Lake Tahoe, on the most eastern edges of California. I had lucked out and scored a campsite just atop the rounded slope that spilled down into Emerald Bay. Just days prior I was in the heat and desolation of the Mojave

Desert and its Death Valley. Although it has its own appeal, it was now so comforting to be aside water, in an air that grew increasingly cool with each passing minute. I felt like I had really arrived somewhere and felt accomplished for again having survived the harshness of the desert.

I took a deep breath of the cool pine-filled air with the knowledge and awareness that I didn't deserve any of this, yet it was lavished upon me. The most striking and comforting feature of the moment was the sunset my eyes beheld. The sun had dipped behind the piney bluffs, sending an arsenal of colors: warm oranges, vibrant pinks, rich purples and blues to jab into the soul and evoke awe.

By this point, in all my travels and wanderings, I had pondered and written quite a bit about natural beauty and the spiritual truths hidden within. Features and phenomena in nature, although they serve their own selfish purposes, also are symbolic and reveal truths about God and man. I had come to adopt a philosophy summed up in a phrase that repeated in my mind: "Beauty is never wasted," meaning that behind every beautiful feature or event in nature there is a message God planted to be found. It was all intentional.

So here I sat, in front of a rich sunset, above an angelic lake framed by dark sweet pines. I've learned a lot from streams and rivers. The moon and sky tell truth. The rainbow holds promise, and even a majestic tree speaks power. What is the meaning behind a sunset? Such beauty is so exquisitely extravagant, it must hold a powerful and prized message. Its display is so moving. I began to think of how some things are universally beautiful. Many differ in opinion, but I do believe beauty is objective. I have never met someone who would deny the beauty of a sunset. It's these things which are universally beautiful that are all the more compelling to me in that they carry a message.

I had to pause and start at surface level. A sunset marks the ending of a day, the closure, the wrapping up. If I were to relate that to human life, well the closure and wrapping up of life is death. But death? Really? Death has so often a negative connotation, and a sunset is beautiful. Does a sunset, something so beautiful, really hold a message about death? Two summers prior, I had lost my Grandpa Hodge. It was his time to die. It was his sunset. He was the first family member I lost as an adult, and, at that time, I was thinking of how death, although often viewed as a loss, is really the completion of something. It is the race fully finished. If you live a life in accordance with God's will, everything that you were meant to do in life, all your purpose, your calling, is complete at death. It is the most glorious of accomplishments! It is the most relieving, freeing, and beautiful of things. There are no more questions to be had, no more searching for purpose, no more toil and pain. There is a richness and completeness. The beauty of a life fully and rightly lived coming to its closure can parallel both the melancholy and celebratory beauty of a sunset.

Then I started thinking of the different colors of the sunset. Why does a sunset have an array of colors? What is the purpose behind this? Why are some sunsets more beautiful than others? For what reason do some have more colors than others, and why can't we see the sunset sometimes?

I started attributing the colors of the sunset to the overarching qualities of a person's life. When a life comes to an end, we can see the summation of a person. We can look at a life in its entirety and identify the qualities that person lived out. As a sunset can be rich in red, orange, pink, blue, purple, so a man's sunset can be marked by his own colors, whether it be kindness, generosity, love, bravery... When a life comes to an end, and we reflect upon the person, these attributes become brightly evident and on display.

Some sunsets are more monotone, as some lives are marked by one outstanding attribute or quality. Other, perhaps more beautiful sunsets, are marked by many colors. Many attributes are on display for the lives which appealed to and touched a multitude of people in a multitude of ways. Then there are the sunsets that, well, aren't. We don't see a beautiful display. Instead there are clouds or storms. There is no beauty to be seen, but just a gradual fading into abysmal darkness. This is the life not rightly lived, the life pursued apart from God. The life that lacked forgiveness; the life that turned cold; the one that was troubled and overcast by its own selfish ambition; the one in which goodness did not take root; and there, in that, death is not a completion nor fullness. There is no beauty to be seen. The palette is dismal and downcast.

When it is my time to go, or to put it frankly, when I die, what will be the colors of my sunset? Will there be a richness and beauty on display? Will my life be complete?

Yes, through God's grace, I will work to make it so. But if I were to pass today, what would my sunset look like? What qualities will summate my life?

At this point in my musings, my mind was on fire and delighted by the richness of thought. I was inspired. I broke open my journal. I could make a list of favorable qualities and consider the evidence in my life that point to each. I wanted to pause and consider the colors of my sunset. I began to think of positive qualities, and then my mind was steered to Scripture: Galatians 5:22-23 reads, "The fruit of the Spirit is love, joy, peace, patience, kindness, goodness, faithfulness, gentleness, self-control." Perhaps these were the things exhibitable in life, things worth nurturing, the ingredients of the most spectacular and beautiful of sunsets. I realized that in these nine things which constitute "the fruit of the Spirit," all other good qualities stem. From **Love** we get self-sacrifice, endurance, forgiveness, trust, humility, and bravery. In **Joy** we find happiness, charm, deep contentment, and hope. In **Peace** we find resolve, resilience, calmness, comfort, acceptance, security, confidence, and unity. In **Patience** there is perseverance, maturity, and knowledge. In **Kindness** there is selflessness, consideration, giving, charity, and thoughtfulness. In **Goodness** there is integrity and trustworthiness. In **Faithfulness** there is loyalty, bravery, and the unwavering. In **Gentleness** there is calm, patience, even-temperament, nurturing, and respect. In **Self-Control** there is wisdom, intention, and perspective. All of these constitute beauty.

If my sun were to set, in all honest and sincere reflection, I think my colors on display would be honesty, integrity, trustworthiness, bravery, comfort, resilience, and intention. These are the positive qualities I most identify with. I do not share this to boast. After all, these all come from the fruit of the Spirit. They are found under the umbrella qualities of love, peace, goodness, and faithfulness. And these are not products of my own being. They are from the Spirit of God which is a gift. In identifying these colors of my sunset, I've also come to find that I am lacking in the display of others. I want my sunset to display the full array of colors, and what I most need to work on is nurturing more joy and kindness in my life. At times my life be plagued by pessimism, unjustified negativity, and unrighteous reflexive acts of self-preservation.

Through this reflection, I was very much intrigued to read up and study the "fruit of the Spirit." When my travels were over and I was home, I did just that. To my surprise I realized these nine things were packaged together in a singular Spirit. There are not separate fruits. They come together. The singular word "fruit" is used with the singular indicative verb of "is," not "are". The Spirit of God living in his people endows us with all these qualities as one gift. They don't need to be planted or harvested individually. They are in every redeemed believer, at our disposal to employ in our lives, to transform this world and point others to Christ. The only thing that keeps some attributes from being more apparent than others in my own life, is my own faulty human nature. As Jesus says in Luke 9:23, we have to "deny" ourselves daily and follow him. Then the Spirit of God can really shine through, bringing fruit to ripen and eventually colors to sunset.

When I consider the colors of my sunset and become preoccupied with all that would entail, I am not just thinking of a display. I am not here thinking of just how I want people to be thinking about me upon my passing. That is missing the point. As we reflect upon the colors of our sunsets, it is really a time to take moral inventory, to examine our lives and see if they align with all the potential we have in the Spirit of God. Then, as we are more aware, we can take action steps to remove more of our selfish being, to weed out the clutter and clean the storeroom of our lives, to allow more colors to shine through in our life and become evident in our sunsets. This is achievable only through an active relationship with God and ceaseless pursuit of Him. These attributes, these colors, don't develop individually or by our own will. Rather, quite contrary, and astounding, they become brighter and richer the more we know and yield to God. The more we come to know God, the more He will be made known in our lives, evident in the fruit throughout. Thus, when the time has come, and our mortal life is passing, there too, beauty can be found in the colors of our sunsets.

Here, aside Lake Tahoe, as all the color faded into the night sky, the sunset complete, I zipped up my tent, shimmied into my sleeping bag, and rested my head on my pillow. *It is true*, I said to myself, *beauty is never wasted*.

# MANZANAR AND
# THE QUESTIONS IT RAISES FOR TODAY

The drive up and out of Death Valley to the west is perhaps the most harrowing drive I have ever been on. The narrow road hugs sheer cliffs, and at times with no guard rail, leaving not even an inch to mechanical error. The road winds and bends quickly and dramatically, and on the opposite side of the road from the cliffs are the hard rock faces of the Panamint Mountains, stern, not the least bit comforting. *There better not be a car coming from the other direction, because I doubt we could both round the curve at the same time successfully.*

Everything was sandy beige, rocky, and dry. Before I climbed this mountain in my vehicle, I was driving across the long low flats of Death Valley. The road zipped across the desert of barren rocks, shrubs, and occasional salt flats. This area was nicknamed the "Devil's Golf Course." The road then gradually ascended the base of the mountains, where it took on another character. There in the valley, beginning this drive, one could see an enormously long stretch of road. It didn't fade from view in the distance, but traversed the full route of the valley perfectly straight, then finally, just barely, escaped into the mountains, like the mining bandits of old bee-lining and then hiding out in the heights.

Up here in the mountains, my hands were tight on the steering wheel and my moves well calculated. Every once in a while I would steal a glance to the right and see the immensity of Death Valley now way down below me. Its white salt flats were now so prominent. Just the sight of it looked piping hot and desolate, and for a moment I wondered how I survived down there.

I've often told people the mountains surrounding Death Valley are some of the most impressive and enormous. It's not that they are the tallest in our nation, but when you view some of the nation's tallest mountains in the lower 48 states, in places like Washington and Colorado, you're already viewing them from thousands of feet above sea level. In Death Valley the mountains stand much taller because you see them from a starting point of 200 feet below sea level. Thus you see much more mountain, and they are breathtakingly enormous.

Driving these curvy mountainous roads, I was reminded of the old Wile E. Coyote and Road Runner cartoons, in which the Coyote runs so fast, chasing the Road Runner, but then he runs off the cliffside, only falling when he eventually notices there is no more road underneath him. I felt like if I wasn't careful, I'd find myself right off the cliff just like Wile E. Coyote.

There was a great deal of relief after I made it up and over the Panamint Mountains and slithered between the In-yo Mountain range, finding myself now in another valley, the Owens Valley. Now I could rest and take a breath at around 3,700 feet. Here there was the comfort from natural greenery and wide open flat spaces. To my right I could see the dry desolate brown peaks of the Inyo and Panamint Mountains which border Death Valley and to my left stood the tall snowcapped, pine-ladened, granite peaks of the Sierra Nevada. It is a place of wild contrast, with mountains of such different character on either side in prime view.

The road up here definitely had me wide-awake this early morning, but now in the quiet tranquil valley my mind could rest again, and I could gracefully and mindlessly zoom across the road. Not far in my journey I saw a sign that im-

mediately grabbed my attention: Manzanar National Historic Site. This was a unit of the National Park Service. I had
seen it on my map. In 2016 the National Park Service, in
honor of their centennial, released a free pamphlet map of
the United States with every National Park unit listed. I had
seen Manzanar on the map but hadn't figured that it was
actually en route. Knowing little about it, I was still excited
to visit, learn, and check it off my list.

I pulled into the parking lot, and no one else was
here. I had gotten such an early start down in Death Valley
that it was now only 8:00am, and I had an hour before the
visitor center and museum would open. I walked up to the
door and found a slot full of park maps and brochures. Almost as important as watching the park film is reading the
park brochure. Because I couldn't go inside and watch the
film, I went back to my car to read the brochure. Later I
would get to watch the film and tour the museum. What did
I learn? In simplified terms, during World War II Manzanar
was a war relocation camp for Japanese-Americans. There
was a broad distrust in the U.S. of those of Japanese ancestry, especially following the bombing of Pearl Harbor on
December 7th, 1941. There was suspicion of who was a spy
or secret operative of the Japanese government, and Democrat president Franklin D. Roosevelt, acting out of caution
for "public safety," signed Executive Order 9066, which
enabled Lieutenant John L Dewitt of the U.S. Army to use
the military to remove everyone of Japanese ancestry from
the West Coast. Dewitt said, "you can't tell one Jap from
another…They all look the same…A Jap's a Jap." Describ-

ing the incarcerated Japanese-Americans, the National Park Service in its brochure states, "They were from cities and farms, young and old, rich and poor. They had only days or weeks to prepare. Businesses closed, classrooms emptied, families and friends separated. Ultimately the government deprived over 120,000 people of their freedom." Manzanar held 10,000 of these people.

To me, this seemed like such a tragedy and stain on American history– a grave mistake or perhaps a willful wrong. I looked across the camp, the Sierra Nevada stood tall and magnificent behind the camp, dramatically rising up from this dry valley. This was a beautiful place, but to think a place of such beauty was also a place where people were so wrongfully deprived of their freedoms was quite the combination. Something so good was contrasted with something so wrong. It was a place where beauty was paired with mel-

ancholy.

I began walking down the pathways. Manzanar was
organized into thirty-six blocks, each one holding about sixteen barracks. Now only a few restored barracks remained.
Nearly all the structures were gone, but looking at the map I
noticed that tucked between some barracks once were com-
munal spaces. There were mess halls, a theater, high school,
elementary school, Catholic church, Protestant church,
Buddist temple, baseball field, hospital, park, and orchard. I
walked around with a sort of sacred reverence for this place.
This was a place where human freedom was taken, where
people really grappled with life, living, and its meaning. It
was a place where people suffered and sought purpose, or
lost purpose in confinement. It was also a place where people sought faith to see them through. With such things in
play, this was ground zero of a spiritual battle zone. I could
feel it. I could sense it, and it wasn't all bad. It wasn't oppressive. There was both physical and spiritual beauty here.

I came to what was labeled Merritt Park on the map.
Here were the small decorative dried up pond basins, river-
ways, and bridges which once helped compose beautiful
Japanese gardens. I saw some pictures on the interpretive
plaques of this place back in the early 1940s. The incarcerated constructed these gardens. I paused in contemplative
surprise. *Why bother?* I thought. *You've lost your freedom, you've
lost everything you had, yet in the midst of a place of such oppression
and darkness you've chosen to make something so beautiful?* It was
once so beautiful that even famous photographer Ansel Ad-
ams made a trip to Manzanar to photograph these gardens.

Throughout my wandering of the camp, I also learned how the incarcerated organized community events, such as community dances, plays, and sporting events. They also planted and harvested crops in the orchard and attended church and school. There was a very distinct beauty to be seen here. Despite their circumstances, many of these people chose to live their lives to the fullest, making the most of their given situations. That was inspiring. To lose so much but to carry on living exhibits a great and inspiring fortitude.

I came to the back of the grounds, the edge of the map, and there were a few flat headstones on the ground marking graves of people who had passed away in the camp and one tall standing obelisk monument inscribed with Japanese Kanji characters reading, "soul consoling tower." The National Park Service states, "Today the monument is a fo-

cal point of the annual pilgrimage, serving as a symbol of solace and hope." This area was ladened with paper cranes—a Japanese symbol of peace, hope, love, and healing in troubled times. There was a Japanese lady kneeling down by the headstones, leaving either paper cranes or flowers herself. I do not know if there is a certain season or pilgrimage which calls for these paper cranes, or if it was a routine gesture.

I eventually made my way back to the visitor center. I toured the museum full of photos and artifacts and watched the park film. It struck me as quite interesting that these people were not forced into this camp. They came willingly without any sort of Due Process. They were convinced it would be a place of safety and security and something they needed to do as a duty to their country. Video footage showed people giddily boarding trains, ready to come to this camp. I think these people were grossly misled, but I also found their sense of loyalty to their country quite profound. I gathered that their coming here was realized to be a sacrifice for a greater good. Some saw themselves as taking one for the team. At the time I thought, *what patriotism!* Later, as I reflected upon this, I wouldn't find it quite as patriotic but rather concerning that these people so blindly followed their government. But also, in regard to patriotism, I saw a photo and read of the students in camp pledging allegiance to the flag of the United States. The incarcerated children would do this every morning. Despite their situation, these people believed in the principles of America, what it stood for. Even if they were being deprived of the American values in the moment, they still believed in them, and did not abandon them nor their allegiance to them.

What I learned and saw at Manzanar would ruminate in my mind for quite some time. Reflecting on what I saw, I have been reminded of how important history is to the present. Learning about what we have done as a nation, and considering the motives behind our actions, can help us immensely in our decision making and discernment in the present and future.

It's quite important to note that the removal of all these people, which included the closings of their business, the loss of their homes, their isolation and ejection from society, was all done in the name of "public safety." Those exact words were uttered by their leaders. Certainly all Japanese-Americans were not infected with disloyalty to their country. Not all Japanese-Americans were spies, but just to play it safe, a blanketed act of oppression was spread out among a whole population. It's become evident, throughout history, that it's easy for people to abandon their moral conscience and fall in line to obedience when it comes to matters of safety. "Whatever you say, I will do," can easily become a mentality towards the government when the term "safety" is thrown around.

In my own lifetime, I've seen safety propped up, become a deeply ingrained value, and then elevated to an idol status. Creation and destruction is conducted in its name. A family's need to put food on the table, to keep the business running, to pay the mortgage, or even to see each other across state and national lines, has in recent times become irrelevant, frivolous, trivial in comparison to the great idol of safety. Safety is a carnivorous beast demanding much sacrifice. I am not advocating recklessness. Being safe to a measure is wise, but there is a great distinction from exercising safety with prudence versus idolizing safety to a god-like status that dictates all of one's actions.

These Japanese-Americans gave up their freedoms and came to these camps willfully, in the name of "public safety," in an unquestionable trust in the government. One may look back and think these people were just naive and assume the government would never do something like that today. I would not be so quick to jump to such conclusions. I think people and governments have the same faults in character and the same potential for corruption as they've always had. What is different today, however, is that we are informed by the past to think more critically of the present and future. We all need to question the sacrifices we make to "public safety," and to other idols in our government and society. As we do, we will be faced with moral questions of, *what is right and what is wrong?* It is easier to not grapple with such philosophical questions and just go along. It is also more natural to want to be taken care of, giving up freedom little by little to the god of "public safety," than to take lead and be free. Freedom is gutsy. It takes toiling through hard questions and taking action backed by principles, even when it goes against the grain of society.

Some, in the study of history, may conclude these relocation camps were needed, that they served their purpose in isolating and deactivating Japanese spies, and the sacrifice of some was worth it for the greater good. I can respect that opinion, and likely there is evidence to it's favor, but I still find the whole incarceration of innocent people to be a moral wrong. However, if one is strongly convinced in their conclusion, that this all was ultimately good in the grand scope of things, I ask him or her to fully own it and attribute it to its source. Give credit where credit is due. The incarceration of all these Japanese-Americans was not a pure American act, for it does not align with American principles or values at all, including equality, freedom, and Due Process. Rather, it was an act of the Democrat party and thus needs to be filed next to the other accolades, including the prolongation of slavery, the creation of the Klu Klux Klan, and the establishment of the Jim Crow Laws.

Another thought I've had as I've reflected on Manzanar is related to the press. It's evident that racism towards the Japanese was prevalent in the times leading up to Executive Order 9066. Photos and artifacts clearly demonstrate this. However, most of these artifacts are out of the press. I find it particularly telling that this racism was propagated, perhaps even created on a large scale, by the press. All this racism doubtfully seemed organic, like it just sprang up in the varying communities throughout the nation. I find it hard to believe. It is more believable that it was sold, planted, and propagated by the news media. Read the newspaper headlines of the time. It was clearly an agenda, and this all served the government's purpose. The press was and is a tool of the government, which makes me question, was there really a sweeping racism in the United States towards Japanese, or was that the narrative of the press? Or did the

press exploit existing racism for greater division to achieve the government's goals? This all leads me to my next questions for our present time: What messages are the press trying to instill in us today? and, What agenda, present or future, might these messages align with? If we can train ourselves to routinely ask this question and be skeptical of the purposes of the media, we won't be so blindly manipulated and divided for political purposes.

Eventually two Republican presidents sought to address this wrong committed by our country. Ronald Reagan signed the Civil Liberties Act of 1988, giving an apology and financial reparations for those who had been detained in these camps. This was my first time ever learning about such a concept as government reparations. Later, George H. W. Bush amended this act to ensure every case was addressed and again gave another apology on behalf of the U.S. government.

Ultimately Manzanar National Historic Site taught me that the corruption we see in our government and news media is not entirely new. We've been down this road before. We must question our government and media. And equally important, let us wake up and realize that when we pledge allegiance to the United States of America, as the school children did in Manzanar, we should not be pledging blind allegiance to the government, but rather an allegiance to the principles that constitute America and an allegiance to our fellow Americans.

Manzanar is a scar on American history, but it can teach us much. Let's not lose sight of our history— the good and the bad.

Before I left Manzanar, I toured the simple barracks

and took a few photos. Some barracks had beds lined up one after another in a military fort alignment. Other barracks housed small family-style apartments. I thought about getting a book in the visitor center to read more about life in Manzanar, because this history intrigued me, but I knew I wouldn't be dwelling too much on this chapter of American history during my trip. I would be moving on to another. Next stop was further back in time to the era of the California Gold Rush, as I would visit Bodie, a mining town, turned ghost town and then a state historic site.

# Ghosts and Gold:
# The Arrested Decay of Bodie and Your Life

I was up on the highlands early in the morning, pulling over to take a photo of the hundreds of sheep grazing in the pasture. I had never seen so many before. It reminded me of John Muir's summer in the Sierra as a shepherd. Maybe this was a familiar view he saw: little fleecy clouds grazing up and down the hillside and the sky a cloudless blue. I was on my way to a ghost town: Bodie State Historic Park. This one had been on the radar for a while. It is the ghost town of all ghost towns. I say this because of it being the largest intact ghost town, boasting over two hundred remaining structures. The citizens once claimed it was the largest city in California, with a population of around 10,000 when it peaked in 1880.

Today it is a thirteen mile drive off the highway to this ghosted metropolis in the heights. The last three miles were dirt and rock, and there was a car before me obstructing my view by spinning up clouds of dust. I was doing the same for the car behind me. I certainly wasn't visiting this place alone, like when visiting many of the other ghost towns throughout my travels. The dusty road finally curved around and spilled into a flat sandy parking lot. There were dozens of other cars. I popped open my trunk to get my backpack and gear up for exploration. The car, which had been trailing me, pulled up beside me and a husband and wife stepped out. "That was quite a drive," the man said.

"It sure was," I agreed. Was he referring to the scenery of treeless pastures, the rocky road, or the hundreds of sheep? I didn't know, but I appreciated his friendliness and no apparent resentment for the clouds of dust I sent billowing their way.

I was enthralled when I stepped foot into the dusty streets of Bodie. It was more than I could have imagined, and by "more," I mean it in the literal sense— so many structures and pathways to explore! The pictures of the place online were quite intriguing, but in reality this place was on the next level, and it was so quintessentially old Wild West. I felt as if I was upon some movie set or propelled back in time. However, the buildings were rightfully weathered by time, telling me this was a rare relic of the past.

I was excited to explore it all, but as disciplined as I am in such matters, I first had to watch the park film. What did I learn? This was a place rich in multiple ways. It mined about $34 million in gold and silver in its time, adjusted to about $100 million today. It is also rich in the history and stories it holds. I felt one must spend a lot of time here to really get to know Bodie. I would only get to brush upon the knowledge of its rich history.

I learned that the gold and silver mines in Bodie were once owned by the Standard Mining Company, and atypical of many other mining towns, the Standard Mining Company did not own the town, just the mines. All the other businesses in town were private. When Bodie was booming, it even had its own town within its town. The influx of Chinese immigrants who worked on the railroad and in lumbering, to support the town, sought to keep their own customs and traditions in their own community within Bodie. Yes, this is a ghost town with a Chinatown that once had its own general store, saloon, and Taoist temple. I would learn many more interesting facts about Bodie, later on a tour. But to set the scene, and frame things in context, Bodie went through many fluxes in population in part due to fires, as-

sumed mineral depletion, and eventual unprofitability of the
mines. It stayed alive until 1942, when the U.S. government's War Production Board passed an order which shut
down all non-essential gold mines in the country. Bodie's
last remaining mine was closed and mining never resumed.
The Cain family, who owned much of the land, was conscious of its historical significance and hired a caretaker to
look after the place in the 1940s, until they transferred it
over to the state of California in 1962, after it was named a
National Historic Landmark.

　　I looked out. Streets intersected with streets everywhere. There were flat lanes and hilly neighborhoods. All
the buildings were in uniform, composed of dark vertical
wooden boards. Out in the distance, forming the Bodie skyline, was the Standard Stamp Mill which I would get to tour
later.

The first structure I saw entering Bodie was the Methodist church. It is perhaps the most iconic feature of the town, despite it wearing the uniform dark wooden boards and not doing much to stick out. It was modest. Along with its simple gable roof were its triangular window peaks, short rising steeple, and protruding foyer. I learned that Bodie was booming for over a full year without a church. It was a lawless place. One of its ministers, Reverend F.M. Warrington described it as "...a sea of sin, lashed by the tempest of lust and passion." I can't imagine how difficult it must have been to minister and feel a sense of obligation to a congregation in such a place.

Traveling down the main streets, most of the buildings were closed and locked, but I could go up to the windows and cup my hands around my eyes against the glass to

peek in. Nearly every building was furnished. In the homes I saw tables and chairs, vanities, sewing machines, beds, rotten mattresses, wallpaper peeling off, canteens, and bottles, and hats sitting about. One building was a pool hall, and the pool table still lay next to a furnace and a bar. One of the general stores was well stocked with just about everything you could imagine a general store to have back then, but everything was just about everywhere, in such a state of disarray and decay, that just the disorder and abandonment gave it a haunting sort of feel.

Ghost towns are not named so because of the supernatural, but simply the term refers to a place that has been abandoned. However, seeing so many things so shamelessly abandoned and rotting away certainly gave a sort of spooked aura. It was especially evident in one building with the way the light filtered in the window, dispersed through a laced curtain, and crept across the warped floorboard, casting natural shadows. If anyplace here was to be truly haunted, though, it would have to be the mortuary. It looked just like one of the many other houses, but I cupped my hands around my eyes and against the window to peek inside. A large coffin lay horizontal in the room, and up against the wall leaned two infant caskets. I felt something distinctly eerie about being at a mortuary in a ghost town, looking at infant coffins. Perhaps it was just a sure reminder of the fallen state of humanity. Here I was in a place left abandoned, rotting away, where life once lived, fixing eyes upon caskets, a reminder of the finite nature of our existence on this earth, and I was looking at infant caskets, symbolic of lives sadly taken prematurely.

I did a bit more wandering myself, peeking in the windows of the school house, which was in near mint condition, and an old gas station with the oldest Shell sign I've ever seen. I stopped for a moment at the old two story hotel which had me imagining people coming to this place and checking into a room. *Why were they here? Was it for business or just visiting? Would they check into their rooms and then maybe head out on the street to find a place to have dinner or stir up ruckus in a saloon? What sort of men would wander over to "Virgin Alley"?* This place once had a lot going on. Now its buildings were void of life and silent.

After a bit of wandering, I went on a guided tour up to the Standard Stamp Mill. The ranger led a group of about fifteen of us up the dusty streets of Bodie. Before coming to the Mill we walked by the once home of Theodore Hoover, the older brother of president Herbert Hoover. I was fascinated that this place had a connection with Herbert Hoover through his brother. I visited Herbert Hoover National Historic Site in Iowa the previous fall and learned all about him. It was there, in the old Quaker meeting house in the Herbert Hoover family's village, that I took time to ponder and reflect upon my last summer's lesson to "be still, calm and quiet." I love, how in visiting National and State Parks, there are so many connections between people and events across the country. In the earlier days of our republic, the people of influence had broad sweeping connections across the nation. One thing that happened here had another effect that happened there. These commonly occurring characters and

connections help tie everything together and paint one grand image of the United States.

Once inside the Standard Stamp Mill, we saw all the powerful mechanics, giant gears, and heavy equipment. The ranger explained the stamping process of this mill– how these giant stamps would literally crash down upon rocks and break the mineral deposits. Then a series of magnets and mesh beds would sort out the gold and silver. The most interesting thing the ranger shared with us here was how early employees in this mill were known for trying to steal gold from the mill. They would hide it in their pockets. So Theodore Hoover, as manager of the mine, established uniform outfits– jumpsuits with no pockets. These thieving employees found other ways to steal, however. In the hot mine a man may stage a wiping of his brow or a hand comb

The Hoover House

through the hair, leaving behind gold dust to later be collected from his hair, eyebrows, or eye lashes.

Here in the mine, the ranger also gave a super fascinating fact: In recent years, a Canadian mining company surveyed the land, finding about $2 trillion worth of gold still deposited in the hills around Bodie. The U.S. government stripped the mining permit from the Canadian company and now the state of California just sits on two trillion dollars of gold beneath its land. At first mention, I thought, *California needs to mine that to pay off its debt*, but the more I've thought about it, I've realized it's better kept reserved, for I don't think the California government is by any means fiscally responsible to handle such a sum of wealth.

History and gold mining aside, I think there is a lot to learn from ghost towns about life. I've written about this before in my book, *Canyonlands: My adventures in the National Parks and beautiful wild,* but Bodie, I find, taught me something different. You see, the park ranger explained how Bodie was in a state of "arrested decay." Meaning, the place was in a state of decay, but they were trying to arrest that decay, so nothing was to be changed, restored, revitalized, or repurposed. The place was simply to be arrested in its state of abandonment and decay. The only intervention was to occasionally add a support to a building to keep it standing. So, because of "arrested decay," in every building dust was collecting, walls were rotting, items were unprotected and weathered by age. Many of the buildings were even left messy inside. Old cans, cartridges, bottles, hats, and books lay about, left abandoned, in the same location, untouched for ages. This had me thinking about life.

As we age, we are prone to find our own lives in a state of arrested decay. I look at all these physical objects left abandoned in Bodie and I see them as metaphors for the non-physical and spiritual things we have accumulated in life. We each have an array of experiences, stories, lessons learned, and passions which we have collected over the years. These are all valuable things, gained for many purposes. But I think, as we age, apathy has a way of arresting some of these things and causing us to abandon them despite their value. We no longer put them to use. We get old and we move past these things, and instead of seeking action and influence, we make excuses. But did you not have these experiences for a purpose, and did you not learn these lessons in life to share them? Did you not develop passion to let it stay dormant, collecting dust? Many have places in their lives that are in arrested decay, and it truly is a great loss. We need to exercise the abilities we've been given, nourish the passions that have been instilled, and share what we have learned in life to build up others.

Dennis Rainey in his book *Stepping Up: A call to courageous manhood,* explains how as we get older we are fed a series of lies which rob us of the perception of our own value and worth. We rely on excuses which deem us irrelevant and rob us of our dignity. He talks about the final years of life as some of the most influential. It is here one has accumulated the most experience, wisdom, and lessons learned. All of these things are great riches to be passed on, but many men keep them to themselves. Rainey writes, "What an opportunity we have as we enter into the final years of life to use the wisdom and influence we've accumulated and reach out to the next generation." He also goes on to say, "God created men not to rust out but to wear out as they stretch toward the finish line." We are to be utilitarian with all we have been given, and, with age, our toolbelt is much more hardy than when we were younger. As written in Job 12:12, "Wisdom belongs to the aged, and understanding to the old."

I'd regret for anyone to cup their hands around your life and peek into your soul finding all the valuable spiritual things of life collected, laying abandoned. It's not an easy question to ask but it is one Bodie beckons: Is your life but a ghost town in arrested decay? It doesn't have to be. Take a look inside. What do you have there in your spiritual storeroom? What can you share? Think about it like this: You are not a state park but a city full of spiritual investments. There are no ghost towns in the Kingdom of God, so dust yourself off and get on with life!

And also, maybe like in Bodie, there's so much more treasure still to be mined from life. Don't just sit on it. Fire up the stamp mill!

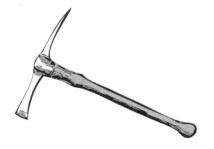

# The Travel Companion

It was the morning of July 7th. I was on my way to pick up Zeke at the airport. He'd be accompanying me for ten days of my summer adventure. I was so excited to share part of this adventure with someone else. These trips were so fun and so meaningful to me. I am always wanting to share my experiences with others, even my day trips into the wilds of Kentucky, but I very rarely can find anyone who is interested. I was so ready to share these experiences of the summer with someone else.

Zeke will be a character in this book for the next many chapters, so I think the reader needs a proper description of him, just as I would provide if I were writing any piece of fiction. Of appearance, he was of a smaller stature, lanky, thin faced, but strong-willed and full of energy despite his meek and mild appearance.

I first met Zeke just the spring prior in the Great

Smoky Mountains National Park while camping at the Cosby campground. We hit it off immediately. He was unlike anyone I'd ever met before, a wild creature of nature, in tune with the environment around him. He could climb trees to great heights by hugging them and shimmying his way up; he'd find wild plants and tie them around his wrists; and he'd go hiking barefoot. There was this wild, back to nature quality about him that was a few steps beyond me. At the time he was one of those people I wished I was more like.

I learned he was also from Kentucky but from Bowling Green, the other side of the state, and he was in school for wildlife and forestry conservation. We went for a hike together in the Great Smoky Mountains and decided we wanted to go on more hikes together.

He first earned my trust when getting ready to leave the Great Smoky Mountains and part ways to our different sides of Kentucky and I lent him my GPS. During the hike, when he sat down at an overlook, he accidentally sat on his phone and smashed it in on a rock. He didn't know how to get home and was relying on his phone to guide him. I lent him my GPS, hesitantly so. This was a stranger. I wasn't sure if I'd ever get it back. I didn't have a smartphone yet and often relied on this device. However, we met up in Kentucky to go on other hikes in the Big South Fork and Zeke returned the GPS to me. He was proving himself trustworthy.

Later in the spring, with Zeke, I explored some things in western Kentucky that I wouldn't have otherwise seen, such as Shanty Hollow, a wild entrance to Mammoth

Cave, and other outdoor places near Nashville, Tennessee. He'd sometimes get up ahead of me on trails, and I'd find him in a tree or down low studying some plant or fungus. I loved his interest in nature! *Finally someone else like me who gets my interest in the natural world.* There was an energy around him that was contagious, which propelled me further into the wild, and a positivity I admired. He was always smiling and always looking on the bright side of things. I'd later learn it wasn't always genuine. It was a facade. It was a means to win people over and not always sincere.

Regretfully, I tiptoed around any deep or serious conversations with Zeke. I don't know why. Perhaps I sensed there would be dissension. So despite our great shared love of nature and outdoor recreation, our friendship was quite shallow. I'd soon learn, on this trip, that our worldviews were entirely different, and he had a habit of telling little white lies here and there that with time eroded trust.

I find superficial "friendships," exhausting. I choose to put my energy into deeper, more meaningful friendships, kindred spirits if you will. We should always be respectful and can be friendly to those from whom we differ greatly. We can choose to spend time with these people and learn a lot, but to invest a great deal of time and energy into a friendship is another thing. I believe a friendship will only be lasting, at least for me, if we have common fundamental views of the world around us. A worldview seeps into all matters of interaction with people and the natural world. We'd get more into this later.

When I picked Zeke up from the airport, the car immediately flooded with the scent of stale cigarettes and sour shoes. He claimed he stopped smoking, but it lingered on all his things. We had a journey ahead of us. This day we needed to cross the Golden Gate Bridge, travel through California's wine valley up to the Redwood National Park. Along the way we'd stop at Battery Spencer, a viewspot of the Golden Gate Bridge. We'd also make a quick visit to Muir Beach to say hello to the Pacific Ocean, and we needed to stop and stock up on food for the days ahead.

For some reason I was very concerned about crossing the Golden Gate Bridge. I thought about it many nights leading up to this day. It was daunting. I think maybe I was scarred by being the passenger on the crowded hectic bridges of New York City. I feared driving through San Francisco would be like driving through New York City. It wasn't. It was a breeze. On the other side, at Battery Spencer, we tried to take some photos with the bridge but they weren't very good. The sky was cloudy and the air was cold and windy. Because the weather was far from ideal, our stop at Muir Beach was extra brief. So we soon hit the open road. Onward to the Redwoods!

It was a drive that kept dragging on. Eventually the arid valley gave way to moist tall dark Redwood Forest. We rolled into Elk Prairie Campground in the Redwood Forest in the dark of night.

# The Inspiration of the Redwood Forest
## Philosophical Implications of Nurse Logs

It was a cool wet morning. This land was moist, damp, dark, and dripping. Beneath my feet the decaying wood on the forest floor was almost sponge-like. This sure wasn't Southern California anymore, where I had just been the day before, where the ground is perpetually thirsty. This was a new place for me– The Redwood Forest of Northern California.

"Wow!" I exclaimed. "You have to come see this. This snail is huge!" I was impressed and also wanted to wake my travel companion, Zeke. I stood outside my tent taking in the misty wet wonderland. We had arrived in the dark the night before, and I wasn't sure of what all comprised the surroundings when we were setting up camp. So I gingerly stepped out of my tent with curiosity. *What is out there?* I thought. The creature I found crawling up my tent was the biggest insect I had ever seen. It was crawling very slowly, easing its way, putting its whole body into it. I had my termi-

nology confused. It was not a snail at all. It was a banana slug. This creature had a dismal sort of earthy yellow, with a rubberlike appearance. It was rightly named, for not only do these slugs have a yellow appearance, but they also are just about the size of a small banana. I'd come to find that Zeke is not an easy one to wake up and get moving in the morning, but my exclamation about a bug got him right out of his tent. He is one fascinated by critters and crawling things of all kinds.

"That's not a snail. That's a slug," he corrected, observing it and soon gently poking it with a twig, inspecting its response. I was a little bit embarrassed by my error. He went on to spy two more crawling around our camp. They are commonly associated with the Redwood Forest, but I had not read up enough about this park to know, and thus these slugs were quite a surprise for me. We had camped in

Elk Prairie Campground, just a short walk from one of the park's visitor centers. After I got the ball rolling to get the day started with my bug exclamation, I made breakfast. I fixed my campfire apple crisp in which I baked apples in a tin cup over a campfire and melted an oat chocolate chip Clif Bar over them. After breakfast, we quickly packed up our camp, then prepared our backpacks for an overnight adventure.

### Redwoods vs. Sequoias

Before embarking on our day's trek, we drove over to the visitor center where we began a stroll through the Redwood Forest on an entanglement of short trails with interpretive signs. We had seen some redwoods, driving between them the evening before. It was spectacular to see the evening sun finding its golden glow between their branches on the pine floor. But now it was a distinctly different experience to be outside and in their habitat. These trees are massive, surely impressive, but they don't quite provide the same *wow* factor and sense of awe as the sequoia's of Southern California. People often assume the redwoods are the world's largest trees. They are the world's tallest trees, but the mighty sequoias are the largest in volume, having girthier trunks and therefore invoking a greater sense of awe and magnitude.

The forest floor was a bed of pine needles and moist wood decay. As we trod on top of the forest's soft bed, we looked up at the high reaches of the redwoods disappearing as their branches covered one another. They cre-

ated a canopy for sure. We were under it. The term
"inside the forest," really is quite appropriate. We were
not quite fully outside. We were *inside,* but a different sort
of inside. We could not see the sky except for small slivers peeking in, and thus the forest was dark, dismal in appearance. Vibrancy was dampened. Looking down from
the forest's tall reaches we encountered our company,
enormous ferns crowding in what otherwise would be
empty space, between the trunks of the trees to the edge
of the paths. I couldn't help but make more comparisons
between the redwoods and the sequoia. The sequoia has
a cleaner, more refined look about it. It has straight edges
and is more dignified. The redwoods are a little more
wild, sloppy, unrefined if you will. They have many knots
and lumpy growths which especially congregate around
their bases. They give a feebler appearance as some are
split and splintering. In a couple instances we climbed up
into some trees which had split, and we took our picture
in the tree cavities.

## Nurse Logs

As we wandered around the interpretive paths, I
could see Zeke's head just barely visibly among the ferns
which grew nearly as tall as him. At one point, with him
ahead, I stopped and read an interpretive sign. It had really invoked some pondering. It was next to a fallen tree.
On top that fallen redwood, or from within it rather, other saplings were growing, and moss and greenery
were laden. I had also seen, along the day's hike, other

instances in which a nearly full grown tree had grown out of the fallen trunk of another. The placard beside this tree read, "Nurse Logs." I read that these fallen trees provide just the right nutrients to foster growth of the next generation of plant life. They are a phenomenon of the forest. I observed this particular fallen tree in front of me. It was as if it was its own world, its own little island or little planet in the universe of the forest. This decaying tree provided so much life and created its own miniature forest. It had its own visible microbiome.

This was very captivating to me. I knew immediately something so spectacular and peculiar is not without a deeper meaning. *What is the message God has for us through "Nurse Logs"?* I truly believe no marvel of nature goes without a message. All of nature is designed to reveal spiritual truths to mankind and point us back to God.

Nurse Log by John Wagner

I began to think about people in relation to trees. To help you follow my train of thought, or perhaps my "tree of thought," as it branches out in many ways, let's take this to my most rudimentary observation. A Nurse Log is dead yet it provides life. There are people who are dead, but yet provide life. This is not in the sense of bodies decaying and providing nutrients for the soil or tree growth. Don't get me wrong. Rather, I mean in the sense that those who have gone on before us enrich our lives through their past lives fully lived. Their legacies, their teachings, their love and efforts are life-giving. We often live off of, or find our life-fuel through, the inspiration and efforts of those who have come before us, and if we don't, we should. There are great people of the past who are true gifts from God, whom He placed in the exact moments of time to enrich our lives.

## Nurse Logs in Scripture

I thought about the lives of those in Scripture whose examples provide such enrichment to our own lives. I think of the faith and commitment of Paul in the face of persecution and suffering; the openness and raw relationship between Job and God in the midst of extreme suffering; the trust of Moses despite feelings of inadequacy; and the courage of Joshua to lead a new generation in battle after their people had gone astray. As I've posed this question to others, there are many females in particular who find strength in Mary for her obedience to, and trust in, God to be the mother of His only Son. There are so many Biblical figures who enrich our lives. However, there is really only One who can truly give life, and that is God through Christ Jesus. For the sake of this Nurse Log analogy, when I talk about "life-giving," I refer to ones who can greatly and profoundly enrich our lives, not literally give life. There are so many life-giving people in Scripture it's overwhelming. God has given us a record of their lives with intention to help bring about the robustness of our own lives and ultimately lead us to Him.

## Nurse Logs in History

With these thoughts, I was overwhelmed in the best sense of the word. My wheels were spinning. I decided to consider other areas of our lives or other categories of "Nurse Logs." I thought about more recent historical figures– the Abraham Lincolns, the George Washingtons, the countless heroes of time, and the men and women who have served in the military whose sacrifices have cleared the forest for our lives to flourish, especially all the lives sacrificed in the Revolutionary War and Civil War that allow for the freedoms we have today in our country. I also considered the theologians and philosophers whose great explorations of truth have informed my own life and enriched it, even those who more tactically have built things and made advancements in medicine. Then I took this down to a more personal level. I asked myself, *Who are the specifically identifiable Nurse Logs in my life— deceased people who truly enrich my life? Whose legacy continues to feed me and provide the nutrients for my own growth?*

## Grandparents as Nurse Logs

First and foremost, one answer is clear: It's my grandparents who are all deceased. It's their efforts, their values, their consistency which influenced the character and values of my own parents. Consequently my parents have passed on those same values to me. There are so many aspects to consider, including ones of which I will never be aware. I can, however, examine some of the obvious ones: faith, creativity, persistence, family, love… Those are some of the nutrients I grow out from, left by their lives. I would surely not be who I am without my grandparents, and as a matter of fact, not for my grandparents parents, and the lineage for generations. My grandparents are surely the most nutrient dense Nurse Logs in my life. Their influence, though most times not direct, is the most profound and interwoven in my life.

My grandparents, Raymond and Betty Hodge, sitting on a log

My grandpa, Lyle Wolf, and me

My grandma, Marian Wolf, reading to me

## Walt Disney: a Nurse Log of creativity and work ethic

I began to think of others, deceased people apart from family, who have enriched my life. When I think about my sense of creativity and work ethic I think of Walt Disney. He influences me as a writer and teacher. The broad gamut of his stories and creative work spur me on in my own creations. He adopted a principle his father gave him: "Any job worth doing is worth doing well." I believe that. It guides me in my own creative endeavors. Walt has had a great influence on the quality of my work, and his example speaks to me and influences my work. He also saw the quality and potential in others. He was a master at bringing talent together. That has influenced me to bring outside talent into my own creative projects. I also am inspired by the value he placed in storytelling, family, and innocence. Even my patriotism is inspired by Walt Disney's love for his country. How sad Walt would be to see how far the company he started has strayed from his values.

Something often overlooked about Walt Disney is that he placed a great importance on reading too. He hoped his storytelling would inspire children to read more, something I am also so passionate about. I've spent a few years writing for Dolly Parton's Dollywood Theme Park, and in that, getting to know more about Dolly Parton than I ever expected or could have imagined in my life. I see how Walt Disney is likely a nurse log to Dolly as well, inspiring her in her theme park, resorts, and storytelling. In her book *Dream More: Celebrate the Dreamer in You,* she really summed up the value in reading that perhaps the three of us share. She writes, "I have noticed that people I've met who love reading tend to be more engaged and more creative."

To top it all off, I am inspired that Walt made the largest entertainment company in the world out of nothing. His story is that of a humble farm boy in middle America, who moved to Kansas City with virtually nothing and was homeless. He started off on his own, taking showers in a train station and sleeping in his office, but in those moments he had fierce determination, which for me is life-giving inspiration. When I feel like I make no progress in my own efforts I think back to Walt's story and find the gumption to keep going.

## John Muir: a Nurse Log of viewing nature

Another man who inspires me, who feeds my life, is the preservationist, writer, and adventurer John Muir. I wrote about him in my book, *Still Calm and Quiet: More adventures in the National Parks and the beautiful wild,* when I visited his family home in Martinez, California. Through reading his work, he has shaped how I view nature— how all of creation is intricately designed with common properties reflective of a common Creator. John Muir cherished all the fine details of nature and that has helped me find delight in the most common, intricate, and most unusual things of nature. Muir has taught me to view all things in nature with awesome wonder, truly privileged to be able to look into the fantastical, artistic mind of God. This has also helped me find the great meaning in all things in nature. If it wasn't for

Muir, a number of my books would not have been written, or at least not the way they have been. I may not even have stopped to ponder the Nurse Logs and really consider what message they hold, and therefore I wouldn't be writing any of this now.

Muir also helped me toughen up. When I brave the elements and my discomfort grows strong, I think about all Muir endured on his adventures: sleeping exposed on a lump of moss or in the bitter colds of Alaska, or even walking a thousand miles across the country.

**Theodore Roosevelt: a Nurse Log of character and strength**

Lastly, one who should not come as a surprise to anyone who knows me and my writing is Theodore Roosevelt.

He inspires me most in terms of his character which was so solid. His commitment to principles, right and wrong, and what is just and righteous was so strong. He did not shrink from hardship but endured it to great extents, compelled by his own moral duty.

I was initially drawn to Roosevelt learning of his childhood illnesses and the immense grief he had as a young man through tragic loss. *How can someone go through such pain and suffering, yet become such a powerful and effective leader, living such a rich life, and become president?* I had to study this man and learn of that which guided and sustained him. Roosevelt, without a doubt, would have said his own father, who passed away when he was a young man, was his greatest Nurse Log, and to me Theodore Roosevelt is certainly one of my greats. I pull great strength from his many hardships and resolve.

In 2022 when I spoke at the *Gathering of the Teddy Roosevelts: Badlands Chautauqua* in North Dakota, I began my talk with this very topic of Roosevelt as a Nurse Log. To my humbling honor, the oldest living Theodore Roosevelt re-priser, the dignified Marty Jonason, told me afterward, "The part about the Nurse Logs really gave me chills." Though I was surprised and felt so honored to receive such words, I thought of it as a challenge. Shouldn't we all feel that sense of chill when we consider how greatly we can impact the lives of others, even when we are gone?

## Roosevelt's Joy

Back to my study of Roosevelt, I'm most recently interested in Roosevelt's joy. He was a man of many outward emotions, but a very prominent one was joy. A quote that often comes to mind is, "The joy of living is his who has the heart to demand it." One could take this to great philosophical lengths, to some interpretations that I may even disagree with. However, for me, and what I believe Roosevelt was saying, was quite simple: There is great joy in this life we are given, but it must be pursued. He follows this with his line, "Life is an adventure, accept it in such a spirit," implying that joy comes from fully embracing the adventure of life. We must remember that God wants us to be joyful, and we can find great joy in Him and his many blessings in life, but as Roosevelt says, we must pursue joy and fully live our lives. Oh, there is so much to unpack when it comes to Roosevelt. I could write a book about him… well, actually, I have.

A very important aspect of living life is also the truth that we cannot fully live our lives apart from God's Spirit gifted through the redeeming power of Jesus. To Roosevelt's point, we cannot fully enjoy our redeemed life without embracing all that lies in our paths and pursuing the opportunities afforded us. As he would say, this is the "adventure." It's so easy to fall into gloom in an aging world which does not seem to be maturing but rather decaying. With so much going on in the world, one may think pursuing joy is but a frivolous and selfish pursuit. It's easy to dismiss it in all our trouble, but joy is so important that God commands us at least twenty-five times in Scripture to rejoice, and joy is mentioned over two hundred times in the Bible. In Philippians 4:4 it is written, "Rejoice in the Lord always, again I say rejoice!"

With all the mention of God, amidst my discussion on Nurse Logs, one might ask, *Are you going to mention Jesus as your Nurse Log?* Surely Jesus is the most influential force in my life. He influences and permeates every corner of my life, and I want His influence to be even greater. If at times that's not true, it's yet a deeper desire to want my heart to long and let God have more control. The reason why I don't call Jesus a Nurse Log, is because He is alive! He is not dead. This I know. Jesus was a human, but he was also divine, God in the flesh. Here I discuss the deceased purely human Nurse Logs who nevertheless I give God all due credit. All Nurse Logs are gifts from God.

## Authors as Nurse Logs

As I've thought all of this over to great depths and have considered my Nurse Logs, I must also credit the countless authors through the ages whose words inspire and give us life. How fortunate we are to live in a time when we have the wisdom of the ages passed down to us in text and so many books in print which can provide so much enrichment. It can be natural for some young people, myself at one time included, to dismiss the writings of the deceased as irrelevant and outdated…but pause. I now unfold such old books with great reverence and an expectancy to learn. Some of the writers of the past were much more thoughtful than the average man today, much more conscious of God and their place in the universe. They may be gone, but the words they have left behind, may be nutrient dense. We must have sacred reverence for the past. The past too is a gift. It is all a part of God's story. Let us cherish the wisdom of the ages and the library filled with countless examples of lives past lived.

The whole phenomenon of Nurse Logs, though fun to ponder, and an instigator of reverence and gratefulness, is also a challenge to us. Will we live lives that count for the next generations? Will they feed off of what we have done with our lives? I'll admit, I don't know what that means for my life. I don't know what it looks like. I have to have faith. It's like trying to see the sky through the limbs of the red-woods. I know it's there, I just can't see it. God has a plan for your life, even though you may not know the specifics. Maybe just like it did for Marty, the reprisor, this should give us goose bumps. I pray that in God's plan we may be those life-giving Nurse Logs of the forest.

## Who Are Your Nurse Logs?

As you venture forward in the wilderness of the un-knowns of life, take a moment to consider, *who are your Nurse Logs?* May you draw inspiration from them.

# An Unexpected Visitor

The sun grew bold, piercing through the forest, creating stark contrast against the dark redwoods. Zeke, and I were backpacking through the Redwood Forest in Northern California on our way to the Pacific Ocean to the Golden Bluffs Campground. The hike in total was to be about seven miles, but after just a few miles, my backpack was getting quite heavy. I kept adjusting the straps, raising it and lowering it on my back, trying to find the most comfortable position. We could have driven to the campground, but I wanted the novelty of hiking across the forest and achieving that great sense of accomplishment.

Along the way it was rather interesting. Many of the

redwoods had hollow cavities or had fallen to make natural bridges. I did cross one such bridge, and poked my head into a few tree cavities, but I wasn't quite as far reaching as Zeke who climbed up into a few trees, reaching great heights. One of the first times we ever went hiking together I noted how much he truly interacts with the forest. In the Big South Fork, back in Kentucky, he'd shimmy his way up a tree trunk, just hugging onto it. He'd be atop a giant boulder in a matter of seconds.

With the light shining so powerfully above and really spilling into the forest, it revealed how the forest wasn't as dense as previously perceived. Yes, there were lots of ferns everywhere, and a redwood can be found in any direction. However, apart from the redwoods, other trees were absent, and the redwoods don't branch and sprawl like some other trees, but more like bloom towards their tops, leaving a vacancy in the forest, a void space between one tree and the next. The path we were on was also a well-worn one, so I didn't quite feel as though I was in the wildest of places I had perhaps expected. It was a pretty well-worn playground.

We were on a path called the John Irvine Loop, and technically we were not in the National Park but a State Park. The area's full name is "Redwood Forest National and State Parks." That's what all the signage proclaimed. It's a conglomerate of State Parks and one limited region of federal land. Its three most comprising parks are Jedediah Smith Redwoods State Park, Del Norte Coast Redwood State Park, and Prairie Creek Redwoods State Park.

In my book, *Canyonlands: My adventures in the National Parks and beautiful wild* I made a lot of Star Wars references. I was a considerable fan at the time, but I'm sad of what has come of the franchise. I do believe, however, it is worth mentioning here that the Redwood Forest is the planet of Endor in Return of the Jedi. It's the land of Ewoks and imperial speeders zooming past redwoods and giant ferns. If anyone has seen the movie, this just helps paint a visual. I was getting a little worn out by the scenery however. It was the weight on my back and the hard worn trail, I believe, getting to me. After a while the landscape was a bit monotonous. I had tried to take many photos, but the great contrast in lighting made it hard for my photos to turn out desirable. I was ready to get to the ocean!

Before we emerged from the forest, we passed by an area called Fern Canyon. It was all according to plan. Fern

Canyon is about a mile hike through a level canyon about as wide as a two lane road. It wanders along Home Creek, and a number of times we hopped over or walked in the creek. We also had to maneuver over a few fallen trees. The canyon walls were about a couple stories high and were sprouting with moisture-loving ferns. In some breaks between the ferns' adornment, I could see water dripping down the canyon walls and mosses hugging tight. It was a unique natural feature but limited in display. The canyon narrowed us in, inhibiting our view of the rest of the forest, and all we could see was green, green ferns, and more green ferns.

Then….

The Pacific Ocean! We ran out onto the sand, dropping our bags and taking off our boots. The hike, though not much to report on, had taken a major part of the day. The excitement to have finally made it to the ocean was real.

I changed into my swim trunks and envisioned a refreshing swim, but when my feet hit the water, I knew I would not be swimming at all. It was very cold! That was enough.

Looking back, I noticed how the forest had abruptly ended and the landscape turned immediately into sand. There was no cohesive graduation of landscape. It was drastic. We had come out of a low line of the forest, but stretching ahead and behind I saw the forest rise and fall on sandy bluffs. Many of the bluffs were covered in greenery with sand patches peeking out. We were in a very wide inlet of the ocean, but we could not see where the ends of the bluffs curved, because the ocean sprayed a fine cool mist, cloaking the landscape. And if it was not spraying it was creeping up from the ocean, giving a hazy appearance. This was not the fun-in-the-sun, warm summer for which I may have been hoping for. This was a damp chilling beach with sand of a dismal gray color. It was a large beach, and I imagined one could walk out very far into shallow water with such a low gradient. The sand here was very fine, except for the patches of small rock and shell shards that showed up every so often.

I realized swimming or basking in the sun just wasn't going to happen, but I did recline on the moist gray sand for a while. Zeke went out into a shallow sliver of ocean, and a large wave came rolling in and really got him good.

I was observing, taking in my surroundings. The way the light hit the water with the reflection of misty opaque sky made the ocean appear as silver– a long stream of tinsel with crescendoing waves of white. After a brief rest, we carried on, boots in hand. There was one more mile south to hike on the sand before arriving at Golden Bluffs Campground. It was a strenuous final stretch, having backpacked for so long, and now our feet were sinking into sand with each step. At some points I walked in the tire grooves of a jeep or some vehicle that had previously been out on the sand. Unfortunately those tracks had adulterated the otherwise wild and natural landscape.

Up ahead we started to see tent domes sticking up among wispy beach grass. Some of the blades were green but most were golden. Here we were at Golden Bluffs! It did indeed look just like it did in the magazine. I had seen this campground in a Sunset Magazine edition on *The West's Best Camping*. When I saw it printed on those pages I knew I wanted to be there in person. I had arrived!

After passing by a number of occupied campsites, we located ours, which I had reserved in advance. All the other campsites had vehicles beside them. We seemed to be the only ones who hiked here. When we reached our campsite, we were surprised to find that it too was already occupied. This has happened to me before in my camping adventures. It's usually some couple not following the rules and feeling a great sense of entitlement. But this instance was very different, for it was not occupied by any human at all. No. It was occupied by an elk— a large bull with a full rack of antlers. It was munching on the wispy grass. We approached. It did not budge nor was it phased. It looked up once to quickly dismiss us and keep eating. It had no cares. "Excuse me, but

I have a reservation for this site," I said. He didn't acknowledge me.

   We plopped our backpacks down by the cement picnic table. The elk was about a mere twelve feet from us, right alongside the area to pitch the tents. It was clear the elk was in no hurry to move, so *maybe we shouldn't be either*. He was by no means threatening. I took out some beef jerky and Gatorade from my backpack. We sat there on the ground, propped against the seat of the picnic tables, just watching our personal elk. I thought we might as well get situated for this spectacle. I had pulled out our hors d'oeuvres and embraced this exquisite evening of dining, oceanside, with an elk at the Golden Bluffs. How fancy!

   When it came time to set up our tents, he was right there with us. After my tent was set I went over to the beach– the pure natural beach of the Northern California

coast. The sun was starting to set, and it was indeed very golden, making the dismal gray sand turn gold, and the bluff behind me, by the tree line, glow. The wispy grass surrounding our tents was radiant. I wanted to enjoy the moment more than I actually did. Everything looked so warm and elegant, but I was freezing cold. I was wearing a flannel shirt over my cut-off and a pair of sweatpants. It was certainly not enough. I wrapped and held my arms close for warmth. I reclined on the sand, not long, but enough to notice the dual tone of the sunset, gold and blue. It was not like the sunset at Lake Tahoe. This was a very distinct two tone sunset, but no two sunsets are the same, just as no two lives are the same.

Back at the campground, we were searching out firewood and noticed our elk had moved on to another site. An
obviously drunk camper walking around offered us one of
his bundles of firewood. "We'll take it." It was enough to
make a fire to heat our cans of chicken noodle soup. After
eating and enjoying the warmth of the fire for a bit, and going over the next day's plan with Zeke, I then secured the
fly of my tent, to shield from any bit of cold and wind, and I
crawled inside. I nestled myself into my sleeping bag, atop
the sand beneath my tent floor, and fell asleep.

# Tide Pools and Tsunamis

We had survived a cold night on the sands of the Pacific coast, and I was ready to start moving and get out of here. When I emerged from my cocoon, unzipped my tent, and peeled back the fly, I saw none other than our resident elk here to grace us with his presence once again. I suppose he liked to come around meal times, although we certainly did not feed him.

At the picnic table, both Zeke and I were sitting, wrapped in our sleeping bags, shivering, and pitifully sneaking our hands out from under our sleeping bags to pinch off a bit of Clif Bar or down a gulp of Muscle Milk. That was our breakfast.

It was a cold gray misty morning at Golden Bluffs. The wind was whipping, the ocean waves were fiercely crashing, and nothing was quite golden this morning. The place was rather hostile to our presence, so I did not want to waste any time in getting packed up and back on the trail. We had taken a different route back through the Redwoods. It was the official "Tsunami Evacuation Route," as one sign proclaimed, but it was also known as the Miner's Ridge Trail on the park map. We hiked it for 4.1 miles out to the car at Prairie Creek Redwood State Park. The trail was rather un-notable, especially after the experiences and observations of the day prior. My mind was set on the objective: get to the car and onto the next leg of the adventure. While we were hiking, we came across a young couple on the trail. Zeke knew them! They were from Auburn, the small town of about 1,600 that Zeke's family is from in southwestern Kentucky. They chatted for a few minutes.

When we reached the car, we drove twelve miles south to the Kuchel Visitor Center. We had already been to one visitor center the day prior, but I like to visit all the visitor centers at a given park. I suppose it's the fear of missing out on something. Plus, this was the visitor center with the park film which is a staple in my visitation of a National Park. I also needed to get a pin to add to my collection and a park sticker for my summer's Nalgene bottle. There, Zeke bought himself a brown Redwood cap. I was glad, for it was a sign he enjoyed the adventure enough to buy a souvenir. I was very concerned about Zeke having a good time. I had convinced him to come on this trip and spend the money to fly to California, and I wanted to make sure it was well worth it for him. Also, all my previous National Park adventures were so special to me. I wanted him to find that joy and fulfillment which I found in my park adventures.

I admit, after finding it very difficult to connect with people after moving to Kentucky, I gave up at trying to include others. I was an outsider, with no real family connections there. Everyone around me was already established in their family and social circles. I could not break in. *I will go do things by myself and enjoy things by myself,* and I did. I had many valuable experiences at the time, but I had been convicted recently to try and share my life again. I found my life to be very rich in experiences which I so desired to share. If I was married, I'd naturally share these experiences with my wife, but, being single, more effort was needed.

One day I was listening to the song "Better Get to Livin'" by Dolly Parton, and it really spoke to me on the topic of sharing my life. It was a pivotal moment in which a paradigm shifted. I was going to intentionally try and share my life again. This resolve was very uplifting for me. My revelation in the desert days prior confirmed this. I can open the book of another and write into his or her story tales of cherished adventures, rich in meaning. I also had the successful experience of sharing a portion of another trip, which I discuss in my first book, with my friend Dom, in Bryce Canyon. I hoped I could help provide Zeke with such a rich experience, but to some extent I was very naive, for much of this ability was out of my control. I should not have carried this weight. Everyone experiences everything differently. Nothing is quite the same for everyone. It was all so well-intentioned, but I was carrying a self-imposed expectation that became a burden to me, which in return became harmful. It would soon become increasingly apparent.

After our detour to the visitor center, we headed northward in the Redwoods by vehicle, parallel to the ocean, on our way to Crescent City and the northernmost unit of the Redwood National and State Parks: Jedediah Smith Redwoods State Park. There we would camp at Mill Creek

Of course there were places on the way to see. One
of the first stops was at High Bluff Overlook. It was one of
the most memorable views of this whole summer's trip. As
the name suggests, we were high up on a rocky craggy bluff,
which used to be part of an old mine quarry. We were 307
feet above the ocean looking down and around at a truly
expansive view of the ocean. We could see the small sandy
shore lines winding around the Redwood Forest and rough
rocks sticking up from the ocean, some as quite enormous

boulders but miniaturized by how high up we were. We could also see breaking waves all over, not just against the shore but out in the blue expanse and against the protruding rocks. The ocean was very much alive and busy in all corners. To add to the beauty, the sky had turned a rich blue, except for the condensation lifting from the forest behind us. With a mostly clear sky, the ocean reflected an array of blues from a light turquoise to a shallow royal. I was really taken away with all the movement of the ocean and all the hundreds of independent waves crashing. I took out my camera to capture a video of the display. I was still using a point-and-shoot. I had not fully graduated to a smartphone.

I then sat there in silence, trying to be still, calm, and quiet for a moment, really taking in the scenery. I had quite an unusual vacancy of thought and would close my eyes, listening to the sounds of the ocean, feeling the warm sun on my face, and then open them every once-in-a-while to be surprised by the view again.

It's not any fault of his own, but with Zeke there was just a different dynamic than what I was used to in such beautiful moments. Typically I'd find myself in places like this, of such beauty, alone with God, communing with Him, speaking with Him. Maybe it was simply Zeke's presence, and adding to the fact that he didn't share the same faith, or that he was talking on the phone with his mom, interrupting the serene, but I was not connecting spiritually as I so desired. I suppose I wanted to be alone.

We continued in the car down to Crescent Beach which was beautiful but not too different from the beach we had camped on, minus a much busier road just behind us. We were there only briefly before we made our way into the town harbor. By description it may not sound charming, but in my memory it is held as just that. There was a simplicity and sincerity about the place that added a great ease. It was not trying to be anything other than what it was. It was a blue-collar harbor and small shipping port. There were lots of small boats in the bay next to a bunch of fishing crates, a U.S. Coast Guard Station, and a small lighthouse. Just across from all that, inland, was a trailer park next to a Super 8 hotel and a local seafood restaurant. That was all on one side. On the other side of Highway 101 was purely the Redwood Forest, which was boxed in on the other side by the Indian reservation.

We were both very hungry, and although I would have just been fine breaking open the snack box in the trunk, Zeke wanted a full proper meal at the restaurant, The Fisherman's, and so we went. It was nice to sit down and have a full meal. Zeke got some oysters, and I got salmon. Our booth was next to a cold window where we could look out and see all the boats in the harbor. There were also dozens of tiny little red ants on the windowsill which kept creeping onto the table as we ate.

Zeke bought my dinner which was very nice of him. It was a bit of relief, as I was starting to get concerned about money. Through some instances already, I was learning it was going to cost more to travel with Zeke. I was used to traveling very economically. I'd survive on Clif Bars, jerky, and dried nuts and berries for days. I would rarely pay for a sit down restaurant on an adventure like this, especially if I wasn't really in between parks but really still situated around one locale.

I think it may be interesting for the record to note how much my trips have cost in the past. My last three summers of National Park adventures, each a month long, cost about $700 each. That includes plane tickets, a rental car, accommodations, gas, food, camping gear, souvenirs, and everything else. That gives a picture of how I travel. It may not sound like a lot for a month of travel, but that actually was a lot of money for me at the time. I had an excellent credit score, and so each summer I opened a credit card with an introductory 0% interest rate for one year. I'd charge everything to that card, and then over the course of about four to five months, I'd pay it off. In the process I'd make some money by receiving cash back rewards. My $700 big summer adventures may sound quite surprising, but it goes to illustrate a few things. First it shows the state of the economy just a few years ago, prior to our grand inflation per Democrat leadership and policies. Then it hints at the salary by which public school teachers live on in Kentucky. Lastly, perhaps it shows how economical of a traveler I was. I have wanted to explain this and be transparent, because I have heard on more than one occasion, "I don't know how you afford to travel so much." Well, it takes planning, roughing it, skipping meals, and sleeping outside. The years of these first four National Park adventures were also lean financial times for me. I was paying off student loan debt from undergrad, paying for mandatory graduate school to keep my job, and paying off medical bills. But where there is a will, there is a way. I digress.

After dinner we parked further in the harbor and walked around in the tide pools. It was quite fun and just fascinating to the curious childhood marine biologist that evidently lived in both of us. We carefully moved from rock to rock, looking down in shallow pools of all sorts of sea urchins, crustaceans, and occasional dark pink and white-laced sea stars. We also walked a peninsula to Battery Point Lighthouse. It was a short stubby little thing, but quaint nevertheless with its little red roof and stout appearance. Around the lighthouse were some rocky cliffs adorned with patches of short pink wildflowers, which had to be rather tough. We climbed around the small rocks cliffs and at one point stopped to observe some pelicans and another sea-

bird, the murre, which was feeding and would nose dive into the water, emerging a few seconds later to do it all again. It was quite entertaining to watch, and its maneuvers were somewhat comical, brandishing a few laughs.

As we walked back to the car, I noticed two dramatic government-issued signs. One was bright red and displayed, "Danger, Deadly Waves at Any Time." Another had five tips for surviving a Tsunami, complete with diagrams and a footnote stating that "cold water can paralyze."

Warning signs for Tsunamis were new to me. That's not something we see in Kentucky or anywhere in the Midwest. We do have some signs labeling tornado shelters however, and I remember the signs about earthquakes from my time in Mexico City, but never Tsunamis.

       After our enjoyable and chill evening in the harbor, we stopped at a local Safeway supermarket to buy a few snacks. We purchased some cherries. This was starting to become a thing here on the fringes of the Pacific North-west. Cherries would become increasingly popular and prevalent in Washington. We also bought the goods to treat ourselves with s'mores over a campfire that evening.

Mill Creek was a nice wooded campground. As we were setting up camp, Zeke became frustrated trying to blow up his air mattress. I had bought these cheap eight dollar air mattresses at Walmart when I arrived out West, but I didn't bother buying a pump. I'm always just used to using my lungs. Yes, it's an inconvenience, but as already evidenced, I was a cheapskate. I'll admit it does take a long while to pump up an air mattress with the power of one's own lungs, and it does make me light-headed. I have to take frequent breaks, but it saves money. I don't think Zeke was quite ready for this, and I hadn't evolved in person and character to the point where I could afford the convenience of an air pump.

So when Zeke was done setting up his part of camp, he was done with everything. He was done with the air mattress, done with me, and done with the day. A tsunami of sueño came over him, and he went right to sleep. It was still early in the evening, and I wanted to maybe go explore a trail near the campground, build a fire, tell stories, and make s'mores. I let him sleep for a while, then I tried to wake him. I documented in my journal that I tried to wake him six times. He would not get up. In retrospect, I under-stand that he was probably just very tired, especially after our two days of backpacking in the Redwood Forest, and it was likely he didn't sleep too well on the brisk Pacific coast.

However, I internally was starting to become frustrated with him. Rest is important, but at the moment I viewed it as him wasting an entire evening. To strengthen my case against him, I started thinking how difficult it was to get him moving in the mornings. The poor guy was tired, but I was full of energy. These sort of trips energize me, and I'm always about packing in as many experiences as I can and seeing as much as I can. Regardless, I resolved that I wouldn't wait for him any longer. I built a campfire solo, and I made s'mores by myself and then went into my tent. I documented that I had hiked 41.2 miles so far on this summer's adventure including a total of 12.5 miles with Zeke. I then turned off my headlamp, let my head sink into my pillow and drifted off to sleep. I had a good evening at the ocean but had a pestering thought that Zeke would probably be somewhat upset with me, making the s'mores without him, but what could I do? He wouldn't respond. I still hoped he was having a good trip.

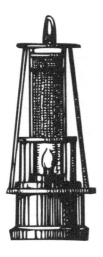

# Oregon Caves and the Creepiest Park Ranger

*He's going to kill us. This is it.* Who? This park ranger. *He is sick, unhinged.*

We were in the pitch black underground of Oregon Caves National Monument. He made the small group of us on his tour extinguish the candles in our lanterns, and now he was talking about the ills of humanity and death. I didn't think he was trying to be playfully spooky at all, for it seemed no conscious effort was pointed in that direction. His gloom seemed to emit so naturally from some deep-seated bitterness and hatred within his soul.

I didn't trust him from the start. There was something impersonal and antisocial about him. He couldn't relate to the guests. He didn't know how to interact with the common pleasantry of any ordinary human, and my spirit was not at ease. I could sense discontentment within him and a resentment towards humanity. It was so evident, and now, at the end of this tour, I felt things had really built to a climax. This would be a sick man's ideal moment to take his disdain for humanity out upon us all, brandishing his weapon of choice.

Let's backtrack. How did I end up in such a situation? Well, in the morning my travel buddy Zeke and I packed up camp at Mill Creek Campground in the Redwood Forest in Northern California. Zeke was not mad I made s'mores after he went to sleep so early the evening before. It was a new day. Today's car trip was only about sixty miles, so we had time to piddle and peruse. We started our day briefly by visiting the Tolowa Dunes State Park next to Crescent City. Essentially it was more beach access and nothing too distinct from what we had already seen, that it doesn't even reside much in my memory. After visiting the dunes, we stopped for some breakfast at Jack-In-the-Box to appease Zeke's ravenous hunger. Though a small skinny guy, he always was the hungry one. Then, after a quick breakfast, we were on our drive into the forests of Oregon on our way to Oregon Caves National Monument and Preserve.

This would be my first trip to Oregon, and I really did not have any preconceived notions about the state other than I just imagined it as a lot of moist, mysterious and deep, pine forests. I was right. I had no judgment on the people. No stereotypes had ever presented themselves to me. I didn't and still don't know what it means to be an Oreganian. The only place in Oregon I had heard of prior was Portland. It had recently become the epicenter for Millennial hipster culture and the Leftist's ideal progressive city. It had received much attention by the media as the place to be. I didn't pay close attention to all that, but I heard the buzz in passing, and I learned of the city eventually showing its true colors. I have learned through my travels that you should never judge a state by its big cities. Chicago is not a reflection of the rest of Illinois, Louisville is antithetical to the rest of Kentucky, and I feel the pain of rural and small town Californians whose reputation is so tarnished by the state's big cities.

That being said, we were nowhere near a big city. We were in the wilds, driving through Klamath National Forest, along the border of California and Oregon. I did feel the need to stop and take my picture by the "Welcome to Oregon" sign to add to my ever-growing collection of state welcome signs. At one point we stopped at a wayside National Forest river access called Myrtle Beach. There were some big boulders on which people were climbing up and jumping off into cold water. Zeke wanted to partake. I knew I would not. It was way too cold for me, and cold water is just something my body doesn't handle well at all. It has no appeal to me, for I turn white and blue and shiver to the greatest extremes. In contrast, I love the heat. Stick me in the scorching desert sun at 120 degrees and I'll revel in it, well at least for a while, until I pass out, but we know that's another story.

It was pleasant and peaceful to sit on the rocky shore of the river within this grand forest this young morn-

ing. Its water was super clear and pure. There was little care this morning, and no pressure on time, so I simply watched the others do flips and dive into the water from the tall rocks.

When we departed and finally reached the turn off to

Oregon Caves National Monument, the road narrowed into a winding, slithering little thing going upwards. One big feature of the monument is the historic Oregon Caves Chateau circa 1934. I had booked a room there far in advance, before I knew Zeke was even coming on this trip. Luckily this room, although small, would be just big enough to accommodate us both. From the outside I admired this dark, elegantly rustic gable roofed masterpiece. It was tucked in the forest alongside a small waterfall and babbling brook which actually ran inside the building. We followed the small wood -railed path that led to the lobby. I loved it. It was so picturesque.

I very much favor the idea of being in a place and leaving the car behind, and this was one of those places. Here we had our accommodations, dinner, trailhead, and the cave all at our disposal. The lobby, though quite large,

Oregon Caves Chateau

felt quite intimate in its very inviting aura. It was "L" shaped. Towards the front was a big stone fireplace with a large pile of chopped wood next to it. Placed throughout the lobby were leather couches, floor lamps, and rustic end tables. An old brown piano stood on dated forest green textured carpet. Through the large old windows, light filtered through the pine trees and into the lodge. The place certainly fit the classic style of the National Park architecture movement, which I've written about before, in which the design aims to blend into the natural environment. Everything about this lodge fit its surrounding forest just perfectly. It's character was just right. At the front desk a friendly attendant checked us into the room, reaching into an old-fashioned wooden cubby behind the desk for a skeleton key.

When we set out to locate the room, it was quite an interesting maneuver. The room was on the very top floor of the Chateau. It required going up the central staircase but then up an additional few flights up stairs, walking to the end of a hallway, making our way across a sitting area and game room, and there at the far end of that common space was a small door which looked to be just a closet. Any casual visitor would never have known there was a staircase here which led to a room, but we opened the door and found our own private small staircase which wound up to this attic room. We had this secret nook high above the Chateau. It felt very much like something out of a book, and it would be a great break from sleeping in the cold damp northern woods.

The attendant at the desk said this was the last sum-

mer to stay in the Chateau in its present state before it would undergo a major renovation and remodeling. The room was certainly dated but in the most charming of ways. Its bathroom features and lighting seemed to be straight out of the 1930s. I felt privileged to be able to be among one of the final people to see the place in its original state and also sad that it wouldn't ever be the same. I like old things, such as decor and amenities, as long as they are kept up. It may be the historian in me that loves the novelty of being passed back in time. Sadly, I learned later that the Chateau closed indefinitely after this summer. Funds and gumption never surfaced to keep it running, despite it being on the National Register of Historic Places. It still could one day open again.

Zeke and I were in the room briefly enough to drop

off our bags, use the bathroom, and scarf down some cherries we had bought the evening before. Then we were off to our first cave tour. We simply walked a few yards outside the front of the Chateau to the small entrance of the cave. I enjoyed the plaque that read "Oregon Caves National Monument set aside by President Taft July 12, 1909." The fall before I visited Taft's home in Cincinnati, Ohio and later learned he was a distant relative of mine. I like being able to connect the dots and locations of people in U.S. history.

The tour was the standard "Discovery Tour." It was very pleasant. The cave was not enormous like Carlsbad Caverns, but had way more character than something like Mammoth Cave, which is very uniform in appearance. Oregon Caves is more miniature in size and wanders and winds through a labyrinth full of a plethora of cave formations and glistening flowstones. When we finished the tour we had a quick turnaround before our second cave tour. I had

booked the Lantern Cavern Tour for the novelty of such an experience. Between the two tours I thought to squeeze in a short hike. It became more of a run, however. We completed the paved Cliff Nature Trail. It led to a beautiful lookout point which presented the pine forest stretching out over the Siskiyou Mountains. It actually resembled the Smoky Mountains in the Appalachian chain in terms of the height of the mountains and how the pine forest just rolls over them. On the way back to the cave there was a friendly dear walking right on the path in front of us. It was not startled but actually turned around and started to approach us. I suppose it was looking for a handout. I'm sure it would have eaten out of our hands.

After our quick run of a hike, we were back in the cave on the Lantern Cave Tour guided by the creepiest of park rangers. There was something so unsettling about this ranger's persona from the beginning. Something was not right. He told dark tales of people dying in caves and about numerous wars that went on in the world while here this cave sat in silence untouched. He talked about how people during the Revolutionary War and Civil War hid out in caves. I'm not going to question the validity or the extensiveness of that, for it's irrelevant. However, he spoke about how people remained in caves because of fear of the world. He talked about how the cave is quiet and peaceful, but the world outside is full of hate and war. He talked about God, and how for ages people were disillusioned by a belief in him. "God is not real," he claimed. "It's a tale to control the masses and keep them living in darkness," he explained. To summarize things, in his beliefs there was no God, no good in humanity, and we were all trapped in the darkness. "There is no light. There is no hope in the world," he said. My heart began to race. *He's going to pull out a gun and murder us all right about now,* I thought.

Then…there was an intense moment of silence. Panic was setting in…

He opened the cave door. "…Then there came the light of science," he said. "Science takes us from darkness to light. Science illuminates our misunderstandings of the world and our fear about life. So as we walk out of this cave, walk into the light of science."

*Phew! Get me out of here! I will gladly walk into the light after being in this dark cave with this creep! Get me out into the Chateau or out into the forest.* I rushed out of there and took a deep breath. That was a stressful fight or flight moment, and I had a lot of thoughts and feelings to express.

First off, I found it extremely audacious to take this analogy of light amidst darkness and apply it to science, while denouncing and attempting to demean the religious faith of so many. It would be one thing to simply use an analogy of light and darkness with science, but to take it a step further and walk on the religious faith of others is grossly disrespectful, especially given that the analogy is so prevalent in the Bible and immersed in religious faith.

I would expect someone representing the United States as a U.S. National Park Service ranger, preserving the nation's natural and cultural treasures, to have a bit more sensitivity than to flippantly disregard the deeply held religious beliefs of so many people of the country he serves.

Going back to the 8th century B.C., the prophet Isaiah, in reference to Jesus' coming, wrote, "The people walking in darkness have seen a great light; on those living in the land of deep darkness a light has dawned," (Isaiah 9:2). Then when the prophecy of Isaiah was fulfilled and Jesus walked this earth, Jesus is quoted in the Gospel of John saying, "I am the light of the world. Whoever follows me will never walk in darkness, but will have the light of life," (John 8:12). Also in Scripture we read, "This is the message we have heard from him and declare to you: God is light; in him there is no darkness at all. If we claim to have fellowship with him and yet walk in the darkness, we lie and do not live out the truth. But if we walk in the light, as he is in the light, we have fellowship with one another, and the blood of Jesus, his Son, purifies us from all sin," (1 John 1:5-10). These are just a few of the Bible's references to light.

The religious analogy of light is certainly deeply entrenched in religious faith, and it does raise a lot more questions than the scientific one. It's multifaceted. What does the Scripture mean by light? And why is Jesus described as light? And at a more personal level, how is Jesus light to me? I did not appreciate this ranger's assault on faith, but I take it as a challenge to examine my own beliefs. I would conclude, God is light, the source of all clarity and Truth. Science can be a search for Truth, but is a human operation and can get things wrong, and even when science gets things right, it points to God.

Freed from the cave and the most worrisome of

rangers, I enjoyed the rest of my time at Oregon Caves National Monument and Preserve and the delightful stay at the Chateau, and I'd have some food for thought and the impetus to unpack some of my beliefs about what is light in the philosophical and spiritual sense.

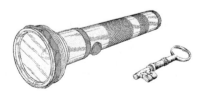

# What is Light?
## God, Science, and Emerging from the Cave

What is the light? Many people are familiar with the famous Hank Williams song, "I Saw the Light." As the first stanza goes, "I wandered so aimless, life filled with sin, I wouldn't let my dear Savior in, Then Jesus came like a stranger in the night, Praise the Lord, I saw the light." A subsequent verse talks about coming to Jesus like a blind man regaining sight. There are countless songs of faith that have reference to light. Those of us who grew up in Sunday school are probably familiar with the classic song, "This Little Light of Mine" and how we are "gonna let it shine." References to seeing the light, and shining that light, are intertwined in not only American culture but universally in regards to God and faith.

I was at Oregon Caves National Monument and Preserve, and I had just finished up a lantern cave tour in which there was an extremely unsettling park ranger who was equating emerging from a cave into the light of day like mankind leaving behind religious faith and walking into the eye-opening light of science. I had to challenge this, as for a while I had entertained the thought that emerging from a cave into the light of day is best served as an analogy of coming to Jesus and realizing there is so much more to life and existence than the darkness we often toil around in.

The Bible is full of passages in reference to light. In John 8:12, Jesus calls himself "the light of the world" and says how his followers will "not walk in darkness." I think this is telling not only of God's character but of our own nature as well. Without Him we are left with nothing but to walk in darkness. Like Hank Williams, we wander aimlessly chasing the wrong things. We are lost in that dark cave of existence. Then comes God as light, providing us clarity, direction, and vision. We can see purpose in life as He leads us out of the cave into an existence so rich in meaning and abundant in spirit, more than we could have ever imagined. When Jesus also says we will "have the light of life," I believe that is not only a reference to clarity, direction, and vision, but also great joy. Light is one thing and life is another. When they are combined together, joy is an outstanding by-product.

In 1 John when we read, "God is light: in him there is no darkness at all," I think the Scripture also uses light to show the great contrast between the perfectness of God and depravity in His absence. He is the direct opposite of the darkness, of the evil so persistent in the world. He is unblemished, without a shadow of sin, incapable of it. It is He and His truth that brings forth the distinction of good and evil. Anything antithetical to God is darkness. Anything of God is of the light. He is the source of all truth and meaning in the world. Darkness is chaos and lostness, a void and emptiness. God reveals meaning, purpose, direction, fulfillment, and wholeness. His light also helps us grow in spiritual maturity, just as a plant needs light to grow, so our spirit needs God's light. If there was an absence of light in our universe, there would be no life on earth, just as without God our souls would not be. He is the source of life.

Another very important aspect of the light of God is that it helps us understand sin and our independent hopelessness. Without God revealing himself, giving us His light, we would not know of our darkness, of our sorry state. We would not know there was salvation to be had. We would be blind slaves of the darkness. But God, who in no way is obligated to reveal Himself to us, through love and the blood of Jesus Christ, revealed His light, thus creating a contrast, allowing us to see we need a savior. Not only does He create this contrast, illuminating our path to salvation, but He also gives us that light to carry as well.

As Christians we believe God's Holy Spirit dwells in God's true followers, and that the Holy Spirit is of the light of God. That's why we read in the Gospel of Matthew, when Jesus is talking to his followers during the Sermon on the Mount, "You are the light of the world. A town built on a hill cannot be hidden. Neither do people light a lamp and put it under a bowl. Instead they put it on its stand, and it gives light to everyone in the house. In the same way, let your light shine before others, so that they may see your good deeds and glorify your Father in heaven," (Matthew 5:14-16).

This light is God, is of God, and is in his followers. This light serves many purposes, and different parts of Scripture focus on different aspects. Some may attribute one specific belief to light, whether it be God the Father, Jesus, the Holy Spirit, the Christian, truth, or salvation. I believe, informed by Scripture, that the light is actually only one thing with many aspects. God is light, and in Him are all these things. In Him is the truth, salvation, and the Holy Trinity with whom the Christian partners with to carry that light.

When Jesus calls his followers "the light of the world," I see it as the Christian channeling God's light, serving as a beacon in a dark world to draw others to the salvation of Jesus Christ. The person in search of truth, or even one whose heart remains open, will naturally be drawn to the light of God's people. He will see this light in others, be drawn to it, only to learn that the light is the light of God beaming through the Christian. The light is not a product of the Christian, but the Christian merely serving as a conduit for God's powerful light.

We are also warned in Scripture that not everyone comprehends this light. No one is too far from the redeeming power of Christ, but those who succumb to darkness, subscribe to it, and are ruled by it, cannot understand the light. Secularism certainly does not have an understanding of it. Those consumed by their own selfish desires and lusts of this world don't get it, for it is written, "In Him was life, and the life was the light of men. And the light shines in the darkness, and the darkness did not comprehend it," (John 1:5).

We live in a world where many people have become hostile to God, have elevated themselves to the center of focus, and have replaced God with other gods. Man himself, too, wants to be his own god. This is a characteristic of humanity's own nature. When man follows that path, putting himself first or false gods first, he sells himself immeasurably short and lives a life depraved and in darkness, whether he fully realizes this or not. Some surely don't realize this at all. They have lived in a cave all their life, unaware of the existence beyond the cave. Others wander in the cave, and their soul does not rest, because they know there is more. They are in search. They know there is something beyond the cave.

I am so blessed to understand this light and to have this light. I know the light of God is so radiant. The clarity, the truth, the guidance, the salvation, the joy is so real, so powerful, so convicting, so life-giving. It makes any sapling on a nurse log become the strong unwavering tree in the forest. It casts beautiful, rich, wonderful colors in one's sunset. It illuminates a path out of the forest in the darkness of night, out of the cave into the full light of His glory.

I do not boast of myself at all when I say this, for this is not of me. No, rather I boast in Him. It is all God, and I desire for His light to be stronger in my life. I want

His light in my life to guide people to Him. I know by my own efforts I always fall short from being the light God so desires for me. His desire for me is bigger than I could ever imagine, but I live by His mercy. I must strive to draw closer to Him, to let His Spirit dwell more richly within me, for He is the light alone.

I feel sorry for the man who replaces God with science. I am not anti-science, but I do warn of making science a God. Science does not have all the answers for life and the human condition. Science does not fulfill man's spirit. Man's ability to perform science is a great gift and a great tool. It has done so much good for humanity, clearly myself included. But science is also a human study, a set of procedures made by man to serve his purposes. To rob the analogy of light from God and place it on science is just not justified nor appropriate by any means. Science can but scratch the surface of the questions we have about what is true. And we must always approach science critically and skeptically, because it has also contributed to a lot of evil in the world. Science proves itself to be wrong time and time again.

A hot button issue in the world today is race, especially in terms of racial injustices of the past. What is often not discussed is that it was a scientific "fact" that degraded some humans over others. In the 1800s it was science that had "proven" superiority and inferiority of races. Harvard's own Louis Agassiz was a great proponent of polygenism, using science and the then "scientific" study of craniology to claim human races were distinct species. Carolus Linnaeus of Sweden was a naturalist who was the father of such studies. His ideas were also propelled by Petrus Camper, a Dutch professor of anatomy. Johann Friedrich Blumenbach, a German scientist, also carried these studies on and invented the term "Caucasian," which was one of the many "scientific" terms used to distinguish the different species of humans. These scientists were no fringe individuals but authoritative voices of the scientific community at distinguished schools. Of course their science has been invalidated today, but we must acknowledge those once "scientific facts'" as a root of racism. Notice I said "a root" and not "the root" for there are many roots on the plant of racism, including pride, fear, and power... I acknowledge all of these, but science was also a major root and a driving justifier behind slavery. Few will ever discuss and acknowledge this, because to reveal this great flaw of the past, tarnishes the god of science whom many worship.

Unlike the light of science, the light of the true God never changes its facts. It has and is always consistent. It reveals to all men that they are all made in His image. We are equally inherently valuable and loved. There is no other "light" in this world that has done more to bring people out of oppression and injustice than the light we find in the Christian faith.

Yes, science when executed rightly can shed some light on some of our questions, and I am grateful for that, but even what science gets right is pointing us to the truth of God's light. He is the source and Creator of that truth. Sadly, the park ranger who emerged from the cave thinking he was walking into the light because of science, I believe sadly was just walking into another spiritual cave chamber. May one day he truly walk into "the light of life."

Just the spring prior to this visit to Oregon Caves, I was exploring an unmarked cave with Zeke back in western Kentucky. We were there for hours. We had grown accustomed to its cool darkness, the cold water rushing through it, and its gloom. It was fun exploring. I quite enjoyed being there, but finally emerging from the cave to the bright richness of spring in Kentucky, to the blooming trees and blossoming flowers, and the radiant sun, my senses had never been so incredibly overwhelmed! At that moment I thought, *this is what it's like coming to know God.*

So many people live life in the cave, unaware there is more, so much more! It also reminds me of a baby in the womb. It lives in that dark place. The womb is its world and existence, but then it's born and awesomely emerges into a whole new consciousness and greatness. It's from that concept Jesus talks about being spiritually born again. Whether it's emerging from a cave into the light of day, from a womb into the world, or from one door into another place, as John Muir taught me, these are all concepts reflective of a common Creator, designed to teach us truth and bring us to Him. May you find and walk into that Light.

# JUMPING IN CRATER LAKE

*I have to do this,* I thought. *I* felt I just had to jump into Crater Lake. I had come this far, but I was full of so much fear. I was staring down off a cliff into Crater Lake, into a seemingly endless abyss. Crater Lake has some of the clearest and purest water in the world. It's a massive lake at about five miles in diameter. With a casual glance the lake is a vibrant bright royal blue, but at the right angle, looking straight down into it, I could see the blue gradually grow deeper in transparency reaching an eternal darkness. The truth is it reaches about two thousand feet in depth. From up here, that seemed like an eternity. My eyes could follow little bubbles that traveled up from the depth, growing bigger as they wobbled and floated up to the surface. I have never in my life been able to see so deep into water. These little bubbles helped show the profundity of what I was looking into. It was unsettling.

I was certainly not alone on jumping into Crater Lake. This was the thing to do. There were dozens of other young people who were doing it, each one taking his or her own turn, and just about everyone reached the rim with hesitation. It wasn't a terribly high cliff, only thirty five feet. That's a little over two stories, but it was the shock of looking into it, and seeing an endless depth, that caused just about everyone to rethink matters.

*What if I don't come back up?* I questioned. The thought was irrational, I know, but it is what seeing such deep waters provoked. If I couldn't see into the water, if it was just murky, like most of the water in Kentucky, I would just have trusted the water to propel me back up. There never would have been a question, but here, something about seeing the depth of the water conjured up this incredible fear.

This one irrational thought wasn't the only fear. There were also two more aspects. Secondly, the temperature of the water was very cold. At the visitor center I learned it was about forty degrees today. That's very cold for water. Also, I had lost trust in myself as a swimmer. The summer prior, while visiting my brother Nathan in New York City, I visited Rockaway Beach at Gateway National Recreation Area on Long Island. I had seen some people jumping around on a sandbar out in the ocean. It didn't look far. *I could swim out there too.* I did and just barely made it. *That was strenuous.* When I lived in Houston, Texas, I went swimming everyday for exercise, and I had really built up my confidence as a swimmer, but it had been a while. My lungs were no longer in quite the swimming shape.

After a fun time of jumping around on the sand bar, it came time to swim back to the mainland, and that's when things got hairy. I felt as if my efforts were fruitless. I kept swimming but wasn't going anywhere. I didn't seem to be making progress. The ocean was just pulling me backward, and I began to panic. In my panic, my limbs grew stiff. I didn't think I was going to make it. It was quite an intense moment. At one point I decided to just give in and see how far it was to the ocean floor. I sank, and I hit rock bottom. It was not far off. So my strategy was to sink, hit the bottom, jump up for air, and gradually progress my way to the mainland. This seemed to be more effective and require less energy than trying to rotate my panic stricken limbs. When I made it to the shore, I collapsed on the sand in relief. This experience was traumatic. When I'd go swimming shortly thereafter in subsequent months, I'd find my heart racing as my mind took me back to that moment.

Now at Crater Lake National Park in Oregon, I knew this jump wouldn't involve much swimming afterward, maybe only fifteen feet back to the rocky shoreline, beside the cliff, but I was still traumatized by my incident in New York. *What if I freeze up in shock of hitting such cold water?* I'm sure I wasn't the only one with such questions. There was one teenage girl, who stood there for a good fifteen minutes. She'd inch her way closer to the rim, peer off it slowly, and cower back, taking a deep breath. Very few people approached the jump with boldness. A number of people, all young guys and girls, regularly offered for each other to cut in front of themselves and go first. I was one of them. "Oh, are you ready? Go ahead….You can go first… please." When someone did cut to the front, that person

would often look off the cliff edge and motion for the next person to go ahead. It was a bit of a pile up. When someone finally mustered up enough confidence to jump in, the rest of us cheered in great applause, for we understood it was a big deal and just what it took to do it. It was a great emotional feat of conquering a fear. We all felt it. We knew how strong that fear could be. It was encouraging, fun, and genuinely so pleasing to cheer each other on. There seemed to grow an instant camaraderie among the people here on this cliff on this June evening.

At one point I decided to just get out of the way. My nerves were only growing. I climbed down alongside the cliff to the water's edge and captured pictures of others jumping in. I captured Zeke's jump on video, and there was another young man whose picture I caught mid-air. His feet looked like they were resting on the mountains across the other side of the lake in the photo. I showed him the photo when he got out of the water. He really liked it and wanted a copy. He introduced me to AirDrop, which is something I never knew was possible before.

I just had to jump in the lake too. There were a few reasons. First, I knew this was a rare opportunity to over-come a fear, and every fear I overcome will make me a stronger person. There is nothing inherently dangerous about this. In all rational observation, deep down I knew I'd be fine. It was my own human instincts and irrational fear getting in the way. I was fully aware of this. Secondly, I ad-mit, I wanted bragging rights to say I jumped into Crater Lake. Thirdly, how could I ever live with myself knowing I was up there on the cliff's edge set out to jump into the lake but chickened out? I had to do this. I climbed back up there. I gave myself just a brief moment of hesitation, in which a man said to me, "If you start to drown I'll come rescue you, I promise." I guess that little bit of assurance was enough to green-light this endeavor, and I jumped.

Crater Lake seemed so wide and huge from my free-fall into it. It was too big, too intimidating. *What am I doing?!* I closed my eyes and hid behind the darkness of my eyelids. The cold mountain air ripped between my feet. I felt so vul-nerable, my little half-bare body exposed to the elements, engulfed in the air. I felt the strange sensation of having lost control. There was nothing I could do to stop that which was before me. There was absolutely no way to stop the fall, no turning back. I was at the mercy of gravity and the forces of nature, exposed and vulnerable. I thought by this point I should have reached the water, but I was still falling.

It was taking a while…but I was doing it! I was already proud of myself for facing my fear and already felt accomplished. I had launched myself off that cliff despite the most paralyzing of fears. If there ever is a chance to face a fear, do it. It's what we all must do to keep growing. Theodore Roosevelt, when talking about being a fearful child, once said, "There were all kinds of things I was afraid of at first, ranging from grizzly bears to 'mean' horses and gunfighters, but by acting as if I was not afraid I gradually ceased to be afraid." He also added, "The worst of all fears is the fear of living." I was living, jumping into Crater Lake!

*Okay, where is the water? Surely I should have hit the water by now,* I thought. *I guess I'm still falling.* I wondered just how cold this water was going to feel, and how deep I would fall into it. *What is it going to feel like? Will Zeke get a good picture of this? I'm glad I could share that one guy's photo with AirDrop. After this we will finish our drive and go check out the lodge. It'll be nice to rest there a bit before we go back to camp. Should we make a fire tonight or just go to sleep? Tomorrow we'll make our way to Mount Saint Helens and stay at a KOA. There are so many cool places left to visit on this trip. I'm hungry. I wonder what kind of food we can find around here. I wonder what kind of fish and creatures live in this lake. I wonder what lurks in its deepest depths. Is there something like the Loch Ness Monster in these waters? One day this will all be…*

*KAPLUNK!*

I was in Crater Lake.

Water was gurgling, bubbling, and ripping around my ears. I felt gravity suck me downward, pressure pound at my skull, and then I began to rise. *Surface, come quickly,* I begged.

*Don't take as long as that fall.*

Gasp! I made it. I opened my eyes and....

I panicked.

My knees locked up.

It was so cold. Too cold. I was numb.

I instantly knew I was not going to make it back to the shoreline. My presupposition was correct. Time for plan B! I didn't have one, but I was going to make one. I was not going to make a scene as to call over the man who promised to rescue me. How embarrassing that would be. Instead I flailed my way over to the craggy cliffside just below the jump-off. There was no real rock ledge or anything to provide footing, but somehow, with the greatest of Spiderman-like moves, I fastened my grasp and curled my toes onto that rock's face. *I will wait here until I catch my breath,* and so I did, and I survived. I was white, blue, shivering cold, slightly traumatized, exhausted, yet adrenaline racing, and I was a champion, I guess you could say. I'm glad I did it. It's a story to tell, but...never again!

## A Day's Journey Around Crater Lake

Before we arrived at Crater Lake National Park, the day had started off waking up at the Oregon Caves Chateau, tucked away in the woods, in our secret little attic space high up in the Chateau. There was no central air system in the Chateau, so I unlatched and swung open up one of the rustic windows in our attic to let the cool night air in. The room was pretty warm during the day, but by the next morning it had certainly cooled off.

We made our way down a few flights of stairs to the diner-style eatery on the main level. It too had its own vintage charm. It had probably not been touched much since the 1930s when the lodge was built, but maybe it was tweaked a bit in the 1960s or 70s to give it its distinct color palette of yellows, browns, yellowish-browns, and oranges. It had a dining counter with swiveling stools that snaked around. It was smaller but very similar to the one in Jackson Lake Lodge in Grand Teton National Park, the one in which the "cougars" bought me dinner. Here I feasted upon some buckwheat pancakes and bacon with a cup of coffee. This was the more economical dining option at the Chateau. Last night, feeling fancy, and knowing this was probably the only time I'd be out this way, I splurged, and Zeke joined me. We ate at the lower level dining room in which the bubbling brook from outside flowed into the dining room in an inlet of rocks.

I'll admit part of me felt guilty for spending so much on a meal, and dining on tablecloths and placemats, while camping during the rest of the trip and trying to be economical, but I also felt like for such an experience it was worth it. I had also planned on eating here, so the cost wasn't unexpected. At the time this was the most expensive meal I had ever purchased at around $30. I had braised pork with sautéed carrots, asparagus, mashed potatoes, and a side salad with dinner rolls. It was very savory and done just right.

Before we left the Chateau in the morning, I hopped on the piano bench in the lobby, and I left a tune for the old place, a song I had written on the piano as a teenager. The piano had been calling out to me every time I passed by, and so I finally responded.

Leaving the Chateau, we uneventfully traveled through the forests of Oregon, and, as we neared the small city of Grants Pass, I decided to browse the radio stations and see If I could get an idea of the local flair. In southeastern Kentucky I can tune into some bluegrass and Southern gospel stations with local news of who died and who got married. When I drove across the Navajo Nation I listened to traditional Navajo music in native tongue. When approaching Chicagoland, there is a wealth of Spanish language stations with a lot of *ranchera* music, indicative of its large Hispanic population.

The number of country music stations, I believe, is also very telling about the overall culture of a place. There are a lot of values embedded in most types of music. In the country genre there largely is a love for country, family, nature, the land, sentimentality, hard work, and blue collar grit. Rap music is another example, very telling about values. It overwhelmingly values pimping and prostituting, debauchery, carnal desires, stealing, raping, disrespecting authority, and killing. The prevalence of such stations in a particular region is a small glimpse into the overall and dominating cultural values. So what did I find in Oregon? Well, I landed on a yodeling station. What does yodeling tell me about the people? What values are embedded in the yodeling genre? I couldn't tell you, but my ears were fixated and pleased. What talent! *How does one even do that? Is yodeling a part of Oregonian culture? Are there little mountain yodelers atop the Cascades?* I still hadn't figured out Oregon and wasn't sure if this was an essential part of it.

After departing Grants Pass, we were traveling along Oregon's Rogue River, which flows western to the sea from its headwaters in the Cascades just next to Crater Lake. We were zipping along Highway 5, the Pacific Highway. We could see mountains ahead and heavy greenery and foliage along the highway, with a glance every once in a while of the river with its craggy natural embankments. When we split from Highway 5, we started to ascend and pine trees took over. They were not giant redwoods from days prior, but thick groves of moderate size pines standing perfectly straight and pointed on a dry, barren, and at times dusty ground.

When we arrived at the park, our first order of business was setting up camp. Crater Lake has two park villages, Mazama Village and the Rim Village. We were staying at Mazama, and we were not going to do any backtracking. We had a lot to see, for we only had one day to experience Crater Lake National Park. Mazama Village comes right after the park's entrance station, thus it was our first stop. The

campground was average, nothing remarkable, with large
flat pine needle-laded tent pads under pine trees. After we
set up camp we went to the visitor center, and from there
we had our first glimpse at the remarkable Crater Lake, but
I didn't want to give it too much attention right away. There
is an order of events for visiting a National Park, at least in
my book(s), quite literally. First I had to orient myself with
the park film to be able to better appreciate and understand
the vista before me. The visitor center was a small cabin,
half built of large chunks of rock, the other half of wood.
Next to the main room was a little side room with an ad
hoc set up with a television playing the film. I learned just
how Crater Lake was created by a volcano. To put it simply,
much simpler than the film's details, a large and powerful
volcanic eruption caused a crater, and then over time rain

Wizard Island

water and melted snow filled the crater, creating the lake. One of the many unique characteristics of Crater Lake is that it has no water flowing into it, making it one of the most pure natural bodies of water in the world. I was really fascinated how something so destructive and violent, such as a volcano, created a place now so beautiful and serene. There was a message here to unpack. There is a universal truth to be explored. I'd get back to that later.

From the visitor center we began the thirty-three mile Rim Drive around Crater Lake. We stopped at just about every wayside overlook. The lake is enormous with a six-mile diameter and about twenty miles of shore line. It is quite serene and truly is just a giant bowl. One can see the rocky and steep rim of the bowl all around and always look at the lake from a great distance above on the rim's tall cliff edges. The most striking feature of the lake is its color. It has the richest blue water I've ever seen. It's so bright, vibrant, deep and royal. Such a particular and unique color almost makes it look artificial, as if the water was dyed, like the color of those faux waterfalls of a mini-golf course of the 1990s or out of a cartoon. But, of course, I knew better than to think it was fake, and it wasn't tacky but beautiful in its surreal display.

Surreal is a word I've landed on to describe the place, for to be surreal something incorporates characteristics of reality combined with fantasy. Crater Lake, though very real, seems to incorporate elements of sheer fantasy. Even apart from simple visual observation, there are names given to the places in the park which give way to fantasy, such as Wizard

Island, Phantom Ship, Castle Point, and Wineglass. Even the visitor center and village buildings look rather fairy-tale-like, reminding me very much of Snow White's cottage.

We took a five-mile side trip from the rim, driving down Pinnacle Valley to an area simply called "The Pinnacles," where large sharp, pointed piles of gray and brown volcanic pumice stick up from the ground like the fingers of a giant beast reaching up to emerge from the depths of the earth. I had never seen anything quite like this before, although they did remind me a little bit of the hoodoos of Bryce Canyon. These did not, however, have the flat capstones as hoodoos. Rather these were pointed, like smooth delicate giant stalagmites. They also didn't have the warm orange and red colors of Bryce Canyon, but rather they were mostly a ghostly pale gray and actually not beautiful at all. They were rather ugly but in nature's most intriguing of ways.

Back on the Rim Drive a very notable stop was at the Phantom Ship Overlook. From here we looked out at the lake at just the right angle to see a small island that looked like an abandoned pirate ship. It had craggy rocks that pointed like the masts of a ship, and a few pines and shrubs adorning it, looking like seaweed or barnacles, as if it had been some sunken ship summoned up from the depths of Davy Jones' locker by some dark magic.

Along the drive we also stopped at the Cleetwood Cove Trail, a one-mile, very steep trail of dramatic switchbacks which led down to the cliff where I jumped into the lake. I was excited to get down to the lake and see this fan-

tastical water up close. So far I had only seen it from high above the lake on the rim. So in excitement I suppose I was walking quickly down the trail. Zeke complained I was walking too fast and then brought to my attention that he thought I always walked too fast and that I should be waiting for him. Initially I felt sorry and was more conscious of trying to walk with him instead of getting ahead, though this was nothing I was doing consciously, and by no means an indicator of me trying to put myself first, elevating myself to a position of superiority. It was just my sheer excitement propelling me forward and putting me ahead of him. This may seem like an unimportant detail, but I only note this because it was the first in a series of complaints, or at least the first I recollect in a pattern that started to develop. This pattern of complaining would eventually really get to me, but with that detail aside…

Crater Lake is by all means beautiful, but there is a very similar view from whatever side of the rim one is at. The terrain surrounding the lake is very uniform with its display of pine trees, rock and arid ground. Minus the novelty of the ghostly pinnacles, this park doesn't provide the

The Pinnacles

diversity which most National Parks do, with varying views, flora, and fauna. The attraction here is not much else other than Crater Lake itself. However, alone, the lake is a great treasure and worthy of the National Park title. I suppose if I had given us more time to spend in this park, we may have discovered more, and thus this view would change, but from my one day visit to the park, this was my impression.

The conclusion of our self-directed tour ended back, full-circle, at the Rim Village. I was looking forward to eating at the Rim Village Cafe. Some National Parks offer great food services, such as the Grand Canyon and Yosemite which have great cafeterias in giant scenic halls. Yellowstone has some really good options as well. Even Oregon Caves National Monument surprised with its Chateau. But at this point, I hadn't fully understood how food service works in the National Parks. Different parks have different contracted concessionaires. Some are small businesses, most are parts of giant conglomerates, and some are certainly better than others. Some are dedicated to the guest experience and quality. They have integrity. Others solely value profit and how to trick and trap the tourists to empty their wallets. This was one of the latter. In my first two National Park adventure books I was very careful not to criticize anything in relation to our beloved National Parks, but I have changed my approach. I believe through honesty and sincere critique about how these parks are managed, we can bring about improvement or preserve that which is good. The National Parks are our great treasures as American citizens. We should not let them become exploited and degraded, and therefore I speak honestly only out of my deep love for, and interest in, these places.

After Zeke and I disappointedly purchased some highly-priced cheap food, we went snooping around to find a place to sit down. We made our way to the second level which was probably used only for special events. It was largely an open space, but at the end of the room there was a couch and coffee table in front of a big window pristinely displaying before us Crater Lake. We found quite a scenic place to dine on our less than desirable food. Thus our dinner experience was redeemed by the view alone.

After we ate and enjoyed the view, we went to Crater Lake Lodge, another lodge on the National Register of Historic Places. It opened in 1915 and was similar in style to the outside of the Oregon Cave Chateau, except maybe

Crater Lake Lodge

three times bigger. Inside there was a lot of wood, giving a very cabin-like feel, especially with its exposed timber frames and large stone fireplace. But its lobby was small and not very notable otherwise. There we sat and rested for about an hour. I used the time to write a postcard to my parents, enter some of the day's events into my journal, and revel in the fact that I had overcome a fear and jumped into Crater Lake. We then went back to our campsite in Mazama Campground, and just like that our visit to Crater Lake National Park was coming to an end. The next day we would get up very early and make our way northward to Washington to Mount Saint Helens, another volcanic wonderland.

## How God's Story is Written Everywhere

The most meaningful take-away from my visit to Crater Lake National Park was not the memory of jumping into the lake itself, although that was a great moment of overcoming fear, nor was it the beautiful vistas now imprinted in my mind and in my photographs. Rather it was what I learned about the creation of the lake in the park film in the visitor center and how it relates to spiritual life.

Typically I'm not captivated with geological presentations on layers of rock, seismic activity, tectonic plates shifting, volcanic eruptions eons ago, etc. On some occasions those things can be interesting, but usually, right off the bat, I'm questioning the validity of the information presented when it all starts off talking about millions and billions of years ago. To the contrary, I believe the Earth to be rather young and that God designed it with the appearance of age.

Also, I believe the Earth was so violently shaken during the Great Flood in Genesis, that so many processes that would have taken, under normal conditions, millions of years, happened quickly in all the trauma.

Surely during the Flood volcanic activity was abundant. The Earth, while covered in stormy waters, shifted rocks dramatically, and sedimentary layers formed quickly, burying things rapidly. Nearly every National Park in the Southwest references a time when the Earth was covered in water or a massive flood. This should influence our understanding of rock layers, geology, and the Earth's age.

However, the geological park film about the physical creation of Crater Lake spurred fascination in other ways. The events that created the lake are believed to have taken place only 7,700 years ago, which would place it at right about the time of the Great Flood. I also learned that Crater Lake was actually Mount Mazama once upon a time. It is believed it stood as tall as 12,000 feet. Then it had a violent eruption spewing over nineteen miles of lava and sending ashes over one thousand miles, some landing in Alberta, Canada. When the volcano erupted, it left a giant cavity in the earth, a crater, which over time filled with melted snow and rain water to a depth of 1,943 feet, making it the nation's deepest lake. The National Park Service in their park brochure describe the volcano which created the lake as "catastrophic."

After learning about such a "catastrophic" event, now one can step outside the visitor center and see a serene, beautiful, mountain gem of a lake. It's pristine, vibrant blue,

and so enjoyed by many. I was captivated with the notion
that something so violent and destructive resulted in something so peaceful and beautiful. *There's a deeper message here,* I
knew. I had to channel my inner John Muir first to examine
how this concept of peace and beauty after destruction is
exhibited across creation. Is it a design element consistent
across existence or an isolated event? Then I could question
what God is teaching or revealing to us about Himself in all
this.

    The preliminary probing question I had to ask was,
*What other destructive things result in beauty?* I was immediately
taken back to my days of being very sick with a trifecta of
intestinal and digestive system destruction. I was battling
ulcerative pan-colitis, pancreatitis, and a bacterial infection.
At the time my body was withering away and wasn't even
breaking down food. I was malnourished and in extreme
pain, losing blood in large amounts. My plans for the future
were ripped away from me. The havoc it created in my life
was real, and as the National Park Service might say,
"catastrophic." But during this whole time of sickness, God
was doing immense work on me, putting me through the
refiner's fire, creating who I am, and teaching me reliance on
Him and trust in His goodness. I emerged stronger in every
way, physically, emotionally, and spiritually. I was also given
a new gratefulness for my life, my body, and the world
around me. After being confined to a hospital room, bed, or
exam table, too weak to move, I was now able to climb
mountains, summit scorching sand dunes in the Mojave,
jump into Crater Lake, and take in a deep breath of fresh

mountain air without pain. This all brought me great joy.

I was able to see profound meaning and beauty in life after the painful time of destructive sickness. Some struggle with coming to terms with the coexistence of God and suffering. *Why does God allow suffering?* After having been through much pain and grappling with the question myself, I don't. I do not believe God brought about the pain or suffering in my life at all, but I believed He used it. He redeemed it to bring about goodness and peace in my life. As Romans 8:28 says, "God uses all things for good for those who love Him and are called according to His purpose." I truly believe God can redeem anything to bring about goodness and spiritual growth, ultimately bringing Him glory. The overall message of Crater Lake was becoming clearer. It is one of the redemptive nature of God.

I then began to think about war, how terrible a thing it is, and how timeless it is in our fallen state of humanity. But then I considered how after war there always comes peace. We see this repeated through the ages. When right prevails, there is good that follows. The destruction of war is not a good thing. It is never desired by the righteous, but eventually it results in, or is redeemed for, peace.

We too, as followers of Christ, wage war in our own spiritual lives. We equip with the spiritual Armor of God as talked about in the book of Ephesians. We take down strongholds and defeat principalities' weight in our lives. As it says, "For our struggle is not against flesh and blood, but against the rulers, against the authorities, against the powers of this dark world and against the spiritual forces of evil in the heavenly realms," (Ephesians 6:12). These battles are fought violently through prayer, Scripture, obedience, reliance on God, and with the name of Jesus. One may question my word choice of "violently" when referring to such things as Scripture and prayer, but yes, I mean it. I believe these are violent and effective weapons in the spiritual realm against the forces of evil. Spiritual war can be ugly. It's sacrifice. It's a shaking up and reordering of one's life, but it ultimately leads to peace and a right relationship with God.

In my thoughts I then came back to the natural world. I looked towards the mountains and thought how, per the words of the experts, all mountains are created by earthquakes and volcanoes, both destructive acts of nature. Now these mountains stand tall, unwavering, and at peace.

Forest fires, too, are another thing that seemingly, on the surface, are all bad, but those destructive events are redeemed as well. The aftermath is a nutrient-dense soil and room in the forest for the next generation of plant life to grow. I have seen many a forest both on fire and recovering from a fire. A forest fire is ugly and can be scary, but, recovering from a fire, the forest floor is always decorated with flowers. There are sprouting berries and mushrooms and new saplings starting to really take root. It's a beautiful thing. There is peace after a ravaging fire.

I also began to think about birth and how it is such a painful and laborious process for the mother, but out of such a mess of pain comes the beauty of new life and the peacefulness of a resting baby. Then I thought of death itself. No one wants to face the process of death. Some will die tragically. Some will fight to cling onto this world. People will grow old and suffer ailments before death, but through death God reaches down and reclaims the life of His follower. Out of the end-of-life turmoil, suffering, and human-instinctive fear, He brings about ultimate peace as He fully restores one's spirit in His very presence.

Ultimately this great design element from a volcano to a serene crater lake, from a forest fire to a flowering grove, from labor pains to a baby's sigh, from war to peace, and from death to life, all show the redemptive nature of God. The message was becoming even clearer, as I realized it was then pointing us to Jesus– the ultimate redeemer. Jesus felt pain on this Earth. He asked for the "cup to pass" from Him when considering his approaching crucifixion, but He then went on to endure the most gruesome of deaths and the most momentous event in all of human history. His great sacrifice, and His own redemptive rising from the grave, conquering death, brought about the possibility for salvation and the redemption of the human soul. He paid the ultimate price for our sin, making us just and acceptable, forgiven and presentable to a pure and perfect God. This event is so great, so important, that God has painted it across His creation. The volcanoes, the forest fires, the wars, the labor pains, they all point us back to the redemptive story of Jesus and salvation.

It is so great and worthy to be written in the fabric of all creation, because it is only through the blood of Jesus that we can be redeemed from the destructive forces of sin in the world and in our lives. God wants to save us eternally, but eternity starts in the present, and God is here to wage war with us against the dark spiritual powers which have a hold on us, from our self-destructive habits, from our mental and spiritual turmoil. God saves. He will deliver and redeem. As He promises, the battle is already won through Him. Through turning to Jesus, accepting His forgiveness, and waging war, God is helping us to be "born again." To do so is not easy. There can be labor pains as one must leave behind his old self, but ultimately we have peace knowing God is fighting our battles with us and will redeem. I think about the violent volcano spewing lava like blood, but then I look at the beauty and peacefulness of Crater Lake, and I find hope. Here God reminds me of who He is and what He does. None of the wonders of nature are without meaning. God has placed His story everywhere and wastes nothing.

If you have not called out to God and sought His forgiveness through Jesus, I hope you do, and I urge you to. If you have not waged spiritual war, arm up! The stakes are high. Your soul and eternity is on the line. May you feel the transformative redemptive power of His love as you come to personally know God, and may one day your pains and trouble be replaced by beautiful crater lakes and alpine streams.

"And he who was seated on the throne said, 'Behold, I am making all things new.' Also He said, 'Write this down, for these words are trustworthy and true,'" (Revelation 21:5).

# WHAT KIND OF MOUNTAIN ARE YOU?

Finally we arrived at Mount Saint Helens National Volcanic Monument. I was in awe of the immensity of the landscape and baffled that something so grandiose and impressive didn't get more attention. I hadn't heard much about this place, and I only came across it while looking at a map of Washington state. Perhaps if I was alive when the volcano erupted in 1980 I may have known more about this place.

After learning about the volcanic eruption in the visitor center, Zeke and I were chasing down even greater views on a small path that led from the Johnston Ridge Observatory on the foothills of the behemoth of a mountain base before us. We were free after being held captive by the journey in the car for much of the day. We were about four miles from the mouth of the beast, when I sat down alongside the path next to some Indian paintbrush and other small mountainous blooms snugly grasping onto the sides of the path

between jumbled rocks. There I beheld what would have been, less than forty years ago, Washington's fifth tallest peak, but now it was just the base of a mountain. It was still tall, nevertheless, slanting upwards to 8,363 feet, but it was missing its peak which would have topped it off at an additional 1,400 feet. Now, instead of a peak, it prominently displayed a giant volcanic crater. Looking at Mount Saint Helens, I knew I wasn't looking at any ordinary mountain. It proclaimed, "volcano" loud and clear, for despite its enormous crater, it displayed its sprawling avenues and canyon ruts where lava once flowed, and much of the mountainside had been ripped barren and replaced by volcanic rocks. In some small crevices, plant life had resumed, but the sprawling directions in which its destructive lava flowed was still very evident.

Adding to the volcanic ambience, this evening a spread of clouds hung just below the crown of the crater, giving the illusion of smoke and adding great perspective. It also made the mountain look very regal with the pointed rock's edges spiking up like the palisades of a king's crown. The clouds also added an element of fantasy, really elevating the scene. Although Washington is a very mountainous state, here no other mountain stood in the background of this one, at least nowhere near her height. Mount Saint Helens stood alone, bold and royally, popping out against the rich blue sky.

I was particularly fascinated by the avenues, ruts, or canyons surrounding and sprawling from the creature-like veins. They were prominently displayed with the evening sun lower in the sky, casting sharp contrasts against the land and allowing the canyons to cast their own dark shadows within. These were "canyonlands" not illuminated by light, as I've discussed before, but ones trapped in darkness. I wondered what animals roamed down there. I wondered how enormous these places would seem on foot. *Have people even explored all of them?* It was fascinating to think that only a handful of decades ago these divots didn't exist. Then the deadliest volcanic eruption in the United States took place, spewing ash in a 250 square mile range and sending billows up to sixteen miles into the sky. Before then, this landscape would have been so different. It had been drastically remolded. As John Muir would see it, it was God at work, still designing his earth, molding the land through natural phenomena.

I was still fixated on the massiveness of this area and how its present landscape was relatively new. Even the divots aside, I was wondering if the whole mountainside in general had been fully explored in its current state. *What is hiding out in all of nature's rubble? What fantastical rock formations and marvels surround this thing in its new design?* It was such an enormous space that I imagined other National Parks I've visited fitting entirely in the space this mountain base encompasses. I thought how even some cities could fit within the crater alone. I wish I had time to roam freely and explore this land without a care. It would be fun to disappear into this thing, getting lost in its immensity and wonder. But I couldn't. I had responsibilities and an itinerary.

As I sat there, I did what I like to do in front of beautiful vistas: I closed my eyes, took a deep breath, and opened my eyes to be re-amazed by what was in front of me. Then the wind started to roll in, and I was getting cold. I crossed my arms, hugging myself in my flannel. Before having to leave, I had to get into the important thoughts. Observing the volcanic mountain, I posed the question: *What does this mean? What is the message of Mount Saint Helens?*

I was looking towards a crater, as I had done just the day prior at Crater Lake National Park, but Crater Lake seemed entirely different from this place. Crater Lake was distinct in appearance and messaging. But there was one commonality. They both started with a volcano, meaning what they are today was birthed by a violent natural event. What made the places so distinct from each other were their outcomes after the explosion. Crater Lake was a place of serenity, of beauty, tranquility and peace. It gave the message that despite great destruction and loss, there is peace and beauty. Mount Saint Helens today could be described as beautiful by some too, but it's for sure a different beauty from Crater Lake. It's impressive and awesome, but beauty is actually not the word I'd use for it at all. It looked very much still like the aftermath of destruction. The rubble was in clear view, the paths of destruction evident. It was like a scab was ripped from a wound not fully healed. It was a raw landscape, not replacing the destruction with the serene, but blatantly announcing its story of violence. The crater was not filled with rich, pure, calming blue waters but was empty, vacant, and void. Where forest once spread across its mountainside was barren rock and pumice.

I then had to think about what I've already concluded about mountains. Two summers prior, when I was at Great Basin National Park in Nevada, I was standing below Wheeler Peak thinking about how solid and strong the mountain was, and I started to think about the word *unwavering*. I wrote, "I observed how the mountain is very bold despite erosion and the rock glacier. It's still not going anywhere. The mountain is firm, steady, resolute, and then I began unpacking the word that would last and linger with me– unwavering. It's been my observation in life that consistency in a person is hard to find. People come and go. They change, they disappoint, and the slightest variation in weather can even disrupt a person. I do not want to be this type of person. I want to stand strong. I want to be a person others can rely on– a constant, a non-variable, dependable, and above all unwavering."

Mount Saint Helens was not unwavering like Wheeler Peak. This mountain had betrayed its surrounding landscape and all the life that had put trust in it. It left damage, took lives, and left voids, and it is said it may eventually erupt again. This mountain did not produce the beauty of Crater Lake nor the security of Wheeler Peak. I began to adopt the notion that there are different types of mountains, and they have different meanings, but that all mountains are representative of different kinds of people. There are the bold unwavering mountains, like Wheeler Peak and the majority of mountains, I've seen but few people I've met. Then there are those volcanic mountains, like people who have gone through pain, suffering, and trauma. Some volcanic mountains return from those dark moments in life with a new found peace, beauty. They are born again into something greater like Crater Lake. But other volcanic mountains, like Mount Saint Helens, are like people who have been badly hurt and haven't gone through the powerful process of redemption. Instead, they have built up resentment and anger to then spew hateful words and actions. They are abusive. Their anger is not controlled, and thus they are explosive, wielding destruction around them. They abuse their children, snap at their coworkers, fight with their spouses. Their anger and discontentment change the life and environment around them. They take the books of others and scribble into them or rip out pages. They also have unfruitful mountainsides, not rich in life, but barren or covered by mistakes, leaving no fertile ground for anything to take root. I know some of these people, and we all have potential to become such volcanic mountains. It is in our nature to be ruled by our human emotions, to become heated in anger and inflict unjust punishment on others. Mount Saint Helens therefore has a message of warning and shows us the weight of our influence when destructive.

I never want to be a Mount Saint Helens, but do I relate to her? Yes I do. I have my moments of anger and frustration, and in the moment I want everyone to feel the agony that I feel. I spew the lava. It's not right, but I'll own it. This is not to say all anger is bad. Some anger is justified. God in His love beholds justified anger. What really matters for us as humans is the outcome of our anger. Is it productive and justified, or impulsive and destructive like the volcano? I also relate to Crater Lake. I see peace and beauty in my life from where there was pain and destruction before. Despite whatever mountain best reflects me, I aspire to be like Wheeler Peak, consistent, unwavering, immoveable, dependable. However, there were yet other mountains to become acquainted with and this wouldn't be the last mountain on this adventure that would hold a message for me. I was just beginning to explore this analogy of mountains and people. I'd come to find that every mountain indeed is a reflection of our own human potential. Some inspire, some challenge, some warn, some seem foreign, some truly are characteristic of our own selves.

I was energized by this growing perspective on mountains. I was ready to explore it further and open to see what else God wanted to teach me through His creation. As

I'd learn about more types of mountains, the wonder would lead me to pose the question to others: *What type of mountain are you?* But before I could consider mountains any further, a moment of intensity befell the situation. Something happened that had me desperately running opposite from the volcanic mountain. This was an emergency...

Mount Saint Helens, May 18, 1980

# My Personal Devastation:
## The Horrific Reality for Me at Mount Saint Helens:

*I'm not gonna make it,* I thought. The moment was intense. I was running down the little path back to the visitor center at Mount Saint Helens National Volcanic Monument. The situation was urgent. I had the strength. I could do this. I made it in the nick of time. It was there, in the visitor center, where I had my own volcanic explosion. I'm not trying to be funny or acting immature. There is a sincerity and solemnity here. This moment was pivotal and not anything to take lightly. As lava spews from a volcano, blood was spewing from me. I was horrified. I can't even say it was a nightmare, because it was unimaginable. I didn't fear this moment, because I never thought I'd have this moment again. I had been through this before, and I thought it was all behind me. The suffering through ulcerative colitis was done, a thing of the past. I outgrew it, I thought, but it was back. In that moment, emotionally I felt I had taken a stab to the gut and the wind knocked out of me. I was devastated. This in no way had been on my mind. It was unimaginable, but the blood was both dark and bright, and it was real.

Two years ago I was at the gastroenterologist. I had been in remission for six years from ulcerative colitis, but the infusion therapy which had saved me and gave me back my health eventually caused drug-induced lupus. I had to stop it. The gastroenterologist wanted to quickly put me on another new infusion therapy. I didn't want to. When ulcerative colitis made its grand debut in my life, I didn't know how to handle stress. I internalized all of it. I didn't get enough sleep. I struggled with depression. I didn't get regular exercise, and I didn't know enough to eat healthy. I was still growing and developing physically as well. Through losing my health I learned a lot about taking care of myself. I had come to cherish moments of calm, moments to relax. I learned to let many things go. I had conquered depression. I was eating very healthy, and exercising regularly every day. I was strict on my sleeping habits, and physically my body had grown and matured. So I told the doctor I didn't want to go on any new medication. I wanted to come off all medication, because I believed my body would hold up and that I'd be just fine. At first I was hesitant when considering this decision, but over the course of a few weeks of prayer, I came to a great peace about it.

The doctor didn't like my decision. "You don't want to lose your colon, do you?" He tried to scare me, intimidate me into taking this new drug. He was just as obstinate in his opinion as I was in mine. I was giving up drug therapy whether he liked it or not. He closed out our appointment with, "I'll give you two months and you'll be back in my office." The truth is I didn't go back to that doctor. I fired him, but actually it was two years in which my body retained remission naturally before I was back in a doctor's office. I proved him wrong. I thought my two years would turn into a lifetime, but now I was discovering that just wasn't the case.

I had become so healthy and almost obsessive about regular exercise, sleep, and what I ate. I came to really love the body and valued my health greatly. So to learn that, despite all my efforts, everything was out of my control, was devastating. I had come to idolize my health so much, and now it was ripped away suddenly from me. Because I'd been through this illness before and knew how quickly it escalated, I knew my energy, my physique, my ability to eat and retain nutrients, to build muscle, to sustain myself, was all on the line. And, in addition to that great sense of loss and the fear of what was to come, came memories of pain from the past.

Ulcerative colitis first beset me in college, and the pain was persistent and at times very intense. It kept me up at night. I'd toss and turn in bed, unable to make myself comfortable. My stomach felt as if it was burning. One thing that seemed to help me a little bit was moving. To stay in bed felt like I was letting the pain swelter and build up. I needed movement. I needed an outlet, if for anything, to distract me. I always had to distract myself from pain. So I'd card out of my dormitory at night, and I'd wander the streets for hours. When everyone else was asleep, I kept moving. Some nights, especially those leading up to being hospitalized, I was in too much pain to walk. Instead, I rolled around on the floor, back and forth, like a crazy caged animal. The night before I was hospitalized, I was in so much pain, I wanted to pray, but my mind was so tortured by the physical pain it couldn't even formulate the words for prayer, so I literally just moaned and wept out to God. In the hospital I was on a morphine pump. Every two minutes morphine was pumped into my blood, so much so that I couldn't even raise my eyelids. Even after my time in the hospital, nothing was truly resolved for a long while. The disease festered. At my six foot three inch stature I weighed only 130 pounds. It took great effort to walk up the three flights of stairs to my dorm room, and one morning, losing a large amount of blood, I passed out in the shower.

I could not go back to this. I just couldn't. It had taken everything out of me, and to go through it again seemed unbearable.

Then, along with the horror, came blame. I never expressed this blame to anyone at the time, but inside I was blaming the family vacation the month prior in New York. At the time the family dynamic was just a bit stressful, and I wasn't able to follow my strict eating, exercise, and sleeping schedule. I believed it was the stress and irregularity of those events which put a toll on my body and flipped this switch from remission to active disease. Then there was Zeke and myself to blame. It had been a strange dynamic between us. I was stressed about trying to make this adventure just as amazing for him as my previous adventures were for myself, but he wasn't having that experience. He was complaining a lot and that really bothered me to the core.

Also, the past few days, I felt like I was rushing around too much. I wasn't taking the time to really relax and let nature's restorative properties work on me. I needed to prioritize relaxing. I was convinced this return of ulcerative colitis was due to stress and not being on my regular schedule, but naturally I thought this at the time, because I had idolized my health. Looking back, maybe there are bits and pieces of these situations that are responsible, but I really don't blame anyone or anything except the fallen state of humanity. I have learned since then that, yes, stress makes the active disease worse, but it will rear its ugly head provoked by stress or not.

Earlier in the day, when I had stopped for gas, I remember getting out of the car. I felt light-headed for a moment, and something within me was not right. There was no way to explain it. I just knew intrinsically something was happening to me. I had no idea what, but looking back it was as if immediately, in that moment, my body flipped a switch and came out of remission.

How was I going to tell Zeke? I knew I had to. This was going to change the dynamic of this trip. He had never even known this was something I dealt with in the past. We never talked about it, and it can be uncomfortable to talk about. A disease that affects the intestines and bowel with lots of blood, just isn't pleasant. There was no casual way to bring it into conversation. It was so deeply personal, and it wasn't easy to bring up such deep pain. *I'm going to have to modify my diet. I'm going to have to relax more. I'm going to have to try and not stress out about any details, and I am potentially going to be making much more frequent trips to the bathroom.* I needed to tell him.

Leaving the visitor center, Zeke bought a key chain which his dad requested as a souvenir. He remembered when the eruption of Mount Saint Helens occurred and had some connection or special fascination with it. Then we got in the car. We had a twenty mile car ride down the mountainous slopes and through the pine valleys. I was awkwardly quiet at first, and then I had to let the dam break. I told Zeke what had happened with my loss of blood. I told him about my past pains and experience with dealing with the disease and all the horrible things it entailed. I knew, in my very gut, that this was not an isolated event, but the beginning of another long period of struggle, and so I wanted him to know why I felt so devastated.

I made a big mistake at this moment. I left God out. I knew Zeke didn't have a relationship with God, and so I thought I just shouldn't bring Him up. I was shamefully weak in this regard. I had not developed the spiritual boldness which I now possess. I had some growing to do, and I was still clinging onto some sort of youthful notion that convinced me I needed to mold in with the audience at hand.

God's work in my life through my first episode of this illness in college was immense. It is my Crater Lake— beautiful now, but painful at the time. God had taught me reliance on Him, dependence on His strength. He also taught me about faithfulness and gratefulness. He had me wrestle with questions of suffering, pain, and death. He also gave me healing and hope. To leave God out of my story of ulcerative colitis is basically lying by omission, and I was guilty of it. Zeke, however, was a good listener, and sympathized with my pain, although I don't think he understood how heavy of a situation this was for me. I missed a great opportunity, though, to give God glory and share of my relationship with Him. Now looking back, perhaps there was more than a lack of spiritual boldness. Maybe there was anger already boiling under the surface, a question arising in the subconscious that would come forth in a matter of weeks. I was mad.

*God, how can you let this happen to me again?*

# The Mystical Beaches of Olympic

It was the morning after visiting Mount Saint Helens, and needless to say, it wasn't a very wild and back-to-nature morning. We had camped at a KOA just outside the park in the town of Castle Rock, Washington. I am a big fan of Kampgrounds of America, but this one just didn't have much to offer in terms of the great outdoors. It wasn't very wooded, was rather crowded, and pavement spread throughout. However, it did provide us a tent pad and shower, and that's all we needed.

After we packed up camp, we headed to McDonalds for a quick McMuffin for breakfast— maybe not the best choice considering my deteriorating gut health at the time. I would have been fine with my nuts and berries for breakfast, but I had to keep Zeke fed. About a half hour drive later we stopped at a Walmart. There I purchased glutamine and cherry juice, two things I thought would be good for my gut.

So after KOA, McDonalds, and Walmart, we were back on our way to pursuing wild things and were on our two and a half hour drive to Olympic National Park.

Planning to visit this park took a long time. The park map is very intimidating. Although it's all one peninsula, the road that goes around the peninsula swerves between National Park boundary and private land frequently. The shoreline is mostly National Park, but between the shoreline and the center of the peninsula is a lot of private land and inconsistent pockets of it. Sprawling from these private lands towards the center of the peninsula are roads that reach and dead-end like branches within the park boundary. Because the Olympic peninsula is a hodgepodge of land designations, with many sprawling roads, it was quite time consuming to figure out how to tackle it. It didn't have one main park road, like many National Parks, nor did it have any outstanding features. There was no Old Faithful, Yosemite Falls, Mount LeConte, or Going-To-The-Sun Road. Instead there were dozens of "must-sees," depending on who you talked to. I was most excited to visit the rainforest, for it'd be a new terrain and biome for me. I also wanted to see the iconic shorelines with their large protruding rocks from the ocean. I just wasn't sure which beach was "the one," for there were perhaps a dozen.

When we reached Chehalis, Washington, we were nearing the peninsula. There was essentially a "T" in the road. It was a right on Highway 207 to Seattle and a left on Highway 12 towards Olympic. If I was ever spontaneously presented with those options, I like to think my decision would be pretty obvious.

Our first stop on the peninsula was on the Quinault Reservation at a fish hatchery. Driving along, I noticed the sign which read, "Quinault National Fish Hatchery Visitor Center." It was the two words, "Visitor Center," which grabbed my attention. I am a real sucker for visitor centers. It turned out to be a very small, unstaffed, one room exhibit. There was a dated film playing on an analog TV. Of course I watched it. I learned that this hatchery was in cooperation between the U.S. Department of Fish and Wildlife and the Quinault Reservation. It hatches and releases about three million fish a year, mostly salmon. What I didn't know was that we were free to explore the actual hatchery and "raceways." This is standard policy at U.S. national fish hatcheries. I didn't know, but it would have been interesting to see all the Pacific salmon in their different stages, especially since I like to eat them, and you can't find salmon in the wilds of Kentucky.

Leaving the fish hatchery, we traveled further up the peninsula. It was very wooded and rather monotone in appearance. There was nothing of which to take particular note, and being so close to the ocean, the terrain was quite level. It was a bit of a mundane drive. I was getting very travel weary. Although this day I hadn't driven that much, it was the collective mileage of the past few days adding up. Then I saw, peeking through the trees, the Pacific Ocean! It was so beautifully framed by the trees, and I could quickly catch a glimpse at the long sandy beach and the crashing waves. Impulsively, I quickly pulled into a small pull-out along the road. This beach was not on my day's itinerary, but I wanted to stop and was excited that the pull-off was just at the right moment when the desire struck me.

On the park map the beach is creatively labeled "Beach 2." I parked the car and ran out onto the shore. I was glad to be out of the car and in a natural space. It felt very freeing. I had been released into the open, after having been in the car driving through snuggly gathered forests. The beach was very much like the beaches alongside the Redwood Forest. The gradient was low, the water shallow. When the waves weren't crashing, the water spilled across the dark sand causing natural white foam. The big difference between here and the beaches of the Redwoods was that

here a flat thick pine forest stood right beside the beach's
edge instead of large green bluffs. Also littered close to the
tree line was an enormous amount of driftwood, but not little odds and ends, but huge tree trunks and entire barren
sun-bleached trees.

After our brief visit to this beach, I drove us a mile
and a half up the road to Kalaloch Campground within the
park boundary. Although the campground backs right up to
the ocean, the only site I had could secure online was one

right next to the entrance to the campground. The ocean
was not in sight. But after we quickly set up camp, I was ex-
citedly-anxious to return to the ocean. On the itinerary we
were supposed to go directly to the Hoh Rainforest today,
but realizing how close we were already to all these beaches,
I decided it would be a beach day. We would visit the rainforest tomorrow.

The next beach we visited was Ruby Beach. It was
just seven miles up the road. Again, approaching the beach,
the small path led to a beach perfectly framed by the trees.
I'd seen this place before in photographs, and so I felt like I
was somewhere famous. Although it does not have name
recognition of many places in the National Parks, many people have seen this beach before on calendars, computer
backgrounds, and the like. It is iconic in this sense with its

tall rocks, not far out in the ocean, pointing upward like shark fins. These rocks were dark and contrasted against the white ocean foam, gray sand, and blue sky. A number of these ginormous rocks rested and stood on the sandy shore as well, apart from the water, at least for the moment. They looked very epic, as if there should be great stories surrounding them– as if a pirate ship on a great voyage should go passing by, or a group of brave men on a grand odyssey finally reach the ocean after weeks of searching, or some mystic message in a bottle will wash up showing us how to find exquisite treasure. It's exactly *that* kind of beach. Although the sky was blue, it was also misty and cool, adding a sense of chilling mystery.

I could not help but smile with the joy of being here, and we weren't the only people enjoying this place. There were many others too. I wouldn't call it crowded, but certainly not isolated either. Zeke had bottled up energy and wanted to climb up the giant rocks with maneuvers that made me nervous. I watched him for a few minutes, wondering, *would he or could he really do that?* Then I decided to just let him be. I didn't need the stress of watching him risk his life. I took off my sweatshirt to make a little pillow and I laid down on the sand. I closed my eyes, took in the ocean air, and relaxed. I felt my body really needed to relax with my current deteriorating health. This would be good. When Zeke found me after climbing around, we went on to the next beach.

It was about an hour drive with an exit from the park into the town of Forks. I started to see a few signs referencing the book and movie saga, *Twilight*. I learned this was the home of Twilight, meaning the town in which the protagonist Bella is from. Although this is apparently directly referenced in the books, and the town's welcome sign is shown in the movies, no other parts of the movies were filmed here. However, some of the townspeople are proud of their mention in the series and have really capitalized on it, housing the world's largest collection of Twilight set props and costumes and an annual "Forever Twilight Festival". I also ran into a little general store and noted the extensive offering of Twilight nick-nacks. I had not followed this series but could not avoid its mention in Forks, Washington.

When the road led back into the park, we made our final stop in the park for the day. We were at Rialto Beach and the highlight of the day! It was similar to Ruby Beach, with its large jutting rocks, and it was like Beach 2, in that it had a lot of enormous pieces of driftwood. It was different from the others in that no one else was here. It was ours, and Rialto Beach had two distinct features to offer. One is informally known as "Split Rock," The best way to describe it is like a giant arrow head was stuck in the ground, but then a bolt of lightning struck it and separated it perfectly in the center, creating two symmetrical pieces of rock, pointing towards the sky and just the slightest bit towards each other. It was another iconic vista. Something I knew I had seen in photos before, and to now see it in person was indeed exhilarating.

I had also done my research well for this trip, and I knew 1.7 miles up the beach was another iconic spot called "Hole-In-Wall," where the ocean carved out a hole in a rock about a story tall, right at ocean level. Although it may be

Split Rock

Hole-In-Wall

remembered as a hole in a giant rock out in the ocean, the rock actually is attached to the mainland. It is a peninsula, and I guess technically it can be considered a narrow rock arch. However, to the layman's eye, and memory, it's a hole in a rock in the ocean. What makes it particularly beautiful is that it is just at sea level and frames an ocean view perfectly.

It wasn't enough to see if from the sand. I had to go out and walk through that hole. The place was only accessible by foot at low tide, I read. During high tide it's straight up out in the ocean. Right now, we were somewhere between low tide and high tide, but where there's a will there's a way…or a concussion. We abandoned the sand, and started carefully placing our feet around tide pools filled with all sorts of strange sea growing things, urchins and the like. Some were bright green, others were dark blood-stained red

and growing tightly to the rocks, looking almost like some
strangely colored sea moss. The sharp things concerned me.
I didn't want to misstep and have one impale my sole. Thus
it was a challenge, and fun game, I suppose. Eventually we
were done with tide pools and moved onto rock-jumping
and scrambling in the ocean. I stood hunched, perched atop
one rock I had just jumped to, when a rogue ocean wave
forcefully crashed against my rock, spraying my face in bitter
salt water, in a very Little Mermaid-esque moment. The assault caused my body to jolt in surprise. I wasn't sure if this
was a good idea at the time. I wasn't sure if getting to Hole-
In-Wall was achievable, but it was, and it was worth the
trouble. We took some photos and marveled at nature's
wonder. The hole in the rock in the ocean was now also, to
us, an island of dark wet rocks serving as a window to the

sea. The musings and observing of all the fine details could have gone on, but we figured we better get on our way before the tide climbed any higher, leaving us stranded on the Pacific Ocean.

Before we left the beach, we had to hike up to the top of the landmass that eventually jutted out to provide Hole-In-Wall. Back on the shore, we brushed through some sea grass and shrubs and found a very narrow unofficial path that led upward very steeply, making the whole body lean forward and using the hands necessary. Alongside this path, the plant life was very jungle-like with long, large, lanky, sprawling ferns and other foreign plants to me. Atop, the views were even better than from the hole. From here we could see the shoreline spread and the large rock formation now below us. It fit all of the immense landscape into one view.

On our walk back down the beach I did not see any sea lions, as I was hoping for, but the sun was setting, adding slivers of silver and gold here and there on a piece of driftwood or a certain wave. When we got back to the car we had to drive back through "Twilightville" and make a quick stop for some styrofoam packaged burger and fries for Zeke's ravenous hunger. Back in the National Park, at our campsite, I noted in my journal that I was very tired of driving. I had seen some great things today, but it involved too much time in the car traveling from one place to another. I desired to be in one place and leave the car behind. That just wouldn't be the case in this park. The car would have to take us from one place to another, but ahead of us were a lot of impressive things yet to see that would make it all worth it. There were epic vistas awaiting and first time wildlife encounters to be had.

# The Rainforest and the Bear

It was right there, a bear, not more than twenty feet in front of me! I had been strolling along a trail in the Hoh Rainforest of Olympic National Park. Bears were not on my mind. Then suddenly, rounding a bend in the path, came the bear. I was headed towards it. It was headed towards me! It all happened so quickly. There wasn't time for keen observation, just reaction…and a photo. The bear seemed not the least bit inhibited by my presence. It just kept walking on the path towards me in the mere seconds this all went down. I, on the other hand, had fear struck into me. I was that tourist taken off guard.

Now this bear was only a black bear, with much less potential of danger than a grizzly bear, but a bear is still a bear, and the visual of a pitch black coat rounding a bend, contrasting with the greenery of the rainforest, was anything but subtle. Unless a domestic pet, animals with no fear towards humans usually should be of concern. This part of the rainforest was thick with ferns, thus there was no space to get out of its way alongside the path, except by braving the wild undergrowth of the rainforest and whatever lurked in there. So I turned and ran. My own human instinct kicked in. When I look back at the photo I managed to capture in the midst of my quick escape, I find this bear to be quite small. Having much more experiences with bears since, I find myself near ready to mock my former self for my own startlement by this bear, but it was a quick matter of instinct and reaction. I had not been expecting to see a bear at all because I had associated bears with thick pine forests, but I was in a rainforest, and in my mind bears were just not associated with rainforests.

Also, despite hiking, I had also been relaxing. I guess you could say I had let my guard down. Recently I found

myself to be rushing too much and allowing myself to be
stressed by trying to make this adventure experience worthwhile for Zeke. Today I thought I'd seize any opportunities
to relax, and this trail would afford one such opportunity to
really do so. We started the hike from the Hoh Rainforest
Visitor Center on the Hall of Mosses, surrounded by not
just tourists, but trees dripping with mosses which hung on
their sprawling branches like drapery, reminding me of some
photos I've seen of the humid deep South and the trees that
rest on some former plantations. Their trunks were also covered, from the forest floor to their highest reaches, in moss.
Among these moss-ladened trees were other deciduous trees
in the forest, and a forest floor nearly covered in ferns. In
any area there weren't ferns, there were other green plants
stretching out to fill the voids. The humidity, the hanging

moss, and the lack of pine trees wasn't something I'd associate with the far North. It'd be more appropriate from my own experiences to believe I was in the United States' deep South or the jungles of South America, but no, I was in the far reaches of the U.S. on the Olympic peninsula.

After we completed the 1.1 mile loop of the Hall of Mosses, Zeke and I took off down the Hoh River Trail. It was very similar in nature to the Hall of Mosses, except instead of a loop, it was a rather straight path parallel to the river. After a few miles on that trail, I saw a small breakaway from the path, an outlet down to the banks of the Hoh River. It was nice to get a break from the thick forest in an area where the river created a natural clearing, where we could see the sky, the mountains, and look out upon a larger landscape. Our attention was also focused downward, because,

in a still pool alongside the river, there was an utterly bustling cloud of tadpoles. They were thick, chunky tadpoles
with well-rounded bodies and quickly moving tales, storm-
ing around each other in sheer chaos. It was really quite a
grotesque display of nature, an unsettling visual, but terribly
unique of an experience and fascinating in that. The size of
these tadpoles spoke of the large frogs or toads they'd become.

After observing those creatures, I noticed the
warmth of the sun on my skin and the peacefulness of the
river. Its nearby ruffle was soothing to the ears. There were
patches of sand amidst the rocks, and in one I set down my
backpack as a pillow. "Let's take a few minutes and just relax," I proposed. I laid down and closed my eyes. I knew the
healing power of the sun when it comes to body inflammation, and I wanted the sun to just envelop me in its healing
power. I closed my eyes and breathed deeply. This is what I
believed I was lacking. I needed more time like this to relax
in nature instead of always being on the move. I prayed for
my health, and I wanted to fall asleep to wake up with a refreshed feeling of renewal. I didn't fall asleep, but I took
time, with my eyes closed, to focus intently on the sounds
around me, trying to distinguish each sound, focusing on
each one at a time. First I tuned into a bird's call, then a
frog's ribbit, then the ruffling of the river. This practice is
something I've found very relaxing. After about twenty
minutes of laying there on the river's shore, we were back
on the trail. I was slow-moving purposely, trying to have a
relaxing stroll through the rainforest, keeping my body

down from its recently normal state of intensity to that of peace and calm...then...suddenly...a bear!

I was the first to spot the bear. I turned around, pushing Zeke who was behind me and urging him to run. "There's a bear!" I pointed my camera behind me as I ran to capture a photo. Eventually the trail opened up where the rainforest floor stood barren around some trees, an obvious place where people have stopped to take breaks. There was also a couple there, hauling their own backpacks. We stopped. "There's a bear just up ahead," we warned. "It's right on the trail." They were going the other way, so it wasn't of much concern to them.

Zeke and I assessed the situation, and decided, since the bear did not make its appearance to us again, and it had plenty of time to catch up to us, it must have ventured off into the forest. So we decided to turn back around and continue on our hike cautiously. We concluded our journey at a beautiful waterfall. It was maybe forty feet tall and was a double fall, in that the water fell into one pool and shortly after down into another. Some limbless fallen tree trunks covered in moss laid at its base, adding size perspective to the scene. Moss also snuggly held onto all the surrounding rocks of the falls as well, making the scene very green. We had seen the falls from the trail, and following Zeke's off-trail lead, we bushwhacked through the ferns and rainforest undergrowth close enough to shake the falls hand.

When I think back to this day and I consider the encounter with the bear, I think there must be a message here, a purpose for this encounter. Maybe the message wasn't evi-

dent then, but the purpose could be found now in reflecting back upon the event. As I've sauntered with this thought, I've come to some great parallels.

Now, first off, I am a big fan of bears. Visually they are stunning. They are such an intelligent creature and one of God's greatest beasts. I respect their strength, their space, and existence, but for the sake of this analogy, I'm going to liken the bear to the enemy. I'm imagining bears as spiritual beasts, things dark, dangerous, and destructive to our spiritual lives.

Now, as for us, we are on a journey through the jun-

gle of life. Some people wander aimlessly in the jungle, lost.
They have no direction. They are riddled with fear, anxiety,
and hopelessness. Spiritually they are hungry and desperate
for they haven't found the spirit sustaining substance of
God's Word. Others don't think they are lost, for they are
on a path, a very wide and well-traveled path. It lures with
the prospect of encountering great treasure buried deep in
the jungle. The travelers think wealth and prosperity is their
destination, but they are lost too, for this wide path leads
really to nowhere of good consequence but rather to destruction. It leads off a cliff edge, down a waterfall, and into
a mountain lion's den, but little do they know this. Then
there is the God fearing man who follows a path that is narrow through the jungle. Its tightly accompanied by flora and
fauna of all kinds which can cause great distraction, but the
man sticks to the straight and narrow along the River of
Life, the flow of God's grace and mercy (or in this case, the
Hoh River). Others have been on this path before. Great
spiritual leaders and people of incredible faith, great "Nurse
Logs" and "Wheeler Peaks," led by God himself, have
helped clear this path with wisdom and knowledge. With
their great machetes, spiritual fortitude, and grit, they have
helped clear the path for us. This spiritual path, though leading to the very physical presence of God and the safest place
to be in the jungle, is not isolated from trouble. It exists yet
in a spiritual realm of all forces, good and evil. There are the
creatures of darkness that try to disrupt our journey, our
progress. Unexpectedly they come onto the path with the
intent to kill, steal, and destroy. They threaten to take us off

the path, or send us backward, running away from the pursuit of God.

Now not all these spiritual creatures are the same. Just as not all bears are the same. Black bears are generally fearful of humans. Of course there are exceptions, like the one I encountered this day, but typically they instinctively fear what man can do to them. They run off in the presence of man, and man can run off from them, as I've done a few times, but then there are grizzlies which are much more territorial. Although their threat is overhyped, they have been known to attack on occasion, and grizzly bears are not to be run away from. When presented with a running human, it is of their nature to chase the human. A grizzly bear must be handled differently from a black bear, and if all strategies fail, you have to fight it.

So first let's examine the spiritual black bears. They are spiritual beasts that cower. They usually get out of the way in fear. They are those animals we never knew were there on trail, because the animals heard or smelled our presence first, and in fear, ran away. There are beasts of the spiritual world that are in great fear of the presence of the Christian who has the Holy Spirit. When we have the Holy Spirit, these spiritual creatures are truly mortified. They simply cannot encounter the presence of God or be touched at all by the light of His glory. They run away. With God's Spirit dwelling in the Christian, so many encounters with spiritual beasts are avoided.

This gives me, and should give you, a great deal of confidence. For example, I'm not one who believes in ghosts, but I most certainly believe in demons and think the two are often confused. I have been in places that are supposedly "haunted" before, but I disregarded these stories as any danger to myself. Because even if people did have chilling encounters with the spiritual in these places, I know I wouldn't because of God living in me. The powers of darkness flee in my presence, but not because of my actual presence, but because of His presence in me. Hence, I have not a single "ghost" story to tell. This also explains why sometimes people say my presence emits a peacefulness and sense of safety. That is not of me. Sometimes my human mind is fraught with concern, but despite that, there is God's presence dwelling in me. The mere presence of a Christian in whom the Spirit of God dwells is very powerful and influential to the spiritual forces at work in the world.

Then, there is another form of spiritual beast. We can call it the grizzly. It's a specifically tailored one. It does not flinch. It is concocted by the devil himself and released on our path strategically. Sometimes it tries to avoid the Christian, for it too is fearful, but when it is encountered, it usually will not flee in our presence but it will approach. It's also very territorial. The territory it wants, which it thinks it is entitled to, is you! It's a stalking creature, and thus, in this aspect, more like a mountain lion than a bear. It also strategically strikes in time of peace. Here's the thing: We are not to fear these creatures either. God has equipped us with the power and tools to defeat them, but sometimes we are not prepared. We are taken off guard.

In times of peace and security, when we have taken a

relaxing break by the riverside, enjoying the sunlight, and strolling pleasantly through life, watching the tadpoles, sometimes we can become very relaxed in our spiritual lives. We become complacent. We drift away from the Word, from daily prayer and devotion to God. We stop asking questions of faith and pursuing the knowledge of God. Subconsciously we default to, *we don't need any of that now because we are traveling along this path just fine.* Then the spiritual beast appears, the bear comes right out of the jungle. It comes near us, and we are unprepared. We are not armed up with the spiritual Armor of God. Our Shield of Faith is in the backpack, we left the Sword of the Spirit at home, and the Belt of Truth is in the car. It's not to say we are hopeless. We are not, but we face a lot more turmoil trying to pull ourselves together, and in the meantime we may experience a lot more headache and heartache than we would have if we had been equipped.

The lesson here is, that in times of peace and comfort, when the sun is shining and the river is just ruffling, we need to work out our faith, to sharpen the sword, to affix that armor. In practical terms, these are times we need to be really delving into His Word, meditating on it day and night, to pray without ceasing, to ask God questions and pursue His truth, to continue to grow and fortify our faith. Imagine a fully armored Christian encountering a spiritual grizzly on the trail. It approaches the Christian, attempting to bring chaos and destruction into his life, but there's not even a match here. Nothing is a threat to a Christian in the fully affixed Armor of God.

This is not all to say that even the fortified devoted Christian is not met with great challenges and pain. Remember this second kind of beast is tailored specifically for its assaultant. The stronger the Christian, the greater the beast. Even the strongest Christians sometimes go through immense heartache and headache, but rooted in Christ, they are standing on a solid rock out in the tumultuous waves of the Pacific. They know the battle is already one. They are able to endure the pain with peace and resolve that is deeper than human understanding, because it is of God and not themselves. In my own life I have a specific tailored beast. It is that of ulcerative colitis. Although some may dismiss it as a purely physical ailment, the physical and spiritual are intertwined. When I am sick, it does affect me spiritually. For someone who is so active and tries to be so healthy, when I lose my health, I feel like my life is ripped from me. It can be devastating. It has the potential to take a serious spiritual toll. I certainly view my sickness as an attack from the enemy. However, during this summer's adventure I'd soon come to the realization that even if I'm not physically healed, I can win the battle spiritually. No physical ailment need have dominion over my life.

Oftentimes when we are strolling along the path in the jungle, at peace, we lose sight that we are in spiritual war. All of life is a spiritual war. There are moments of peace between battles which we are to enjoy, but just because we are not engaged in a battle at the moment, does not mean the war itself is over and we have the luxury of letting our guard down. In any war, you use the in-between time to train, fortify, plan, and strategize for the next move.

To liken all of life to spiritual war may sound pessimistic, but I don't think it is so. Even if it sounds so, it's an unavoidable reality that I've come to terms with. But I don't view it as pessimistic, because there is a great Hope. It is knowing through Christ Jesus the battle is already won and we have the presence of God with us! When we engage in spiritual battle, we participate in this victory. What an incredible honor and responsibility. It also brings us back to Scripture and prayer. We should never take such things merely casually or as ineffective. Our sincere time in Scripture and our prayers are never wasted. God is using them to fulfill His will. It is all a part of His plan, the same victorious plan of Christ Jesus! We also know that one day, in His eternal presence, not only will all our battles be over, but we will be on the other side of the war, on the other side of eternity, living in complete peace in His presence in His new Heaven and new Earth. "Thus we run forward with perseverance on a path that is marked for us," (Hebrews 12:1). "We press on toward the goal to win the prize for which God has called us heavenward in Christ Jesus," ( Philippians 3:14).

During the in-between times of peace on the trail, it's so important we don't let our guards down, that we don't become too comfortable with the numbing narcotics of life's pleasures and distractions. When considering the war, I also think about our spiritual storerooms. In Matthew 12:35, Jesus says, " A good man produces good things from his storeroom of good, and an evil man produces evil things from his storeroom of evil." This begs the question: *What is in my storeroom?* We place in our storerooms our own amusements, distractions, our selfish thoughts and pursuits, and just flat out a lot of junk. Many of us need some serious spring cleaning, and we shouldn't take these things to the Goodwill either. Much just needs to be burned.

So what needs to be in our storerooms? The things of God, what He values, what He loves, and chiefly, His Scripture. His Word is the most powerful of our weapons. A dear friend and pastor of mine, Steve, in his teachings has called this our "arsenal of Scripture." I like this analogy because so much of Scripture is like ammunition. Immediately it paralyzes fear and stops the enemy. When true pessimism does sneak into my life, often connected with my own health, one of my very effective weapons is the truth of a two verse harmony of 1 Peter 5:10 and Philippians 4:7, "After you have suffered a while, the God of grace Himself, whose knowledge surpasses all understanding, will restore you and make you strong in Christ Jesus." I say it, sometimes out loud. It lifts my own spirit, as the assaulting beast of pessimism and hopelessness is paralyzed when the promises of God are declared and the name of Jesus is invoked. Yes, sometimes it is that simple. We are all in a war. We fight battles that look very different for each of us, but we are all in the same spiritual war and we all reach victory by the same means. So I raise the same question Steve does, "What do you have in your arsenal of Scripture?" and as Jesus asks, "What is in your storeroom?"

Next time a spiritual beast approaches me on the

path of life, I don't want to run away backwards in fear, like I did with the bear in the Hoh Rainforest. Instead I want to be so fortified with the Word of God and His presence that I can approach that beast confidently and leave it behind victoriously. I can rebuke it with Scripture and with the name of Jesus. God gives us the power to slay whatever comes in our path, but we must fortify ourselves in faith and knowledge of His Word. Do not let your guard down in times of peace. God warns in Hosea 4:6, "My people perish for lack of knowledge." Instead, be in His Word, build that arsenal, polish the armor. The more ready you are, the more beasts will also just stay off your path. When they smell that blood of Christ, they stay away, but be ready, for despite His protection, a next battle is always inevitable until He calls us home.

# GAS PUMP IN THE WILD

I wasn't going to let this happen again– the stress of nearly
running out of gas. We were still on our visit in Olympic
National Park in Washington, but as access to the park was
split up by various types of land designations, now we were
on a small piece of Indian reservation at a gas station in
front of a casino. I noticed the price was $3.19 per gallon
which seemed cheap after braving the gas prices elsewhere
in the Pacific Northwest. I'd witness, in a few days, gas prices plummet when leaving Washington into Idaho and Montana. This was not much of a surprise considering the states'
politics and their effects on their economies. Here at the Indian reservation casino gas station I filled up. When I went
inside the gas station convenience store I was surprised by
free coffee and tea. I got a cup of orange spice tea to calmly
ease into the morning. Then we were back in the car for a
short drive into the park to the Hurricane Ridge area.

A few days prior, leaving the Chateau at Oregon
Caves National Monument, driving through the long expanse of National Forest, we were low on gas. We were also
in a very remote area, and when we finally reached an isolated gas station there was a sign that read "cash only." We had
the cash, but perhaps we were here too early for no one was
working. Zeke couldn't use his phone to look up the next
nearest gas station either, because we were out of service
range. I was able to search with my GPS, finding the next
nearest gas station was thirty miles away! I wasn't sure if we
would make it, or if it was even en route, but it was the only
option unless we were to wait a few hours to see if someone
would show up to work at this gas station. *What if they didn't?*
It would be a morning wasted.

So we journeyed on. There was an uncomfortable
silence in the car. I probably wasn't the only one questioning
my judgment. Out the window was mere pine tree after pine
tree– no people, no cars, no buildings, just the forest and us.
Mile after mile, it was all in uniform, and the road was
straight and unending in the dark morning forest. It made
me wonder if we were getting deeper into the wild, further
from any civilization. Normally I'd like this, but not without
gas. There was more and more of the same dragging on,
and, according to the vehicle's interface, we were out of gas.
Yet we were still moving. I was starting to feel the regret and
dread of relying on this GPS. It seemed to be leading us
astray, then...

"You have reached your destination," the GPS
sounded. As my journal details, I didn't think this was in op-

eration, but I pulled up to the singular pump. There was no store and no booth, but attached to the gas pump was a curly coiled wire phone. Zeke pointed to the sign.

"For gas dial 1," it read. We looked at each other with probably the same thought. We were puzzled. *What's going to happen?* We hadn't seen anyone, just trees for dozens of miles. Was someone or something going to pop out of the forest and pump our gas? *Is this sasquatch's gas pump?* I opened the car door and stepped out. The forest was silent. I lifted the phone and held it to my ear. To my surprise there was a dial tone. I punched in a "1". It rang!

"*Hello,*" the muffled voice came through the receiver.

"Hi. I was wondering if I could get some gas." I believe I was too puzzled and confused to have even considered the pleasantry of bidding a "good morning."

"I'll be right there."

*This might actually work.*

We waited, looking around with suspicious anticipation in every direction.

After just a couple minutes we saw a golf cart coming down the road— our rescue!

A pleasant older man in flannel and blue jean overalls asked how much gas we wanted. I handed him a $20. "Sorry about the wait," he apologized, although it wasn't much of a wait at all. "I had to find my keys at the lodge." I concluded there was some lodge I was unaware of, and this was their gas pump. The golf cart was used to travel around their property.

"No problem," I responded. "Thank you."

And we were on our merry way.

That was four days earlier, and I wasn't going to find myself stuck in that sort of situation again, and that is why I filled up at the casino gas station. In the far remote West, with distances so grand and gas stations so rare, every opportunity to fill up should be carefully considered. Take advantage of any gas pump in the wild.

We eventually reached the Hurricane Ridge section of the park. We were getting ready to hike about seven miles to Klahhane Ridge. There was a visitor center, and of course I had to go in. There wasn't much to see for it was a small place. I was engrossed in the literature, the books for sale, while Zeke found a binder on display with pictures and information to identify wild flowers. He studied up on the flora for the day. I ended up buying a book about wolves. The cover of the wolf's piercing stare drew me in. Back at the car, we geared up for a beautiful hike on a trail loaded with wild flowers, majestic views, and lots of wildlife (but no wolves).

And the experience with the gas pump inspired me to write this song...

# Ode to the Gas Pump in the Wild

Driving through the wild, beneath the towering trees,
Feeling the stress as the gasoline quickly depletes.
In Siskiyou National Forest, a land so vast and grand,
But stranded in the woods, was not what we had planned.
Miles of pine trees, stretching, nothing in sight,
Will anyone be our rescue, or will our day turn into night?

O gas pump in the wild, like a lifeboat in the sea,
Rescue us from drowning, would you pretty please?

Then a glimmer of hope, a steeple in the pines,
A chance to refuel? Hopeful as a child.
With a phone on the pole we dialed for our need,
And from the forest's depths, came our lovely savior's steed.
A golf cart in the distance, rolling into sight,
An old man with a smile, making everything alright.
In flannel and overalls, this man helped save the day,
He powered up the gas pump and sent us on our way.

O gas pump in the wild, like a lifeboat in the sea,
Rescue us from drowning, would you pretty please?

In the remote West, where gas is rare and few,
Seize every opportunity to safely see you through.
If it's just a little gas pump, hidden in the trees,
It may be a lifeline, setting you at ease.

So now we hike the trails, where the wildflowers
abound,
Learning of the animals of which us surround.
Here at Hurricane Ridge is where we will happily be
With gratitude to the gas pump forever endlessly.

O gas pump in the wild, like a lifeboat in the sea,
Rescue us from drowning, would you pretty please?

Gas pump in the wild, a sanctuary found,
In the midst of nature's bounty, you wear the crown
With this adventure's end, there's a story to compile,
Of a journey's uncertain detour forever worthwhile.
So here's to the gas pump, a tale to be told,
Along the Rogue River, where memories unfold.
Of a certain lonely gas pump, that will always be
In my adventurous heart forever endlessly.

# The Mountain Goats of Hurricane Ridge

When their procession was over, there were nineteen mountain goats in total just a stone's throw away. We were on the trail to Klahhane Ridge in Olympic National Park. The path was just a small one, trodden into the side of the mountainous ridge. To detour left from the trail would be dangerous, as the mountainside was sloped so steeply, and to the right it would be perilous as well. Although it was pretty and ladened in wild grasses and flowers, it too was steep and plummeted down into the valley. The truth is, this path was probably the mountain goats' path before it ever was a trail in the National Park. The mountain goats were loyal to this path. One by one they rounded the bend and emerged from a pocket of pine forest to this open mountainside. I've heard they can be aggressive when approached, and I noticed a few patriarchs of the band with tall sharp black dag-

gers for horns. Behind them were the women and children,
or I guess technically the "nannies" and their "kids". They
were all so beautiful with their long coats of fur. Some of the
more mature goats had strands of fur dangling from them,
like the moss laid on the trees. Some of the strands of fur
caught in the breeze and wisped around. It was summer
shedding season, and it was obvious these goats had been
carrying fur to the max. They were drenched in it, except for
the young kids. Their fur was short, fluffy, and perfectly
white and pure.

     Enough observing, a decision had to be made on the
part of Zeke and myself. The mountain goats were not the
least bit inhibited by our presence, and they continued walking toward us, potentially posing a threat. They had to have
noticed us, but they didn't acknowledge us. They continued

about their parade, walking along their path, although not with a prideful march. They were certainly not pompous, nor were they timid. They seemed to not have a care and continued on with a quiet and steady confidence.

I had learned from the *Rock the Park* show that making spitting noises can deter mountain goats. I didn't know at the time why, but later I looked into this and learned that it's the sound male mountain goats make to warn aggressors to retreat. So, per my lead, Zeke and I started making spitting noises. The goats showed no alarm, but it did work perhaps, for casually they climbed off the trail and down onto the steep grassy slope, an area Zeke and I could not have gone down, for we don't have that sort of mountain goat balance and maneuvering ability. Here they were on full display as a band. I was thrilled at the spectacle of nature:

mountain goats, in white shaggy fur, on a steep mountain-side, contrasting the dark rich blue of the forested mountains behind them capped with snow; and the innocent little kids, taking careful steps in the wild grasses alongside wild mountain flowers. Once we felt at ease seeing the goats travel off the path, Zeke and I paused to revel in the moment, exclaim to each other how cool it was, and take photos.

This wasn't our first wildlife encounter on this hike. When I parked the car at the Hurricane Ridge Visitor Center, right along the parking lot, were four deer grazing in the grass. One was a buck with its young rack of fuzzy antlers. He was lying down but had his head propped up, alert, as if looking out for the female's feasting in the grass nearby who also came very close to us as we were observing them. I suppose this event was foreshadowing the richness of wildlife, and close encounters we'd experience, on this trail.

The trail was 7.6 miles in total, starting from the visitor center and ending for us at Klahhane Ridge, although this was just a segment of a much larger network of trails. The path held snug to the side of the mountain nearly the whole time, not on a ridge but close to one. It meandered through open grassy slopes and patches of pines. Some of the pines had very shaggy bark and were laden with moss, especially as we gradually climbed higher.

In the open grassy areas, we would see the trail ahead snake among the mountain side. To see it slither along added great perspective to the mountainous scene. To our right, in the distance, the Cascade Mountain range sprawled. It was an overcast day, but the clouds were high enough that even the tallest mountain peaks were not covered. The clouds darkened the forest, making the mountains a deep navy blue with their snowy peaks really popping. No mountain really stood out from another. Instead it was one after another, rather uniformly, with short divots and valleys between them, and each mountain peaking at about the same height. They stood tall like soldiers in uniform, guarding the way eastward.

Alongside our path, and down the grassy mountainside, were a plethora of wildflowers. As Zeke had studied up on them in the visitor center, he was able to identify and call some out by name. There was one with many delicate little white petals that were brushed with pink at their veins and fine edges. Its leaves were stringy pale yellow and green, and they sprawled out like spaghetti. They were a region specific plant called *Olympic onion,* actually producing a bulb that is edible and produced commercially. Another wildflower spotted was *white avalanche lily* with its bursting star bloom

Olympic onion

and dotted with yellow at its pistil. Each one stood in its own space, seeming very independent, spaced out from its counterparts. They weren't like some wild flowers that seem more like city-dwellers, crammed into a small space together. These lilies were country folk. They had their own space, their own plot of land, their own hardy independence. At one point we came across patches of a stalky plant bearing multiple tubular bright purple blooms. They are called *penstemon* and remind me a lot of blue bells. These were all subalpine flowers.

This hike really made me aware of how far north we were, and not just in terms of the nation's edge and proximity to Canada, but also in terms of elevation with mountains, goats, patches of snow, deep mountainous ravines, subalpine blooms, and an arctic touch in the breeze every once in a while. As we climbed in elevation on our windy path, at one point we ascended a series of switchbacks. There at the higher elevation were marmots, those funny whistling flopping, nervous little guys– those beavers of the mountain, as I call them, for their flabby appearance and prominent two front incisors. They smile and run, call out in a loud beeping sort of whistle, or lounge around when it's sunny. To me they are just simply a funny animal in appearance and behavior. They are delightful.

When we reached our journey's farthest peak, we beheld an incredible vista! We could see out to the ocean, an inlet of the Pacific called the Salish Sea, which gives way to numerous straits around Vancouver and the San Juan islands. Also, boldly and majestically stood Mt. Baker, on the edge of North Cascades National Park, between Seattle and Vancouver, although neither city was visible. The mountain was still around 150 miles away, but it was clearly visible with one enormous rounded peak covered in snow and another jutting peak down its side. We sat down and beheld the vista. What an enormous view! We could see so far and even see the ocean, yet felt nowhere near it.

As we were sitting there, enjoying the view and pointing things out, from the corner of my eye I spotted something moving. I looked down to see a chipmunk getting a little too close to my backpack lying on the ground by my feet. I grabbed the backpack up, knowing the critter probably wouldn't think twice of going inside in search of food. This chipmunk was familiar with humans. I could tell. I had no plans of carrying a chipmunk down off Klahhane Ridge. No one should feed wildlife, and there are rules and even laws against it, but before I had time to say anything, Zeke had a piece of a Clif Bar in his hand, which the chipmunk was eating from. Zeke then reached down with his other hand to pet the little rodent's back. After one swift swoop down the back of its coat with his finger, the chipmunk took off.

I planned to stay here a while. I had no rush to get away from this great view, so I settled in the spot I was sitting, clearing away some small uncomfortable rocks beneath me. From my backpack I was guarding from the chipmunk, I took out my new book: *The Wisdom of Wolves*. "Storytime?" I proposed. I proceeded to read the introduction of the book out loud, and Zeke listened.

On our hike back down Klahhane Ridge, we saw more marmots, deer, and wildflowers. When we reached the car, we could agree, we had completed a truly satisfying and rewarding hike. It had some of the greatest elements that make for a good hike: great wildlife spotting, diversity of plants to observe, mountainous views the entire way, and a majestic overlook at its furthest reach. Although the day was a great one, night was soon coming, and things would take another turn. Things were about to get rocky.

# Life Taken Too Soon

I had thought so much about life on this trip. I always do this on my travels, but this time was different because I was looking more outward, particularly considering the influence of one life upon another. As I observed the wonderful phenomena of nature, including the beautiful sunsets, and the towering mountains and volcanoes, God was showing me the weight of a life and the value of influence it possesses.

The sunset showed me how beautiful a life can be at completion, with a display of all the wonderful qualities of a person, what I called "the colors of a sunset." A life fully lived is a beautiful completion at its end, just as the sunset beautifully wraps up a day. I also was captivated by nurse logs in the Redwood Forest. Those fallen decaying tree trunks provide the nourishment for the life of the next generation. People too, when they pass away, can be nurse logs.

Their examples, values they instill, and legacies can all greatly enrich the life of many people to come. I also considered
mountains, how some people are steady unwavering mountains, dependable and a constant for people in a changing
world; and how others are explosive mountains, causing
harm to those around them. However, whatever volcanic
explosions are in one's life, there may be beauty to be found
in the aftermath, like the beauty created from the volcanic
explosion that made Crater Lake.

I started this journey with a dream of all the characters of my various unfinished stories together. They were
disgruntled that I hadn't completed their stories as the author. I took away from the dream the notion that we all are
authors of our own individual stories. We hold the pen to
write into our lives, and we also have the power to reach
over and write great influence and meaning into another's
life with our words and actions.

The concept of life was also so fresh on my mind, as
I was losing my health and revisiting memories of when I
was so sick in college. My life was fragile, and I wanted so
badly to hang onto it and keep on living.

Oh, how rich life is to be able to climb mountains,
to stand on a rock in the sea, behold the wonders of the
forest, and observe the artistry in a sunset. It's such a privilege to write influence upon others, to be a mountain for
another, to experience the painful volcanoes of life and find
beauty in the aftermath. How great it is to grow in the legacies and teachings of those gone on before and provide enrichment for those yet to come. How beautiful it is to ulti-

mately leave a lingering sunset of many colors. Some never experience any of this, however. None of it. They see no light, climb no mountains, and experience no hardship. They are robbed of the opportunity to provide their own sweeping sunset. Their life is unjustly taken too soon.

This robbing of life is called abortion. My strong views on this are greatly influenced by my faith but also by logic and the value I find in life. In the midst of pondering the richness that is the gift of life, a conversation came up with Zeke about the topic of abortion, and it really struck a chord with me, creating a deep reverberating sound I just couldn't drown out.

A big day's adventure had been completed prior. We had conquered Khahhane Ridge and had experienced all its beautiful vistas and its abundance of flora and fauna. Now it was time for a relaxing soak at Sol Duc Hot Springs, also in Olympic National Park. When we arrived, I observed the crowded cement pool supplied by natural springs. I smelled the natural pungent smell of nature's sulfuric acid, and that would be fine in a natural spring, but that paired with saggy, sweaty, steamy bodies, packed in like sardines in the pool, with an occasional peeking plumbers crack, left me with little desire to go in. I was looking for a relaxing soak in nature's pure spring. This just wasn't it. Zeke and I went ahead and each paid a few dollars to use the locker room to take a shower.

When we left, the conversation of abortion came up after both seeing a bumper sticker on the car in front of us. Zeke expressed his opinion that he is pro-abortion. I choose my terminology thoughtfully here. I didn't say "pro-choice" because we weren't even talking about choice. I label his stance as "pro-abortion," because he believed we needed more abortions to take place, because the world was over-populated. He also expressed his view that a child may be born into poverty or to an abusive mother, and therefore, it's better for the child to be aborted than to face those hardships. Of course he didn't state it exactly in those words, but that's exactly the belief, and I couldn't disagree more. I didn't have the words to articulate my view and where this passionate perspective came from at the moment, but now I do.

We can't abort children, because life is sacred. I know the response: "a fetus is not a life," they say. "It's just a clump of cells." But there's no denying these are human cells, and they are living with unique genetic makeup in their human DNA, which naturally, are on the projection to become a fully developed human being. Despite all these truths, some still claim the fetus, though in a stage of human development, does not have personhood until it magically becomes a human being when it passes through the birth canal. I use the word "magically," because there is no scientific explanation describing what fundamentally changes the essence and make up of the fetus, or "clump of cells," one moment before birth and one moment after. Others claim there's a certain week period during pregnancy when a clump of cells obtains its personhood, but no one can give an exact moment and definitive time in which the clump becomes a human, and furthermore what does one day be-

fore personhood look like? How do you measure personhood? If a unique genetic makeup in DNA, and the compo-
sition of living human cells, does not constitute a human
life, when can we consider the formation of a human life to
begin, and when does the human life become valuable? To
me it is always sacred, and no one should be able to discriminate who gets to live and who doesn't based on which stage
of human development one's in, or one's location in or out
of the womb.

"It's about viability," some claim. The fetus, which is
the Latin word for "offspring," they believe is a part of the
woman's body until it is a viable baby outside the womb.
There is a scientific and logical fallacy here. First of all, sci-
entifically the fetus simply is not a part of the mother's body,
for it has unique DNA and unique organs, or at least the
unique genetic code to develop separate organs. The logical
fallacy is there is no baby at any point of infancy that is inde-
pendently viable outside the womb. Yes, there is a point in
which a baby can survive outside the womb, but every baby
is still going to be dependent on the mother or another human being for everything. The baby cannot feed him or herself or conduct many of the necessary functions for survival
alone. Viability outside the womb cannot be a measure of
human life. This would mean the severely handicapped and
incapacitated elderly are no longer "human" or at least not
worthy of human life. We cannot discriminate based on ability.

Others don't believe life is inherently valuable. It
gives way to the belief that some lives are more valuable

than others. This is because, in their view, value is something that can only be assigned. Just as some Leftists believe in the concept that gender is something that is assigned, they also believe worth is not something inherent but is something assigned. Thus a baby is not valuable until it is assigned worth by the mother. Abortion is justified at any moment, even post birth as a moral "healthcare" right because, if the mother does not value the baby, it's life has no worth. This sounds harsh, but I believe it is the most popular stance and reasoning behind those in support of abortion. This is also a very empowering notion for Leftist women, because no longer is life something gifted and created by God, but something they alone preside over. It falls in line with the Left's beloved Black Lives Matter belief that "black women are divine." Women are seen as goddesses and justly determine who is allowed to live and who is not allowed to live, based on who they deem as valuable and who they deem as material waste.

Some acknowledge the baby is a human life and does have value, but they argue that it might be born into hardship, less than ideal circumstances, maybe poverty and abuse. Somehow, if I follow their train of thought, it's seen as doing the baby a favor by ending his or her life instead of exposing him or her to hardships. I find this ridiculous. Hardship is a part of the human experience. It is a part of life, and even if the baby is born into a horrific living situation, he or she can eventually rise above and prosper. Many people have done this. We do not rob people of the opportunity to live simply because they will experience hardship.

Others claim a baby can be a hindrance to the mother's career and life goals. What greater honor or more meaningful thing can one do in life than rear and raise children? I know this is called outdated and sexist. I simply disagree. People who value education, careers, and work before their children, are sad sorry people. I say this for both men and women. It takes both to rise to the occasion of parenthood. A career should never take precedence over human life and the incredible honor bestowed upon a man and woman to bring a life into this world. But this all boils down to a difference in values. One viewpoint is that human life is more valuable than work; the other, that work is more valuable than human life. I wonder what is the idol behind work. Is it money? Approval or fame? Is it a false sense of fulfillment? I know the argument here: "It's not about values. It's just all about timing. Sometimes it's not the right time to have a baby." Well, it may not occur according to your plan, but I circle back to my view that still it doesn't justify ending a human life. That would be an incredibly selfish view.

I am thoroughly pro-life. I am also pro-choice too. I am pro-choice in the regard that one should have the freedom to choose whether to engage in the activity, which by natural consequence, may result in the creation of a unique living human being. Women do not mysteriously become pregnant, or catch pregnancy on a whim, such as catching a cold, like the Left wants us to believe. Women become pregnant through sexual intercourse. The natural consequence of sex is the creation of a living human being. The Left argues sex is a human right for both men and women. Sex is not a human right. It should take two consenting adults. No one is entitled to sex whenever they feel so inclined. They view sex as a human right, disposable in any circumstance for one's own pleasure. It is the very barbaric philosophy which leads to rape and incest, which in return, some use to justify abortion. It is an extraordinarily sick and evil philosophy at play. This should be alarming to everyone.

"What about incest and rape?" This is always deferred to. Well, I still don't budge. Abortion does not solve the trauma of rape. It's been shown to make it worse. Women who suffer abortions report greater levels of depression and anxiety. To perform an abortion here is to take a situation with one victim and create two. Also, I don't believe we should discriminate against human life based on one's means of conception. The conception could be out of horrific, painful circumstances, and my heart does go out for the hurt the woman feels, but we can't start discriminating based on means of conception. The offspring has no say in the matter and is not responsible for the choices of his or her parents.

I hadn't thought so thoroughly and hadn't organized my thoughts as I have now, so when Zeke argued that, "we need more abortions because the world is overpopulated," I will admit, I was offended, and I didn't know how to deal with him. So I folded in on myself and became quiet as frustration festered within me. I was so focused on life and its great potential, all during this trip, so this all hit me hard. I also have a very soft spot for the vulnerable among us. Babies are the most vulnerable of human beings.

With all my frustration, I had pulled the car rashly in a parking space at the Sol Duc Falls trailhead. I wasted no time grabbing my backpack, closing the car door, and starting the hike. It's embarrassing in retrospect, how it all went down. I started running down the trail to get ahead of Zeke, because I wanted to get away from him. I was sick of him.

He had also bothered me a few days before, pretty bad. Now, more mature, I could have dealt with this much better, but in my younger and less experienced state, I didn't know what to do. We had stopped at iconic Multnomah Falls in Oregon. It's a beautiful two part falls separated by a bridge, famous in many photographs. This was not on our itinerary. We didn't know it was on route, but we were so excited to see it. It's always depicted as being this beautiful, remote wild place, but it was really right off the highway, and it was very crowded. Also near the base of the falls was a little soft serve ice cream shop. To me, all the people added a fun energy, and admittedly I wanted some ice cream along with all of them. Zeke was utterly repulsed by the number of people and the fact it had been commercialized with an ice cream shop. I understand his viewpoint, and I did feel a little bit guilty for just being so excited and rather giddy, unaware of his observation. In the excitement I just hadn't thought about it that way. *It is a shame,* I thought. It would have been better if it was kept as a wild place and didn't become quite the tourist catch, but I accepted it for what it was. I also liked the fact that so many people were enjoying something so beautiful. Humans should be drawn to beauty. It is in our good nature. I understood two different ways to look at this situation, but it wasn't a big deal to me. *It is what it is. It could be a better experience, but I'll enjoy what it is.*

Conversely, Zeke seemed bothered by the state of humanity as a whole, and this place had really triggered him. He turned angry, exhibited in a painful silence that just oozed discontentment or bitter comments. I didn't know what to do with this. I had never seen him like this before. I wanted so bad for Zeke to have an amazing and meaningful trip like I had experienced the past three summers venturing solo. I was seeing in this moment, along with many others, he was not happy. I carefully walked on eggshells around him. If I said the wrong thing, or tried to dismiss his emotions as no big deal, I was afraid he'd unleash some greater display of discontentment, and I'd be so crushed. I couldn't handle that stress.

Fast forward, back to Olympic National Park, I ran ahead of Zeke on the trail to the Sol Duc Falls. I guess we both dealt with our anger and frustration primarily in the same way: silence. This was not good, but we learn from our past mistakes. When I got to the falls he approached me with, "what's wrong?" Of course I responded with the most honest and sincere answer:

"Nothing!"

*I am not going to let this little punk ruin my trip, and there's no use in trying to save it for him. It's already ruined for him.* Zeke had been complaining a lot the past few days over trivial things. I failed at creating this ideal trip for him, and I was trying to not care.

When we got back to the campground in Olympic National Park, we had a nice campsite up on a little embankment by a river. It was dark now. By flashlight and burning fire, I broke open my food container from the trunk. I was ready for a feast. Our time together was coming to an end and we had food to eat up. We did eat a strange conglomeration of foods, perhaps some canned soup, marshmallows, crackers, chips, dried nuts and berries.

Then, I addressed the elephant at the campsite.

I was over our discussion on human life, but still focused on how negative he had been lately. I said something like this: "I have tried so hard to make this trip perfect for you. I really wanted you to have an awesome experience, but after everything I've done for you, all I get are complaints and ungratefulness. It makes me literally feel sick!" I may have raised my voice a little bit. My tone was harsh.

I keep things real. I realize a fault in my character is that I'm prone to be very blunt and hurtful when something bothers me. I don't sugar coat anything. Zeke, to my surprise, was actually understanding and apologized. He recognized his negativity, apologized for it, and thanked me for everything I had done for him on this trip. This was also personally justifying for me. I was critical of myself, examining myself inwardly and thinking maybe I was letting things bother me that shouldn't. Maybe half of what I was feeling was imagined. He validated my feelings by confirming he acted out of line. *Phew, It's not just me.* This is rare. It's natural, I think, for many to justify their actions and shift blame. The fact that Zeke owned his shortcomings is very admirable and a mark of maturity.

I felt incredibly better. This conversation needed to happen. People commonly say, jokingly, when two friends embark on a road trip or any major endeavor, they will either end up as best friends or hate each other. It's only funny because there's truth to that. I by no means hate Zeke. I still have great respect for him and no grudges, but I was starting to see that our friendship wouldn't survive much past this trip. We lived in the same world, and we loved it. We both loved the outdoors and nature, but we saw it so differently. I had no kindred spirit here. He was but a stranger just visiting my life, and I suppose just another character in one of my books. *Could I still write something good into his life?* Honestly, I don't think that at the time I was thinking this, but I should have been. I was still too young, immature, and insecure to realize the opportunity I had to be a good influence.

# MOUNT RAINIER: THE NOBLEST OF PEAKS

*Of all the fine mountains which like beacons, once blazed along the*
*Pacific Coast, Mount Rainier is the noblest." – John Muir*

Cars were backed up to get into this park. I could see just a
little bit up the forested road to the entrance gate. A large
wooden sign hanging down from a rustic pine log, propped
up by other pines on either side, had constructed an arch-
way– a portal into the park. Its letters were all upper-case,
bold, and carved simply into the sign. The grooves painted
white displayed, "MT. RAINIER NATIONAL PARK."

This was a top tier National Park, our nation's third
behind Yellowstone and Yosemite, created in 1899 by President William McKinley signing a bill passed by Congress.
This park is named and centered around one mountain
peak, and deservingly so. Mount Rainier is a giant at 14,411
feet. It is visible throughout most of the state of Washing-

ton and has the most glaciers than any other peak in the contiguous United States, with a whopping total of twenty-six glaciers. We had seen this mountain much earlier in the day, traveling from the Olympic peninsula around Tacoma. It was a magnificent bold giant standing in the distance. Over the course of hours, we noticed it growing bigger as we drew closer to it. Now we were at the mountain's base about to enter the National Park!

Once officially inside, passing beneath the enormous sign and log beams, flashing my park pass, and getting my park map, the road immediately began to gradually ascend. We were on our way to the Paradise village of the park on the side of the mountain. There in Paradise was a visitor center, a lodge, and a network of trails. On our ascent through the thick rich forest, I stopped at one point to hop out onto a short path to a platform overlook nestled be-

Nisqually Glacier

tween the dark pines. There at the platform's edge, I beheld the amazing wonder of Nisqually Glacier tearing down the mountainside. Up until this point, this was one of the most impressive views in nature. It was my first time observing a glacier– the breaking ripples of ice, deep grooves, sharp edges rolling over and tearing down the mountainside, but all seemingly still. It was action frozen in time to my eyes. I observed a depth of snow and ice I had never witnessed before, and, as the glacier spread down the mountain, I saw the enormous gorge it had created over many years, carving away at the mountainside. Although there was a plaque labeling Nisqually Glacier, I believe, after considering the park map, I was also looking at two other glaciers in the same view: Wilson Glacier and Von Trump Glacier. It's hard to differentiate between all the glaciers, as they run so close to each other and at times converge.

Van Trump Glacier was named after Philemon Beacher Van Trump, an American pioneering mountaineer who made the first recorded summit of Mount Rainier. He wrote: "That first true vision of the mountain, revealing so much of its glorious beauty and grandeur, its mighty and sublime form filling up nearly all of the field of direct vision, swelling up from the plain and out of the green forest till its lofty triple summit towered immeasurably above the picturesque foothills, the westering sun flooding with golden light and softening tints its lofty summit, rugged sides and far-sweeping flanks – all this impressed me so indescribably, enthused me so thoroughly, that I then and there vowed, almost with fervency, that I would some day stand upon its glorious summit, if that feat were possible to human effort and endurance."

Unlike P.B. Van Trump, I would not be summiting Mount Rainier, but I shared in his admiration of the mountain, and around its base, and on its mountainside, I would experience many of its rich wonders. With just one up-close and unobstructed view, it was love at first sight!

"Let's go!"

We got back in the car and continued on our way to Paradise. It was about twenty miles of meandering parkway that climbed and switch-backed up to 5,400 feet. At Paradise the mountain peak was on full display. The terrain had leveled, to an extent, allowing the construction of the large visitor center, lodge, and ample parking. I was anxious to get outside. Breaking my usual protocol, I took to a trail before even watching the park film. We'd do that later.

Zeke and I started on Nisqually Vista Loop. It's supposed to be a casual paved loop, but pavement was only visible for a few yards. The rest was buried under multiple feet of snow. We slid, ran, trudged, fell, and laughed our way around the loop. The mountain peak, with its great and scarring glaciers, came into view every once in a while through the lodge-pole pine trees. At the trail's furthest reach, we had an unobstructed view of the mountain, while we were on an enormous continuous icescape that stretched up the mountainside connecting to the glacier's ripples. Although it was summer, and I was wearing gym shorts, this place had so much ice and so much snow, that I felt so far in the North, in an arctic landscape. The one thing I had to

overlook, however, was the air temperature, as it wasn't very cold out at all.

At one point on our hike we heard water rushing. We paused and tried to figure out where it was coming from, just to come to the realization that it was beneath us. A mountain stream was flowing beneath the snow. We then encountered a few cavities in the snow just wide enough to fit a body. So taking turns we both hopped down, our boots landing in the shallow stream, and we raised our hands up out of the hole, taking each other's photo, trying for the illusion that we had been buried in snow.

When we completed the loop, we went into the visitor center. It was quite large, with ample space for sitting in its spacious lobby beneath a combination of timber and iron framework that supported a vaulted ceiling. Its walls were almost entirely glass, giving way to much light, especially with all the sun reflecting off the snowy landscape outside. The visitor center had exhibits of the park on its second floor which was a combination of loft and balcony. We went into the theater to see the park film of which I remember nothing, probably because this mountain did not need a film to speak for it. It was so grandiose and commanding of attention, that any measly park film was greatly overshadowed. After the park film, we had a quick bite to eat in the cafeteria there in the visitor center, and then we were back on the trails to visit Myrtle Falls.

Henry M. Jackson Memorial Visitor Center

Our short hike to Myrtle Falls was lovely. I think typically it's only about a half mile walk one way on pavement, but it was a bit more of hike for use trudging over snow banks, perhaps wandering off the official route at times, observing the many marmots lounging and flopping around, and admiring the alpine meadows full of blooming glacier lilies. We concluded our hike at around two miles. Here we weren't exactly above the tree line, for small groupings of pines could be seen at the fringe edges of the meadows, but largely we were above the trees in rolling meadows of the mountainside covered in snow.

Despite it being a sunny day, with a nice rich blue sky, we were cast in the shadow of a foothill. As we approached the falls, we saw it sprawling down into Edith Creek Gorge, chillingly cold in the shadows, water falling

and tumbling over water, streams cascading upon protruding rocks creating many pathways of water. It was a rather simple, but beautiful water fall, as from the creek it sort of bloomed as it fell, branching out in many streams down into the gorge. Just above the falls, the trail led to a pedestrian polebridge perhaps about thirty feet long, made of timber from the forest. Behind the view of the falls, the bridge, the creek, the snow banks, and the flower laden meadows, was the towering Mount Rainier. Its highest reaches were adorned with the silver lining from the sun, peeking out from behind some adjoining ridge, with a cast stretching just far enough to barely reach the top of the mountain.

With all the movement of water sprawling in every which way, falling, and cascading, and glacier lilies feeding off the melting snow, the marmots flopping around, the tourists delighted on meandering paths and trudging through snow, I thought about how rich of a place this was. I also considered how we were up high on the mountainside, and below was a rich forest, full of more waterfalls and streams, thick pines and forest growth, with bears, mountain lions, bobcats, foxes, minks, and all the other wild animals and tweeting birds of the forest. This mountain provided so much life! It was truly rich. I've written about how we can liken mountains to people. There are so many different types of mountains exhibiting the different kinds of influence and character of which a person can posses.

I started this summer's journey in the Mojave Desert where the mountains surrounding are largely dry, harsh, and bare. They lack the richness of a place like this. They do not support an abundance of life. There is no richness of the forest like on this mountainside.

Mount Rainier, with its glaciers melting, feeds the forest around it. Not only can I liken this mountain to Wheeler Peak, being bold and unwavering, but this mountain is also very life-giving. Like a nurse log, it provides rich nutrients, giving life to the forest around it, through its supply of melting ice and its delicate balance of sunlight and shade. However, unlike a nurse log, this mountain is not dead. It's alive. I say it's alive on the basis that it is an active volcano. Thus here lies the message: Though nurse logs provide great insight, showing us how even when we are dead we can provide life to future generations, we provide life to others while still alive as well, just like Mount Rainier. I know this may seem maybe even more obvious than the nurse log analogy, but I think we ought to be aware, we should not over focus on our efforts of what we can leave behind., while ignoring who we are and what we can do in

the present. We have the immeasurable benefit and advantage of our present life. We can use it to take hold of the life books of others and write into them powerful influence, whether it be in the

Paradise Inn

form of encouragement, instruction, giving… Whatever it is
we do, we do not do it alone, as to do so would be in vain.
We do everything through the power of Christ in our lives.
We may be the mountains that provide for the richness of
life around us, but who provides the weather to bring snow
upon our mountains? Who causes the sun to shine on our
side? Who causes the water to melt and fall? Who brings the
flowers to bloom? This makes me think of Scripture, of all
the mentions of bearing fruit spiritually. To bear fruit spiritually is to be like Mount Rainier. Look at the life flourishing
around it. There is evidence of God at work here, and there
would be much more to consider and write about in regards
to the powerful symbolism of Mount Rainier.

When we were done with our hike, we went back to
Paradise Inn next to the visitor center. It was an inn of
beautiful rustic National Park architecture style, cozy and
woodsy, with wood log beams stretching in every direction,
an "A frame" roof, dangling Native American style lanterns,
a blazing fireplace, and inviting little nooks to relax in. It
was a great sanctuary from the snow and the evening cold
outside. There I bought some tea and wrote some postcards.

Leaving the lodge, getting ready to head down the
mountainside to our campsite at Cougar Rock
Campground, a beautiful sunset was on display with deep
rich pinks and purples. The sunset reflected off the snow on
the mountain peaks, providing colorful stretches of snow.
*Wow!* It was a sunset so perfectly reflective of a mountain so
rich in life. Its colors were so vibrant and deep. Most of the

tourists were gone. The area was silent and serene. I had to pause a moment to take it in. John Muir knew what he was saying when he said Mount Rainier was the noblest of peaks.

What kind of mountain are you?

# Skyline, Longmire, and My Walk of Shame

More snow, more glacier lilies, more flopping marmots, more blue sky, more wandering mountain streams, more astounding views– they were all here. It was day two at Mount Rainier National Park in Washington state, and Zeke and I were on our way to Panorama Point. This point was not on my itinerary for the day, but much had been shifted and changed. For the most part, my printed itinerary was ignored for this leg of the trip, and we were just feeling it out. I wasn't going to stress about it either. I was learning to be more carefree, trying to lessen my level of stress and go with the flow, as I was still concerned about my health. So once arriving at the park and observing the maps, a trail named the "Skyline Trail," reaching a "Panorama Point," stuck out to me. I figured places with such names would surely deliver satisfying views.

     As we started off on the hike, we had to leave from

the Paradise hub of the park and hike past Myrtle Falls again, which we had seen the evening before. The entirety of the hike was uphill, and "hill" is quite an appropriate term to describe the terrain, although we were on a mountainside, for this mountainside was composed of various hills and was a very wavy landscape. We'd round one hill, and the incline would lessen greatly for just a moment, and then we were traveling up another. The path we were on had been trodden enough, that for the most part, I could see the path clear from the snow with its natural gravel surface. Much of the trail was also outlined with rocks, but surrounding us, apart from the meadows of glacier lilies, we were surrounded by snow. Slowly but surely we climbed higher, and Paradise was becoming smaller behind us. Reaching the higher snowy elevation of the hike, I noticed to our left a giant gray rock canyon carved by a glacier. The glacier was no longer there. It had melted down into Paradise, but its pathway was clearly visible.

The most astounding view of the trip was not the actual Panorama Point, but when out in a fair distance from us, on the snowy sloping landscape, with a giant rocks wall behind them, and glaciers looming over them, trekked a group of mountaineers. They were traveling all in a line, as in a train pointed upward diagonally. Each mountaineer was bundled up with winter gear: hoods, gloves, and large packs on their backs. They all had trekking poles, and it was obvious they were on their journey to summit Mount Rainier. The view of this train of mountaineers, so tiny and miniscule compared to the immensity of the mountain, added great

perspective; and considering the notion they were on their way to the mountain peak on an impressive journey, sparked in me an exciting admiration for adventure. To be in their presence, if just for a moment, and yet at a distance, helped create this climate of sheer adventure! I wanted to summit Mount Rainier too!...but not this time.

When we reached Panorama Point, after about three miles, there was a leveled area of gravel outlined with rocks. It was also fenced in with a steel cable strung between some stakes. The National Park Service obviously didn't want people on this trail going beyond this point. From here there was a 360 degree view. Looking southward, the main attractions were the sharp peaks of the Tatoosh Range. Although still quite grand in their rugged and sharp attire, they looked like miniature Tetons. From Paradise, the Tatoosh mountains stood tall, but from up here, we looked about level to them or down upon their peaks. Here we could also look down and see the Paradise Inn and the whole village far below. The marmots were trying to steal the show and grab everyone's attention, posing majestically in the most dignified and stately ways, as if suddenly ignoring their rather goofy nature.

Turning to the east, I saw many layers of mountains far in the distance, stretching on immensely. They were of various dark blue shades. The closer ranges appeared darkest, and the further ones lightened up just slightly enough to create a contrast. Thus I could see there were four layers of mountain ranges on display, one in front of another. Behind us, to the north, was a mountain on display as well. First was a snowy stretch of mountainside, but behind it stood the mighty Mount Rainier, ever so boldly, with its crumbling

glaciers. Completing the 360 panorama and turning to the west, two main features came into view: The entire glacier rock canyon I had seen climbing up was in prominent display as a gouge or scar on the mountainside, and then next to it, down in the depths of a valley, was the Paradise River snaking around the forest.

The views were nice, but I believe better views were seen elsewhere in the park. The greatest highlight of this hike was not in the views but was in the journey back down to Paradise. We decided not to complete the entire loop, as it would be a little bit longer and we wanted to preserve time to see some other places in the park, so we went back the same way we came... sort of. This time we did not stick to the path at all. Instead we slipped and slid down the mountainside, surfing all the wavy declining hills. We did so standing up on our feet. There was such a lack of friction between

Longmire

my boots and the snow, and such a perfect uniform slippery
slushy icy consistency of the snow, that I was speeding
down this mountainside. I'd launch myself forward and see
how far I could keep the momentum. It was reminiscent of
sliding across the newly polished wooden floor in socks as a
kid, but here we were sliding down over great expanses, and
it was exhilarating! I was surprised at the physics of this oc-
currence, in that it was even possible. The fun icy descent
had us back in Paradise in no time.

After a quick stop in the cafeteria for some burritos,
we were back in the car. At eleven miles west on the park
road, we stopped at Longmire, a historic section of the park
with tales to be told. Here was a small flat prairie surrounded by trees, and somewhere tucked away were mineral
springs. This was the site where a man named John Longmire and his family had a homestead in the 1800s. It is also
here where the Longmire's opened a mineral springs resort.
People with all sorts of illnesses came from all around the
country to stay at the Longmire's hotel and soak in the mineral springs. It was believed the waters had healing properties. Even doctors would prescribe patients to soak in these
springs. *Where are these springs?* I questioned. *I need to find them.*
*Maybe the springs can heal my ulcerative colitis.* It was unlikely, but
I was willing to try anything. If only I was here about two
hundred years ago. The closest thing I found to a spring was
some sort of water source pooling in bright orange. It very
much resembled the leakage of abandoned coal mines I see
in the forests of Kentucky, but it was likely the minerals of
the spring oxidizing and changing color. It was not very ap-

pealing.

In this Longmire area was also a short path called the Trail of Shadows, which traced a meadow. Next to it stood a small collection of historic buildings from the Longmire's resort days. They were all built in the rustic National Park architecture style. Today, the Longmire's hotel stands as the functional National Park Inn. Next to it was an old rustic gas station and "comfort station," as they called it back in the day, with a tall stone foundation and an overhang with two old gas pumps that were probably once just gas pumps in the wild. Another building, which used to be the park headquarters, is now a small museum on Longmire. It's most fascinating feature to me were some antique taxidermied animals. Maybe it was their age or the way they

were poorly put together, but to me they were funny, especially this taxidermied pine marten flaring its nostrils and showing its teeth, very territorial. As we meandered around the Trail of Shadows, at one point we veered off onto an unmarked path. We ended up crossing a suspension bridge and found a village of unmarked cabins. These weren't on the map. There seemed to be one central building among them. We walked inside just for a moment. Then I quickly realized we weren't supposed to be here. There were couches, tables with board games, and a kitchenette. This was part of a staff lodging complex, I concluded. It was like a community center. *How cool it would be to work in a National Park for the summer,* I thought. What a foreshadowing moment!

Just a couple miles up the road in the park was our campground at Cougar Rock, where we had spent the night before. I thought of taking a break, hanging out at camp, maybe relaxing in the tent, perhaps doing some reading, regrouping and planning the rest of the evening. Our campsite was number twenty, so there was a bit of slow driving through the campground to get to our site. When we arrived, I was stunned to see our tents were not there. Someone else's bright orange-colored dome tent was there instead. All our stuff was gone! I was completely taken off guard. *Did someone steal our stuff? Did someone rob our campsite? How dare they! What a nightmare!* I got out of the car because I was going to confront these imposters, but no one was there. The feeling of offense grew stronger. Then I looked to my right. Our tents and all our camping gear had been thrown alongside the campground road. The audacity! Then

I vaguely remembered something. *I think at one park we are to switch sites in the middle of our stay… It isn't this one, already. Is it?* I pulled out my itinerary. I wanted to prove my suspicion wrong and reclaim my site with my reservation document. I unfolded my itinerary, and embarrassment immediately set in. I was the one at fault. We were the trespassers. We were the squatters. We were the offenders. We were at site twenty, but we were supposed to have moved to site two. I was embarrassed in front of Zeke, to myself, and to whoever else might be in the campground watching us. We got back in the car and I drove to site two. It wasn't that far, only eighteen sites away. I didn't want to deflate my air mattress and deconstruct my tent, pack it in the car, only to reassemble everything. Instead, I decided to take a walk of shame, picking up my tent with the air mattress and all inside. The tent floor was sagging greatly as I was walking it down the road to our new site. I succeeded at trying not to notice anyone else around me, for my head hung low in shame. Back at the site, I situated everything in its place, and carried on, hoping to blend back in among the other campers in the campground.

I don't recall what Zeke was up to at this moment. I was probably too inner focused on my own embarrassment, but when camp was reassembled, I proceeded to seek out some firewood to purchase for a fire we'd have at night to cook our soup. I then rested my head in my tent and read some more of my book on wolves. After a brief rest, we took the short trail from our campground to Carter Falls. The trail was a 1.3 mile segment of the Wonderland Trail,

which in its entirety is over ninety miles. We rushed along
the path beside Paradise River to the falls, which spilled
down from about fifty feet in height. It's described as a
"horse-tail" falls, but the falls splits in two over protruding
rocks near its top to create almost two side-by-side falls. So
I guess it's a horse-tail falls if the horse has two tails. It was a
pleasant fall for such a short hike from camp but nothing to
really write home about. It reminded me much of falls I'd
seen in the Great Smoky Mountains.

After our quick visit to the falls, we drove back to
Paradise. I wanted to hang out in the Paradise Inn again like
we did the evening before. There was a balcony up by the
rafters, in the eves of the roof, with wooden desks and
warm lamps. I bought some hot tea from the inn's cafe and
a few more postcards. I'd fill them out as well as update our
happenings in my journal. When I went to purchase my
postcards, I also bought a green bandana that itself was an
artistic map of the National Parks of the Pacific Northwest,
of Olympic, Mount Rainier, and the North Cascades. It was
a perfect souvenir covering all these parks.

When night set in, we headed back to the campsite,
and this time our tents were still there. *Phew!* I started a fire.
I peeled the label off my can of soup and opened its lid. I
set it just aside from the fire. It was time for supper. This
would be the concluding night of our stay in Mount Rainier
National Park. This was also the last full day of Zeke on this
summer's adventure. The next day, as planned, I'd take him
to the airport in Seattle to travel back to Kentucky. Though
this leg of the adventure was over, I had much still before

me as a solo traveler. I would go on a backpacking adventure in North Cascades National Park, venture on to Lake Roosevelt, and would make my acquaintance with the National Park of all National Parks: Glacier. My health was also about to take a turn for the worse. I'd struggle physically, have to come to terms with reality, learn how to accept it, and find the resolve to carry on amidst hardship.

# REALLY, WHAT KIND OF MOUNTAIN ARE YOU?

Mountains are some of those things in nature seen as universally beautiful. How many photographs capture mountain peaks? How many souvenirs depict their reaches? There's a great wonderment surrounding them as well. How many stories are there about mountains? How many wondrous works of art magnify their glory, and why is there a desire, in so many adventurers, to conquer such heights? Mountains are not just happenstance. They are designed with the richest of meanings. I've talked about them before, but it's time to recap with new findings, bring it all together, and explore them further.

I believe mountains are reflections of mankind, reflecting different types of people. They serve as inspiration and something to reach for, but they also serve as warnings of what not to become. Because mountains have a powerful reflective property, they call for us to stop and check who we are, to see who we have become. Therefore, the question I raise for myself and all my readers is, *What kind of mountain are you?* Of course first we must examine the different types of mountains:

### The Unwavering Mountain

My first relation of mountains to people was at Wheeler Peak in Great Basin National Park in Nevada. I beheld the mountain from below. I just looked up at it and thought, *that is going nowhere,* and then the word, "unwavering," was sent my way. In a world where so much is constantly changing, dependable, consistent, reliable people are rare. I wish to be that constant reliable anchor of a person on the landscape of life. This is our first type of mountain.

*I wish to be that constant reliable anchor of a person on the landscape of life.*

### The Glacial Mountain

It is great to strive to be an unwavering mountain, but an unwavering mountain can also be much more. Let's take a look at the most recent mountain I observed: Mount Rainier. It is a glacial mountain. It's been through many storms and trials of life, which as a result has left ice and glaciers at its peak. This mountain takes all it has experienced, the richness of life, those storms which in the moment might seem bad but in the end are used for good, for wisdom and opportunity, and creates glaciers. Then this mountain helps deliver the life-giving waters to the forest and communities downstream. It does so through self-sacrifice. The glaciers wear the mountain down and erodes it, yet the mountain never forfeits its integrity. Through its glaciers, it creates rivers of life, providing so much enrichment, making things around it grow and prosper. The glacier lilies, the flopping marmots, the forest with all its trees and wildlife are a testament to the character of the mountain.

I believe we read about this mountain in Scripture as Jesus talks about it as the fruit-bearing Christian. He says, "Thus, by their fruit you will recognize them." This mountain is very fruitful. This mountain is also one of the "priests." When God tells Moses His people will be a "kingdom of priests," I believe he is talking about this kind of mountain. No, this doesn't mean this type of person or "mountain" has to be ordained, but it means this person is connected to the Father and intercedes on behalf of others, to draw them to the salvation of Christ. This mountain has responsibility and jurisdiction over the life around it. It is a leader, a giver modeled after the Creator Himself. This mountain develops with age and wisdom, thus it wears a

*This mountain develops with age and experience, thus it wears a 'crown of splendor.'*

"crown of splendor." Like the hairs of a wise and righteous man, it's capped in white. And beneath its snow cap, the mountain wears wrinkles and scars on its face, but it's revered for such things. It's dignified through age and experience.

## The Wooded Mountain

Another type of mountain is the wooded mountain. A glacial mountain can also be a wooden mountain, but not all wooded mountains are glacial. Take for example the Great Smoky Mountains or any of the mountains in the Appalachian chain. There are no glaciers, yet these mountains are extremely fruitful. The Smokies boast one of the most diverse and bountiful biospheres in the world. These mountains, too, are unwavering, but what truly sets them apart is the very thick and rich forest which stretches all over them. These deep woods are filled with many secrets and stories. It's not to say this type of mountain or person is secretive, but it is to say this person is a confidant. It has the trust of others. Life comes to these mountains with all their stories and scars and these mountains become a sanctuary for others. I look at how much life calls these types of mountains home. These mountains are like safe people to confide in.

*These deep woods are filled with many secrets and stories.*

They are nurturers. These people have a forest of knowledge of all who have put trust in them. These "mountains" care and thus remember and retain all that comes their way. They may not be as wise and tall as the glacial mountains, but these mountains are true friends who value all you share with them. You can trust anything with them. They will fold you up in their branches.

## The Desert Mountain

Opposite of the wooded mountain is the desert mountain. Much like the Panamint Mountains bordering Death Valley, these mountains are not fruitful. They are bitter and barren. They do not like to feed life around them. It's evident in the lack of life around them. They are not confidants nor sanctuaries for life, for they have no forest at all. They are harsh. Their existence in life produces little, and what it does produce is prickly. Yes, they are still unwavering, but in the sense that you can depend on the mountains not for anything other than to take up space and maybe create a spectacle. It's sad, but look around. There are a lot of desert mountains. They have nothing to show for the life they've been given. They are also very thirsty for truth, whether they know it or not. All the signs are there.

*They are thirsty for truth whether they know it or not.*

## The Explosive Volcanic Mountain

Another type of undesirable mountain is the explosive volcanic mountain. They are destructive and inclined to harmful anger. They spew lava. Unlike the glacial and wooden mountains, which produce much fruit, these mountains take it away. They tear others down and scorch them with words and actions. They are harassers, spewing bitter words and setting friendships up in flames. These explosive volcanic mountains can erupt because of many different things, but it's almost always because of self-centeredness at the core and the inability to adapt to the forces around them. They easily disregard the life on their mountainsides. They are not unwavering, for their nature is changing. They have great influence but in a negative way, changing the landscape of life for the worse. They are not safe people, yet many people are prone to become volcanic mountains. Let's beware.

These explosive volcanic mountains can erupt because of many different things...

## The Inactive Volcanic Mountain

The word "inactive" might come with a negative connotation, but this doesn't have to do with laziness or obsoletion at all. This has to do with exhibiting a great deal of self-control, regulation, and discipline. This mountain has overcome its nature. Sometimes this mountain may become active, but, in doing so, is not explosive, and it's not defined by being active. This type of mountain can let off steam and fumaroles without destruction, without exploding with lava. This mountain knows of its destructive nature and potential, but overcomes it. It takes its bad nature, or bad habit, and renders it "inactive," whenever it starts to boil beneath the surface. I think of Popocatepetl next to Mexico City. It is active, but it is not feared, for it's not destructive. It lets off steam and returns to calm, allowing forests to thrive around it. From time to time it messes up. It does have minor explosions, but it's not defined by a destructive nature. It yet is reliable and life-giving. It longs to be made new, and that is a righteous pursuit.

*It longs to be made new, and that is a righteous pursuit.*

## The Crater Lake

I veer from mountains to a lake here, but Crater Lake was once a mountain, so it is to be considered among the mountains. Crater Lake has a history. It has been through a lot, but it is on the other side of explosion and now at peace. It is in a state of beauty. It's a survivor. It's redeemed. It has suffered to great extent and been through great pain, but now there is beauty from pain. It is born again and is a new creation, and therefore it is a testimony of redemption. Many can relate to Crater Lake for different aspects of their life that have been redeemed. For some it is their whole person who has been redeemed through forgiveness in the love of Christ. Crater Lake may be calm and not as commanding as the highest peaks, but its resolve and peace is a strong testimony. It does not go unnoticed. In a world of chaos, a countenance of peace is powerful.

*In a world of chaos, a countenance of peace is powerful.*

## The Rock-Slide Mountain

There's a last type of mountain I can identify as of now. It's the rock-slide mountain. It's a weak mountain. When the earthquakes of life come, which are inevitable, it cowers and tumbles. It doesn't mean to, but on account of its weakness, it becomes destructive to those around it. On my later travels in Canada I would come acquainted with Turtle Mountain, where Canada's most deadly rockslide occurred. The event has come to be called, "Frank Slide." This mountain essentially buried the whole town of Frank, taking many lives with it, rendering the landscape lifeless and fruitless. This type of mountain is pitiful, for it lacks fortitude and strength. Cowardice and weakness come natural to man, but courage and strength must be fought for and pursued. The rock-slide mountain, or person, is responsible for its sorry state. It has lacked to build itself up, to form a foundation. It must be known that the foundation to weather any storm and any earthquake in life is only that found in God's Word and through Jesus Christ. This Word also can't just reside on the mountainside, or surface, either. It must live at the very base and core of a person. It is foundational for fortitude in this life and to become unwavering.

So now that I've discussed the mountains in full, let me pose the question yet again: *What kind of mountain are you?* You may have attributes of a few different types of mountains. I believe many people do. Step back from yourself for a moment and observe. What do you see? What does your mountain look like? Take a photograph. Do you see affirmation? Do you see a warning? Do you see conviction? May this help steer you to strive to be a better mountain and encourage you onward in the great adventure of life.

It doesn't mean to, but on account of its weakness, it becomes destructive to those around it.

# Strange Faces, Strange Places

It was the hour to get organized, for it was time to head toward the airport and return Zeke to Kentucky where he came from. So we began first-thing this morning. The trunk of the car was just a grand mess of all our things sort of mixed together: the boots, the backpacks, the flannels, the flashlights, the park maps, the souvenirs. We handed things back and forth as we got organized. "This is yours…..This is mine." We also had to take down the tents and pack up the sleeping bags. It was quite an operation. I wasn't sure how to feel about all this. Was I to be sad to send Zeke off, continuing the adventure by myself? How would that feel after all this time together? Or should I feel happy and relieved to be able to have my solo freedom, to do everything as I wanted to and not have the stress of the complaining and the concern of trying to appease. I guess I sort of shrugged it off. *I'll find out when he's gone,* I concluded.

Leaving Mount Rainier National Park, we stopped just outside at a little "backpacker lodge." That's how I described it in my journal. I didn't bother to write down its name or provide any details, except that I bought a cup of hot tea and a scone for breakfast. I described it as a "backpacker lodge," by the part-grungy, part-artsy nature of the place and the few patrons around sporting large backpacks. In writing about this place, I've examined maps and have tried to locate this place to give it a name here, but I simply cannot find it. Perhaps it doesn't exist anymore, or perhaps it is just well hidden on the maps.

In recalling my adventures in the National Parks and the beautiful wild, this is not the only place I visited I haven't been able to relocate. The very day I picked Zeke up from the airport, and we were traveling our way up California on Highway 101 in the semi-arid lands, passing by many a vineyard, I came to a sign boasting some sort of self-sustaining community. It was advertised as an all-natural farm working on renewable energy. Its signage read "visitors welcome." I knew this was the kind of place Zeke would like to see. So I pulled off the road. This was for him. He seemed excited to see it. We pulled onto a dusty driveway. The land was dry and the sun was harsh. A box stood at a post with a suggested donation listed. We threw in a few dollars. I should have known better…Well, honestly I had no idea what was in store.

So, this was a little commune of various buildings and paths between them we could walk around on. We weren't quite sure where we could go or what we should see. There was some interesting makeshift infrastructure, networks of homemade irrigation systems, green houses, lots of plants hanging around, buildings that were construct-ed…um…what's the word… creatively. It was kind of intri-guing, but then we came across a local. He was a middle-aged man, leathery, wrinkly skin from too much sun expo-sure. His hair was dirty and matted; his shirt only buttoned up halfway to show off his collection of hippie necklaces. He was super friendly and talkative…because he was drunk. The first piece of evidence was the smell on his breath. He welcomed us and gave a slurred introduction to the grounds. He wanted to show us his home that he built him-self. It was a hut made of dirt clay and glass bottles. I'll ad-mit it was impressive. It even had some nice windows built into it. It had to have been a lot of work, but after I briefly saw it, I was done. I was done listening to him curse like a sailor so casually. I was ready to go, but he kept talking and talking.

When we did get away, I made a comment to Zeke about how drunk he was, "…and high," Zeke added. I had-n't picked up on that, but it's because I hadn't been exposed to enough high people to know what that sort of behavior looks like. Then a notion started to dawn on me: *I think we are on a marijuana farm.* Again, I was done. I wanted to get out of here. Before we left we did go into a gift shop, which was surprisingly nice and put together, not very reflective of the jury-rigged nature of the rest of the place. By observing the type of merchandise, my suspicion grew stronger.

That was weird. We carried on.

As I've gone back to maps and the internet to try and find this place, learn more about it to confirm what exactly it was, and to give it a name, I can't find anything. Perhaps that's intentional, and that's fine, because I really don't care to know more. What I do know is that it was in California, and they can have it, and they can keep it. I suppose all I'll ever know about it is what I remember. Just like the backpacker lodge outside Mount Rainier National Park, that's all I got.

After our brief stop for breakfast, we only had a couple hour drive to the Seattle-Tacoma International Airport, so as we got close we made a few stops. Zeke wanted to visit a Target to return a Nalgene bottle he had bought toward the beginning of our trip together. I have a tradition on my summer-long vacations to get a Nalgene bottle and sticker it up with stickers from each park I visit. I had a neon yellow bottle for stickers from my Southwest adventures I write about in my book *Canyonlands: My adventures in the National Parks and beautiful wild.* I have a dark green one with stickers from the *Still, Calm, and Quiet: More adventures in the National Parks and beautiful wild* summer, and I have two classic blue ones from parks I've visited on various smaller trips back in the eastern United States. For this trip I had a dark turquoise bottle sporting my stickers. Zeke had learned of my ways and wanted to do the same. Imitation is the sincerest form of flattery, as they say, so I liked that he wanted to copy me, but the Nalgene he had bought earlier on the trip had a plastic casing around it that must have, at some point, melted onto the bottle and now could not be fully separated. So he wanted to exchange it.

I also let Zeke pick where to have lunch, since it was his last day on the trip, and he was always the one with the large and urgent appetite. It's definitely telling that we were no longer in the wild when he chose IHOP. We were in the city of Tacoma next to Seattle. It was my first time eating at an IHOP. I was surprised to learn there was more on the menu than just pancakes.

In the late afternoon, it came time to take Zeke to the Seattle-Tacoma International Airport. I parked and we went inside. He checked his bag, we said goodbye, and he quickly made it through the TSA security checkpoint. I did feel a poignant sadness. As much as he frustrated me, I felt this heavy aloneness set in. It was the realization that I was so far away from home and now all alone. *Why should this bother me? I've traveled so far away so alone so many times.* But as I saw him move past security towards his gate, I knew deep within me, our friendship wouldn't recover from this trip. Our friendship was built over a love for the outdoors and recreation. Those are great things, but they can also be superficial, especially when we view nature so differently. I view it as God's design with purpose, intention, and messages which it beholds for mankind to draw us closer to Him. Zeke didn't share that view. I also value human life so greatly, much differently than Zeke. We argued about this. He saw human life as too abundant and in need of being lessened. This sat so incredibly unwell with me. I saw it all as sacred and designed by God with great purpose. Redeemed humanity is God's most prized possession. Yes, possession. We are His. I felt I couldn't bring up these deeply held views of mine. They would cause further arguments.

There also was no peace in this friendship. There was complaining and conflict and never a sense of security. We were not kindred spirits. We didn't share any weightier values. At this time in my life I was too young and immature to realize that perhaps I could be an influence upon Zeke's life, but when it comes to forming friendships it takes a great deal of effort for me to form them. I also don't throw the word *friend* around casually. I take the term friendship quite seriously. In recent years I've been very conscious of my use of the term "friend" versus "acquaintance." I will only use that term friend for a true kindred spirit, for someone I can rely on, whom I share great values with, whom I am willing to get behind and advocate for in life, and someone who is willing to do the same for me.

I also believe friendship is a design of God for us to build each other up spiritually. The Bible has a lot to say about friendship. Take into account Proverbs 18:24, "One who has unreliable friends soon comes to ruin, but there is a friend who sticks closer than a brother." Then Proverbs 17:17 reads, "A friend loves at all times, and a brother is born for a time of adversity." Lastly, I'd like to mention Proverbs 27:17, which I also think has a lot to do with friendship. It reads, "As iron sharpens iron, so one person sharpens another." What I thought was a friendship between Zeke and I was not reflective of any of these verses.

We are all wired differently. It takes a deal of effort for me to create friendships. There's this effort of really putting myself out there, and sharing of myself, that doesn't always come naturally. I do it, and delightfully so, when I see the potential for a fruitful and lasting friendship. In such instances it encourages me. I get a great deal of energy from it, and my life is enriched, but to put forth the effort for a friendship based over a mere superficial hobby for nothing of substance, is exhausting. I am not saying that the way I maneuver friendship is the best, and that my views are even the best for me. I find myself often to be solitary, lonely quite often. I suppose if I didn't take friendship building so seriously, but more casually, and I put forth effort to connect even over the shallow and superficial things in life, I may have more people around me. Maybe I'd be less lonely, but also being surrounded by people on a shallow level of commonality I think is exhausting. I would probably feel even more lonely to be surrounded by people who do not share my values and outlook. I do say, that because I do take friendship so seriously, the people I do invest in, whom I truly call friends, mean a lot to me. I am very rich because of them, and maybe I feel a richness of friendship some people do not, and for that I am very thankful.

As Zeke was now gone on his way back to Kentucky, a whole different mindset had to set in. I had to shift from accommodating another traveler to just looking out for myself. I was free! Not gonna lie, this is what I wanted.

Leaving the airport, I was able to quickly adopt the new mindset of being alone and free! The next leg of my journey would take me to North Cascades National Park, but tonight all I had to do was drive two and a half hours to a KOA northwest of Seattle, so I didn't have to be in a rush. Therefore in Marysville, Washington, a suburb of Seattle, I stopped at a Planet Fitness. The original plan was to take a shower there, but then I realized I could just shower at the KOA tonight, and so I just enjoyed a workout. Normally I focus on one certain muscle group per day at the gym, but since I hadn't been to a gym in a while, I decided to just do a little bit of everything.

At this point in my life, I still hadn't made the switch from the flip phone to the smartphone. I had an iPhone, a cheap one, just to take photos and connect to wifi when the opportunity allowed. I needed to take the iPhone into Planet Fitness and connect to the wifi to make a payment through mobile banking. In between sets I was trying to remember a password, reset a password, select all the images of stop-lights, get a confirmation code through the flip phone, translate that over— all of those technicalities.

Next to the gym was a local thrift store. It was pretty large, and I was excited to check it out. *Maybe I can find some fun camping gear. I'd really like to find a skateboard.* That isn't something I could have packed in my suitcase. *Maybe I can find some good CDs for some different travel tunes.* Since I hadn't made the migration from flip-phone to smartphone, I also hadn't made the switch over to digital media. I had no such luck with any of these hopes, but I did find an Under Armour base layer that would come in handy during the cold nights and mornings up in Glacier National Park. Leaving

the thrift store, I did notice a couple homeless people loiter-
ing around the parking lot, one pushing a shopping cart as if
it was a caravan. The way they acted, their demeanor, made
me suspicious they were drug abusers. It was nice to get a
workout in, and to wander around the thrift store, but the
druggies were a stark reminder I was in the city, and I wanted to be back in the wild.

I got in the car and made my few hour drive to the
KOA campground. After zipping up Interstate 5, I was on
Highway 20 heading east along the Skagit River. Urbaniza-
tion waned, and gradually more forest set in. I knew the
KOA wasn't going to be anything fancy in terms of KOAs.
It was just a basic one, but all my experience with KOAs
thus far had been good. Making the turn into the KOA, I
was surprised to find that it was gated, and I had to press a
button to open the gate. I went to the office to check in.
The host seemed a bit frustrated. She went over the usual
rules and explained how the gate will be locked after 10pm.
I wondered why this KOA needed such a security measure
as a locked gate. We seemed to be in a pretty rural area, and
back in nature, which is generally a safer place to be. It's not
like we were in a city. She pointed on the map where my
campsite was. It was the furthest away at a dead-end road.
"There was a picnic table at your campsite, but we've been
having a problem. Some people entered in from the woods
and stole the picnic table, dragging it off into the forest."
This explained her frustration, and now I knew why there
was a locked gate. But who comes from out of the woods
and steals a picnic table? It seemed so odd. I wasn't both-

ered by the fact I wouldn't have a picnic table, but it was unsettling that people come from out of the woods and steal things.

I drove down the gravel path where it dead-ended at my campsite. I was farthest away I could be from any other camper in this campground, isolated. I stood there at my site and looked into the forest, imagining some strange forest people emerging and scoping out what they could glean. *Where were they coming from? What's in those forests?* Not having made the smartphone migration, I wasn't accustomed to using any digital maps to check out my surroundings, so I just looked at that forest with a mysterious wonder, imagining people dragging picnic tables into its depths. Those were unsettling thoughts.

I drove back to the "recreation center," as it was called. It was like a community center in the campground next to the pool. There was a water dispenser and plastic KOA cups. I was a KOA fan and had never seen a KOA cup before. They were obviously meant to be taken. Souvenir! There I sat at a folding table, cracked open my Chromebook, connected to the wifi, and began transferring some of the photos from my point-and-shoot camera's SD card to the Chromebook for backup and also to share some photos online. What an adventure thus far, from the Mojave Desert to Mount Rainier in the Pacific Northwest. It was very relaxing to sit there for a while, and I was at great peace while looking at all these beautiful photos I had taken on my journey. I also proceeded to take a shower and was all refreshed and reset. Then I hopped back in my car and drove back down the dead-end to my campsite.

It was dark now, so there was a certain mysterious ambiance in the air. I stood there on the tent pad in the silence, alone, looking at the forest again. The host's words reverberated in my ears, "Some people came from out of the woods…and stole the picnic table, hauling it into the forest." I imagined them now hauling a body into the forest. I did not procrastinate over a decision. There was an unsettling vibe here. It was not strange enough to cause me to leave, but I was going to sleep in my car, and so I did.

# Traveling Across North Cascades

I got an early start, because I had slept in the car. There was no deconstructing the tent and packing up. I was ready to go. I went from sleep to the turn of the car key and I was on the road. Now it was time to pay a visit to another National Park: North Cascades National Park, which was only about an hour away. When people refer to the North Cascades, it's similar to when referring to the Redwoods. As the Redwoods constitute a collection of state parks, North Cascades too is a collection. There are three major entities: Ross Lake National Recreation Area, Lake Chelan National Recreation Area, and North Cascades National Park proper, though the latter name is just used to refer to all in the trio collectively.

I had big plans for this visit: an overnight backpacking adventure the following day in the Lake Chelan area. Today I would just be traversing the heart of the parks on

Highway 20, stopping at the visitor center, all the overlooks, and seeing what I could see. I had noticed, in my investigation, all the iconic views of North Cascades were roadside viewpoints, so I figured I wouldn't be missing anything essential. When visiting parks I've got to make sure I don't miss out on the essential views. What a shame it would be to go to Yosemite and never see Tunnel View, or go to Yellowstone and fail to see Old Faithful.

My first stop was at the visitor center by the west entrance of the park. There I watched the park film and a series of other films on smaller screens throughout the visitor center. The three National Park units which make up this area were all created in 1968. This park has glacial mountains consisting of over three hundred glaciers. Although it's famous for its sharp mountainous peaks, called the Cascades, it got its name, North Cascades, from all the water cascading from the peaks, forming many streams and rivers. The water sources of the area were used for hydroelectric power, but the development of the National Park stopped the further industrial development. The park's two most famous lakes, Diablo Lake and Lake Ross, are the result of man-made dams. Both lakes are extravagant in their bright turquoise color, which is created from rock particles. The National Park Service describes it best: "The distinctive turquoise color of the lake is the result of suspended fine rock particles refracting sunlight. These rock particles, called glacial flour, enter the lake when rock from the surrounding mountains is eroded by ice and flows into the water through glacial streams."

After learning about everything in the visitor center, it was time to experience it all first hand. About ten minutes up the road I made my first stop. Nestled closely by mountains on either side, within a gorge, and right along the Skagit River, was this little town with modest homes and a few small businesses. It was strange to see manicured lawns, and intentional landscaping around buildings, in a National Park. The only other thing it reminded me of was the town of Mammoth Hot Springs in Yellowstone, where many park rangers and staff take residence. But this town looked rather industrial with lots of electrical wires and utility infrastructure. I know this had to do with the dams and hydroelectric power, but it didn't even cross my mind that the waterways in this park were still being used to generate electricity. I had assumed this was all a relic of the past, that it was a company town of a hydroelectric power company, but the homes left over from that bygone era were now ranger residences. I thought this was a little ranger and park employee village. I'd soon learn I was wrong. The town of New Haven is surrounded by federal National Park land, but this mile long community is owned by Seattle City Light, and all the residents of the town are exclusively employees of Seattle City Light, working on the Skagit River Hydroelectric Project, a series of dams and hydroelectric stations. Altogether this operation provides about 90% of Seattle's electricity. I was surprised to find a currently operating utility company situated within a National Park. Operations of the hydroelectric project began in 1924 with president Calvin Coolidge formally initiating it all, and the National Park designation came more than forty years later. I suppose the value of the hydroelectric power was too valuable to eliminate. I'm sure there is quite an interesting and complex relationship between Seattle City Light and the National Park Service.

In town, I wandered around a bit reading a few historical placards. Prior to World War II this town was quite a tourist destination. The tourists would come in on a twenty-three mile train ride, stay in the Gorge Inn, and go on tours of the Hydroelectric Project on boats. It was quite a thing to see. But after the war it lost its status as a tourist destination.

While in town, I saw an old steam engine on display, and crossed a foot bridge, and I bought a brown sack lunch at Skagit General Store. This town wasn't particularly charming or quaint. It wasn't rustic, and it lacked any defining character. The proximity of the mountains and river were its

most prominent features, but it wasn't trying to be a tourist destination anymore, for it was only a functioning company town. The city dwellers need their electricity. I wasn't expecting this, but I learned that hydroelectricity is a part of the experience when visiting North Cascades National Park.

Just a little bit up the road I passed a dam, one of a series, but this one was the most visible and creatively named, "The Gorge Dam". It had to be old. Observing the architectural design of the powerhouse, you could say, "They just don't make them like that anymore." It was designed with attention to the image it would portray. It was a work of art. Not knowing much about architectural terminology, I would say it was a fusion of Roman and Art Deco design. It had long rectangular windows, boxy features, pillars, and a regal boldness.

Suddenly everything changed past the dam. I was back in the National Park and back in nature's beauty. I was a little disappointed, at the time, to learn that the lakes of the National Park were not natural but were the result of dams. Don't get me wrong. I love a good dam, and I admire human ingenuity to harness power through water, but to know the National Park was not all natural just kind of tainted it a bit in my mind. The only dam I wanted to see here was a beaver dam. *Of course if a beaver dam is a part of nature, then isn't a human dam a part of nature too?* I asked myself. *Is man himself not a part of nature?*

As I continued my journey on the park road, climbing upward in the mountain reaches, I made my next stop at the overlook of Diablo Lake, and oh my! What a sight! Pristine! I was surprised to see that such a vibrant turquoise color could even exist in nature. It was such a bright and vibrant color. Although perplexing, in its surrealness, it yet looked so natural and believable. Mountains dramatically sloped down into the milky turquoise water, which curved around into many bays. To the right side of the lake, before the inlet of a bay, sat two small islands. The middle of the lake spread up to the foot of Davis Peak, a jagged snow-capped mountain. From behind the mountainscape delicate clouds wisped forward, as if imitating beams of sunlight. The dark richness of the pine forests on the mountainsides, contrasting with the turquoise lake and the blue sky, created

a unique Pacific Northwest color scheme. There at the over-look, I also noticed a pine tree whose needles were turning red. It was probably a sickly tree, but in my photos I was able to add a splash of red, creating such a colorful capture. From here the mountains were dramatic and tall, but there were only a few to behold. Mountains didn't stretch on in layers in the distance. Only the immediate ones were seen, giving the accurate impression that I was up very high. All other peaks were below and hidden. Only here could I see the highest reaches, and I did feel on top of the world.

Just a few miles up the road I also came to an over-

look for Ross Lake. It too was stunning. It was similar in
color and nature to Diablo Lake but much longer, and the
way the mountains were situated, and the lesser number of
immediate bays, made it just the slightest bit less picturesque, but still beautiful and magnificent nevertheless.

The rest of my drive provided great views of

sharp craggy peaks, jutting up from the mountains, as if mountains were upon mountains.
These weren't rounded or flowing mountains
but dramatic sudden reaches. And they were
immediate reaches, right there, with snow
caught in their veiny rivets. There was a
definite character to these mountains,
and if these mountains were music,

they'd be crescendoing cymbals of a regal nature. It was as if I could hear the mountains. I stopped at one overlook of the mountain valley and beheld the mountain peaks beside me, so tall. It was truly a moment of awe, and I thought, *I'm back. I'm in my element. The awesome wonder that befell me my first great summer adventures is here to recapture my spirit.* The sense of adventure was on fire again, a blazing campfire, with sparks igniting the night sky. I was coming back in my spirit to a place I so longed to be.

About twenty miles outside of the park I arrived into the town of Winthrop, Washington. None of the campsites in the National Park were reservable online, and, planning my trip, I wanted to have the security of a place to stay. I wasn't sure how busy North Cascades would be. It didn't prove to be very busy at all. Arriving in Winthrop, I was sur-

prised. The land was very arid. There were hillsides surrounding which were very dry and barren. I could have been
fooled that I was in a desert of the Southwest. I had never
before associated the desert with Washington. On the way
to the KOA I drove through the little downtown. It was a
quintessential Wild West downtown of not just Western facades, but the real deal. Nothing was too bold or boisterous
but rather small and charming. The businesses displayed
names such as "General Merchandise," "Emporium," and
"Saloon." A functional vintage gas station with two pumps
sat next to the road where people walked on the sidewalks. I
realized this place was a tourist draw, but not overly so. It
wasn't crowded. It wasn't flashy. It was just right. After being in the remote brisky north reaches of the Cascades, it
was comforting to be in this warm little welcoming Western
frontier town. I'd later learn that Owen Wister, the Harvard
roommate of one of the original settlers in the area, Guy

Winthrop, wrote his famous Western novel, *The Virginian,* after a visit to Winthrop.

The KOA was only a mile from the downtown stretch. I drove across the Chewach River, noticing a bike path parallel to the road and also crossing over the river which was shimmering in the evening sun. Everything around here looked well taken care of. Right next to the entrance to the KOA was a long wooden Western style building named "Winthrop Dry-Goods." *Perfect!* I went inside the small grocery store and bought some yogurt, Frosted Flakes, and milk.

I checked into the KOA, and it was so nice. It sat right at the Methow River, at the foot of a desert hill. I had reserved a camping cabin, which had plenty of space around it, and I felt like I had so much space to breathe in this nice dry, warm, and welcoming place. I took off my boots and trod around barefoot. Relaxed, I organized the trunk of my car. Now that Zeke was not here, I had full reign. I also did a load of laundry and packed for my upcoming backpacking trip to Stehekin. While the clothes were spinning, I took a warm shower in the nicest KOA bathroom I have ever experienced. When I checked in, the host even bragged about how new it was. It was a log cabin style building and inside there were about a half dozen little individual private bathrooms. Each had their own shower and little changing area separate from the sink, mirror, and the rest of the bathroom. They also each had their own skylight, letting in warm sunlight. They all had that nice new building smell, but not just any new building, but a fresh-wood log cabin smell about them.

When I gathered my laundry and went back to the cabin, I noticed a few items hadn't dried completely, so I laid them out on the railing of the porch. I then poured myself a cup of Frosted Flakes into my KOA cup from the night before and reveled in the sweet crunch. As I sat on the porch swing, I updated my journal and read a little bit of John Muir. This was a simple yet blissful moment.

I then drove back into town, first stopping at the cable bridge alongside the bike path to cross over and look down into the river. In downtown, I parked my car and walked down the main street. There wasn't as much to see as I expected from the initial perception driving in, but it was all pleasant. I ate dinner in an old turn of the century schoolhouse, rightly named "Old Schoolhouse Brewery." I had a chicken sandwich on the back porch overlooking the river.

Back at my little cabin, at great peace from a quiet and productive evening, and after having a day full of great vistas and travel, I slept soundly, anticipating the adventure that lay ahead: backpacking into Stehekin.

# STEHEKIN:
## THE MOST REMOTE COMMUNITY IN WASHINGTON

I was very much looking forward to this next leg of my adventure. Never before had I done something quite like this. I was going to board a boat on Lake Chelan, take it forty miles to the other end of the lake, and get dropped off in the isolated community of Stehekin on the fringe edges of North Cascades National Park in Northern Washington. The plan was to camp there for two nights, explore the area, and enjoy the remoteness. Let's go!

I woke up at the KOA campground in Winthrop, Washington and left by 6:30 am, giving myself plenty of time to drive an hour south to the town of Chelan to board the boat at 8 am. I drove through the arid grassy hills of the region speckled with pine trees. Passing through the outskirts of the town of Chelan, I reached the harbor. There sat the vessel, "The Lady Express," alongside a single small dock. She was a moderate vessel, with a holding capacity of one hundred people. The entrance to the dock was sandwiched between two small harbor buildings. Behind it sky-blue waters lay and great mountainous peaks stood in the distance. I rounded a bend to reach the fenced-in parking lot across the street from the boat dock. It was free to park, but it looked like, because of the fence and gate, it was locked up at night. *How should I take this?* I thought. *Does this mean it's a safe area to leave my car, because it'll be fenced up, or is this a crime-ridden area, because it has to be locked up at night?* It just seemed like a small town to me, nothing that should produce much in crime, but having witnessed Seattle area a few days prior, and being a rather skeptical and untrusting person to begin with, the thought of safety did cross my mind, but I concluded I liked the fact the car would be left fenced in.

Now it was time to pack! I had made a list of what to bring with, the night prior, and I had begun packing but hadn't quite put everything together. First, I needed to get dressed for the day. I just rolled out of bed and left the campground. I figured I'd put myself together once I had the security of being where I knew I needed to be in time. After changing clothes in the car, I fetched my overnight backpack from the depths of the trunk and finished gearing up. I needed quite a bit– not only layers for the drastically changing temperatures of the mountainous far North, but also all my camping gear for two nights. My final step was changing out from my flip-flips into my hiking boots. Putting on those boots and tying those laces really puts me in the spirit for adventure. I was ready!

I checked in at the little building beside the dock where they issued my boarding pass, and soon I was on the boat and on my way! The boat was very simple. It maybe was at only a fourth of its capacity. I sat toward the front end. Most of the passenger access was enclosed, but I opened the window to look outside. I noticed the hills immediately surrounding the lake, here by the town of Chelan, were brown from dry grasses, and buildings congregated down at the water's edge. The further we floated from town and out in the lake, the less and less buildings there were. Just a few lavish luxury homes every once in a while dotted the surrounding hills. Then the hills grew larger and greener, becoming increasingly mountainous. The boat rounded a few curves in the lake, and civilization was all left behind. Now on either side of the lake stood the mountains of the

North Cascades with their craggy peaks. With each passing minute, I realized we were becoming more and more remote, and curiosity grew of what this place, Stehekin, would actually be like. *What sort of place can exist so far away from any other civilization?*

The boat ride in total was two and a half hours. I knew it was coming to an end when the lake narrowed and became darker, as the sun was hidden behind the mountain peaks. Then the boat couldn't go much further, because up ahead was just a large mountain and the great wilderness. The boat pulled up to a dock. I spotted a few structures, including the prominent North Cascades Lodge at Stehekin, a modest timber constructed building lying beneath the trees. There were a few vehicles too, and I knew the vehicles were resident vehicles. They didn't go elsewhere, because they couldn't. Stehekin only has one road. It stretches for thirteen miles but does not connect to any other road. It starts here by the lodge and ends at wilderness access. Just the sight of the lodge and the vehicles assured me that perhaps this was a bit more civilized than I had imagined. *I won't be roughing it by any challenging means. I see infrastructure, if primitive, and there will be running water since there's a lodge.*

Once I got off the boat, I made a beeline for the National Park's Golden West Visitor Center to get a camping permit. I had no experience or insight to know if it would be hard to find an open campsite here. *Would this be a popular place, or is this too off the beaten path?* I would find it to be the latter. With ease, I got a camping permit and was directed to the Lakeview Campground, just steps away. It was a rather developed campground, with picnic tables and fire rings, of little sites nestled into the mountainside, overlooking the lake through the pine trees. It was not busy, just a few other tents were set up. I found a site that backed up to some trees climbing up the mountain. I pitched my tent and unpacked. I realized I could not lock anything up. I would have to be trusting. I did take my day pack with me and walked just steps away to "downtown" which consisted solely of the visitor center, lodge, post office, and bike rental shop. There I rented a bike for twenty-four hours. With this I could see it all, and I wasted no time in beginning to do so. I was ready to bike the full expanse of the road and see all the things. I had received a map from the bike concessioners that had all the points of interest along the road, and so I took off.

*How cool!* Just the thought of being in this isolated community that connects to nowhere, but tucked away in the North Cascades, was so novel and exciting. I was also relieved everything worked out to be here. I made it! The place was quiet, serene, and beautiful. The freedom to explore on bike, propelled by my own effort, zooming through the pine filled mountain air, was invigorating. To my left was largely the mountainside and forest, to my right were a few private cabins dispersed alongside the lake. They were picturesque, small, simple, with immaculate little landscaped green grass yards, decorated with flowers, that backed right up to the lake with their little docks. The glassy reflective lake waters spread behind, and mountains stood beyond. A few were of a rustic pioneer cabin style, with

their little stone chimneys standing aside their wooden frames. One looked like a miniature Swiss chalet.

Just about a mile from where I started my bike ride, the lake came to an end and was replaced by the Stehekin River. There at the convergence lies the river delta. The road curves just enough to position the traveler right at the head of the lake by the wispy marshy grasses of the delta lands. The view was gorgeous, looking out into the valley with layers of mountains spilling into the lake. I paused to take in the beauty and serenity.

On the other side of the road was "The Garden." It was on the map. I stopped to find the large garden surrounded by forest and with rows and rows of produce and flowers precisely organized and sectioned. It was bountiful and flourishing. I wasn't sure if I was welcome to explore

the grounds or not. Nevertheless, I'd be back later. There were other things to see.

About a half-mile up the road was the Stehekin Pastry Company. I knew nothing about this place. I hadn't come across it in my research, or at least I hadn't taken particular note of it. Its name was painted on a wood sign propped up against a stone fence. Just behind that was a lush, shady, decorative garden. Most of the building, which looked like a home, was overshadowed by large trees with limbs sprawling above it. I walked the little path, amidst the stone fence and garden, into the most delightful bakery. Cinnamon rolls, pies, and cookies stood in the display case proudly. Behind the counter, visible to all patrons, was the kitchen. I saw enormous mounds of dough on the tables, and people crafting delicious things to eat. The customer side of the establishment was rather dim, but in a cozy cab-in-like feel, with wooden walls and fixtures everywhere. The bakery's kitchen was bright and sleek. I bought myself a nice big piece of peach pie and enjoyed it. As I was waiting to check out, I was observing the bakers busy at work. They seemed to really know what they were doing and enjoyed their work. *How cool it would be to work and live in such a remote place and have the National Park and wilderness a stone's throw away!* I Imagined going to work in a bakery, making the dough for the pastries, and for my pocket, and then leaving work to be immersed in the natural beauty of the wild. I was a bit envious. I wanted to be making pastries, sharpening a new skill and living within a community in the remote stretches of the wild. It seemed just fanciful, just a fun thought to entertain, trying to envision myself in such a setting. I had no idea that this moment, these thoughts, were all foreshadowing of what the future had in store for me. Something like this was not unreachable for me.

I got back on my bike, and just about a mile up the road, I stopped at the Stehekin School, a rustic one-room log cabin schoolhouse in the National Register of Historic Places. Two wooden beams served as steps up to the front porch which was shaded by a long roof overhang. The door was open. I entered. Inside I saw an old chalkboard in the front and a little podium for the teacher. There were old fashioned wooden and steel student desks, where behind the seat of one was attached the desk of another. I saw the little wood burning stove, the oil lanterns, maps and faded student drawings hung up on the walls, and stacks of text-

books on a table against the window. At first I was con-fused. *Is this still in operation? It sort of looks like it's still lived in.* Then I figured it was probably frozen in time as a historical site. Arrested decay?

The map of the sites along the road also had descrip-tions of each. I learned that the school was built in 1921 and was used until 1988 when the new school was built. The population had outgrown their one-room schoolhouse and thus they built a new two-room schoolhouse. Just up the road I checked out the newer school. It had a sign next to the road and a mound of freshly chopped firewood which looked like it had just been delivered. The new school was still a log structure, but it didn't have the rustic look of the original. It looked more like a large hut, in that it had a long drooping roof, but it was very nice, aesthetically construct-

ed, beautiful in its own 1980s design. Around it was a small school yard of well cut green grass, and, beside it, the woods of pines standing tall. In that moment my heart yearned to be able to be a teacher in such a place. I had been entertaining the thought of working in a bakery in the wild, but I had no such experience as a baker. However, the schoolhouse was just up my alley. I am a teacher. *I wonder if they are hiring? I bet it's hard to get a position in such a place.* The reality also hit me that I'm a Spanish teacher, not certified as a general education teacher. The teacher here probably had to teach all subjects to all grades. I wouldn't be cut out for it, but I longed to live in a place like Stehekin already. Even though I was still making acquaintance, it was all so appealing.

Next point of interest was Rainbow Falls. A short path off the road led to it. It was very impressive. Water dropped straight down in a picturesque 312 foot tall fall. I was surprised I hadn't heard anything about this waterfall before. It was so beautiful, and definitely a site worth seeking out. It certainly wasn't as tall as Yosemite Falls, but it dropped in the same horsetail elegance of those falls. It reminded me much of the Sierra Nevada.

After the falls, the road eventually turned to complete gravel and stretched on for about five miles without any other point of interest, just forest, and dispersed cabins. Then I came to Stehekin Valley Ranch. I knew it was a ranch, but wasn't sure what that meant in this context. There was one main structure, a few other outposts, a garden, and a field tucked between the forest. There were some horses grazing, including a large clydesdale of which I snapped a photo.

I was nearing the end of the road when I had completed eleven miles, but it didn't seem so long. It was so enjoyable to stop and see all the things along the way. I liked

how, in Stehekin, everything was on the same road. Everything was in a linear progression. It was so simple, so not overwhelming. Near the end of the road, I crossed a short steel and wooden framed bridge, over the river, and came upon the trailhead for Agnes Gorge. I parked my bike, not worrying about it not being locked up and disappearing. I hadn't seen anybody in forever. I enjoyed the freedom of not having to worry about my things, like I often have to in the more overdeveloped and sophisticated world. As I began the trail, I saw a sign nailed to a tree. Along with the official emblem were the words, "The Pacific Crest Trail." I was surprised that the national trail came through this area. I ended up hiking five miles in the Agnes Gorge. The trail led through the forest to cliff edges up high, looking down at the river gorge. The forest here was very lush with greenery of all kinds, and the forest floor was hidden by growth.

At one point, it did hit me that this was probably the most remote I had ever been, if not to include my adventures in the middle of Nevada. Not only was I in Stehekin and its own remoteness to begin with, but I was way down the road at the far end, removed from everyone, now miles in on a trail. I also hadn't seen anyone since maybe eight miles ago at the bakery. I actually reveled in the solitude. In the physical sense, there was the forest and me. That was it. This world was mine. For some this notion might bring about a bit of anxiety, but for me it brought incredible peace. I never feel completely alone or vulnerable, for I know I'm always in God's presence even when no other human is present. I also am the type of person who can have fun in a group of people or amidst the crowds, but I so cherish, and value moreso, one-on-one time with a friend or individual. It gives me the ability to really get to know a person and connect on a deeper level, to know that person and to be known and heard by that person. So, here at the end of the road, in the Agnes Gorge, removed from everyone else, it was one-on-one time with just me and God. That brought me incredible peace. Let me wander and revel in that.

After I biked the eleven miles back to the other end of the road to my campsite, evening was setting in, and I noticed I had a neighbor. I don't recall how, but she struck up a conversation with me. Her name was Luna Lu. She was a young Asian lady with bleached blonde hair. As we got to talking, she explained how she was from Los Angeles and was a photographer. She invited me to come sit over at her picnic table. We talked about National Parks, Los Angeles, and my day's journey through Stehekin. Of course, as the conversation progressed, I was trying to figure out just why she was taking interest in me. She explained how she loved traveling and taking photos of nature. She had just come from Yosemite and was going to be here for two days, just like myself. She was hoping to capture some good night sky photos, especially of the Milky Way tonight, with virtually zero light pollution. She explained how she was going to go about walking at around midnight to see what kind of night sky views she could behold. She invited me to go explore with her at night. The thought did seem intriguing and she was proving herself to be good company, but clouds were rolling in and I knew I'd be asleep by then. *I could always wake up.* I wasn't convinced it was a good idea. I bid her goodnight, crawled into my tent, and quickly drifted to sleep. What a good day. I loved this place and had a whole additional day in Stehekin to look forward to.

# PASTRIES, GROUSE AND GREATNESS

I woke up to the strangest most intrusive sound in my campsite, just beside my tent. I could not place this sound. I was so perplexed. It sounded like a drumming, but too soft, and coming from too low-down to the ground to be that of a human. *A gnome? An alien? That's ridiculous!* It was so close, approaching my tent. *This is bizarre.* I rolled over and pushed myself up quickly to unzip my tent. There stood the funniest looking bird. I would describe it as looking like some sort of wild chicken, but it was strutting with its feathers on full display and its chest puffed out, like a miniature turkey. It looked so proud and pompous, yet it was so small and ridiculous, especially with its little feather tufts sticking up on the top of its head like some punk-rock motorcyclist. It was trying to be tough, but had big curious infant-like eyes. My initial thought: *What the heck is that?* Upon locking eyes, his feathers shrank close to his body, in what I perceived as a reaction of embarrassment, and then he scurried off into the forest in fright.

I had never seen this type of bird before, and I don't know how I knew, but somehow it's name was on the tip of my tongue. As I exited my tent and slipped on my boots, I kept trying to fish this word out of my memory. I was so close. I gathered my water bottle and my new book on Stehekin and threw them into my backpack. I began walking down the hill and it hit me: *It's a grouse!*...then, *Is the plural form of grouse, grease?*

This was day two of camping in Stehekin, the most remote community in Washington. My encounter with the grouse was midday. When I woke up and unzipped my tent for the first time of the day, I was greeted by the tall pines, the serene lake below, and the mountains standing mightily on the other side of the lake. My camping neighbor Luna Lu was already up as well, fixing things about her camp.

"Good morning," I greeted. "Did you get some pictures of the Milky Way?" I asked.

"No. I didn't end up going. It was cloudy last night," she explained.

It's what I had suspected.

This morning my first order of business was to go to the bakery for some breakfast. I invited her to come along, but she had her own hiking plans. After quickly putting myself together, I hopped on my bike and took off down the road toward the Stehekin Pastry Company. The mountain morning air was brisk and refreshing, and there was no morning bustle about this place, as is common in so many places. Here the few people that were around eased into their morning. It was relaxing, moving at the gradual pace of the rising sun, slowly, growing with every passing moment more alive.

Opening the bakery door, I was bombarded with the enticing smells of cinnamon and coffee, blended with all the other aromas of the fine craftsmanship of the Pastry Company. After camping outside in the cold Northern night, and biking through the brisk mountain air, I knew it was going to be so relaxing and perfect to sit down with a cup of something hot to drink and a great big fresh cinnamon roll dripping with house-made icing. I sat by a window, glancing outside to watch the forest slowly wake up and be illuminated by the morning light. I was in peaceful bliss doing just so.

After a while, I got up to browse the nearby shelf of merchandise. There were hats, stickers, and books. A particular book caught my attention, *Stehekin: A Valley in Time,* the true story of the valley through the eyes of Grant McConnel, a man who lived here from the 1940s until the 1990s. I bought it, along with a sticker. I wanted to learn more about this place, and this book seemed perfect. I also noticed a number of other books by local authors. I realized this was somewhat of an author community. I understood why. The place was ripe for inspiration with its natural beauty, and its remoteness and solitude eliminates all the distractions for the writer. I would love to live in such a place and dedicate my time to writing.

So far I'd imagined myself living here as a baker, then a teacher, and now an author. I had no idea that in less than a year I'd find myself spending my whole summer on the edge of Glacier National Park, in the remote community of Polebridge, sandwiched in between parkland and National Forest, in the wildest river valley in the lower forty-eight states. There I'd live and work amidst the beautiful Rocky Mountains, off the grid, in the beloved Polebridge Mercantile and Bakery. I guess we could say it was a dream come true, after looking at the dreams occupying my mind during my time in Stehekin.

When I was interviewing for the job in Polebridge, over the phone in the winter, the owner told me how he wanted to place me at the front of the store as a closing cashier. In that moment, and in fact all through the interview, in my mind I kept seeing the Stehekin Pastry Compa-

ny. It was my only point of reference to such a job. I re-
called seeing the bakers back in the kitchen with their
mounds of dough, working so diligently but seeming to
have fun. "What about putting me in the role of a baker?" I
asked. The owner, Will, explained how he believed that with
my skill set as a teacher, I'd be best suited for the front of
the house. He was right. He told me that if things work out,
he'd like for me to keep a relationship with the business and
return for more than just a summer. I worked there for
many summers, and I continue to do so. My time working
at the Polebridge Mercantile and Bakery are some of the
richest of my life. Although oftentimes rustic and primitive,
it's my summer paradise. I love it!

After my morning cinnamon bun, I got back on my
bike and traveled non-stop to the other end of the road,
past all the sites I had stopped at the day before: the one-

room schoolhouse, the two-room schoolhouse, Rainbow
Falls, Stehekin Ranch, and then bearing off the main road I
rolled down a path to the Stehekin Airstrip, a field amidst
the pines. *Is this really an airstrip?...I guess it would do.* I could
imagine a little private plane landing and rattling atop this
field. I supposed boat access wasn't the only way to arrive at
Stehekin, but plane access had to be private. There were no
commercial or charter flights. Biking past the "airstrip" I
sought out "The River Trail," from my map. When I leaned
my bike against a tree, and started on the trail, I realized it
was not a very frequently trafficked area, for it was mostly
overgrown and had just a narrow space barely big enough
for my feet. My ankles were brushing up against the growth
of the forest floor. This was a rich lush forest, more characteristic of those back East. At one point, the path came
close enough to the river, so that I could see the water. At
this location, I'd call it more of a creek than a river. I veered
off the path and stepped down onto the river bed. It was so
shallow the water didn't even reach as tall as the top of my
boots. The water was also not high enough to cover all of
the riverbed. The middle of the river was dry, so it was there
I sat down. With my eyes closed and listening to the trickling water around me, I prayed a prayer of thankfulness for
being here. I also prayed about my health. I had enough distractions from all I was seeing and experiencing in Stehekin
that I hadn't been focusing on it, but it was still, in its own
aching way, always present on my mind and felt in my weak-
ening body.

    *This is good for me,* I thought, to relax by the river, to

take in the soothing sounds of the water and the lights beaming through between the tree branches. This was a gift from God. I had been feeling that my body was caught in this state of high tension and if I could get it to calm down, escape this state of being, I'd be okay, but it felt like a lot to do. I was up against my very self. I concluded every moment should be used to help bring my body out of this state of tension. This was one such moment. Relaxing was now a priority of mine. In my relaxed state, I broke open my journal and began to write.

When I got back on my bike, calmed, settled, grounded into this time and space, I leisurely began biking back to the other end of the road. Of course I had to pass by the bakery again, and it was time for lunch. I was hungry and there were many great things on the menu for lunch. I couldn't make up my mind of what to order, so I just decided to buy two lunches, a salad with salmon and a roast beef sandwich. They were delectable– especially the salmon. I thought it was fitting to eat salmon in the Pacific Northwest. Once back in "town," I realized it had been about twenty-four hours since I had rented my bike, so it was time to turn it in. Then feeling mildly handicapped without my wheels, I walked back up to my campsite. It was time for a nap. It was only afternoon, yet I had already covered great ground this morning and felt it was fine to give up some of my day to sleep. After all, relaxing was now a priority. I fell into a deep sleep in my tent, wrapped in this fold of nature, and then I woke up to the drumming grouse just outside my tent.

I ended up spending a large portion of the evening sitting on a rock, up on the mountainside, behind the campground, looking down at the lake. There I read the book I had bought about Stehekin. It was a very entertaining read. Between this evening and the following morning I read the whole book. That's very fast for me. It was *that* good. I enjoyed learning about the community back in earlier times. I read how delivering mail along the stretch of road was a shared responsibility. People took turns. In the winter, the author delivered the mail on skis. It was customary for him to stop by and visit with everyone along route. It sounded kind of nice, skiing out in the cold of winter, stopping occasionally every few miles, stepping into a warm house with a warm fire in the hearth, greeted with a cup of coffee or tea, and engaging in conversation about the latest news of the valley. It also stuck out to me, the part discussing how there was only one phone in Stehekin in the post office brought in by the National Forest Service. That was the only immediate communication to the outside world, and it wasn't very reliable. It also struck me as comical, the part about the aftermath of a plane crash up in the woods, and how the locals, given they had very limited resources, stripped that plane and used it for building materials in their homes, and even parts of it were used for dinnerware. Remnants of the plane could be seen showing up all over the community in people's houses.

The author talked about how, for so long, Stehekin was frozen in time, and a unique and very personal community. Whenever someone had to take the boat down the valley into Chelan, people were often repulsed by the chaos and lifestyle of those "down lake." Reading this book, everything seemed like such a far-off, foreign, yet intriguing concept. However, later in my own time working at the Polebridge Mercantile and Bakery in Montana, I would live through similar experiences. It too is, at this time, a one phone community. The contrast between our life up the North Fork River valley couldn't be more stark against the developing society down stream.

The following morning, day three in Stehekin, it was time for me to go "down lake," back into the real world, but I wouldn't be spending much time in society. It was time for the next leg of my adventure and off to other wild places, soon approaching the behemoth of National Parks: Glacier National Park. Before I boarded the boat, I walked to "The Garden." This morning the gardener was there. From my

understanding this was all his. I bought some sugar snap peas and cherries from him. I stood there in the garden and spoke with him for a few minutes. He told me some of his story and how he ended up here. At the time, it struck me as sort of weak, running away from society and life's problems to live up here in remoteness. I had perceived it as a negative thing, but with the evolution of society "down lake", and after my own experience living in a similar remote community, I have grown in perspective, thinking back on his story. There is a healthier way of living that is lost in the bustle of growing society. I get it.

Back on the boat, I was munching on my delicious sugar snap peas, so sweet and crisp, mixing things up every-so-often with a nice tart juicy cherry. *This is going to be good for me,* I was thinking, for my body and fighting the inflammation I was feeling. *Some nice fresh produce, a few days in Stehekin with moments of great relaxation, and now sitting in the sunlight on the open water is going to make me just fine,* I thought. *My ulcerative colitis was just some strange nightmare. I'm going to put this illness behind me. It's over. I'm okay now.*

I was wrong, very wrong. This was only the beginning. Things were going to get much worse... and much more beautiful.

# LAKE ROOSEVELT AND THE
## CONSERVATIONIST VS. THE PRESERVATIONIST

"Okay, I look alright." I said to myself while looking at my picture with the sign to Lake Roosevelt National Recreation Area. It was a relief. I was not feeling well at all. I thought my relaxing time in Stehekin would be good for the body. It was certainly good for the soul, those two nights up in the forest, in the most remote community in Washington, surrounded by nature. Yet inside my intestines and my immune system were still angry. I felt as if I was entering that stage where my body was starting to reject food altogether. Anything I would eat would make me feel unwell, and I felt weak and withering. This was devastating to me at the time, for a number of reasons, but especially because in recent years I had really focused on my health and building my body up. I was so disciplined and persistent with my daily workouts. I was very strict on my diet. My body was my most valuable thing in life. We should all treat our bodies as the valuable things they are, but I believe I had become over preoccupied with it.

I could see the natural process that played its course for me to arrive at such a place. I had spent much of my teens and young twenties very ill. Then my body healed. I regained strength and began to feel healthy after a long period of sickness. As my body began to once again absorb nutrients from food, it was exciting, and I held such an appreciation and gratefulness for my health. Slowly that evolved into being over-concerned and over-consumed with it. It was about more than health too. It was also about building muscle and maintaining a certain physique. It was building an image and maintaining it. That doesn't have to be a bad thing, but... Did I let that consume me, so losing my health was now unnecessarily devastating? This is what I was thinking.

Now I felt like everything I had built was crumbling down. I was living to build my body. I had put so much value in that, and now I did not have it. My muscles were withering away and I was feeling weak and ill. It was a punch to the gut that was already wounded…. But in the photo I just took, I thought I looked good. I still looked healthy. I still looked strong. I certainly was feeling worse on the inside than I looked on the outside. Sometimes, with ulcerative colitis, it is apparent when someone is ill, but it is also a silent illness, in that one can be very sick and feel utterly miserable, but on the outside everything may look fine.

The photo I took gave me a little pick-me-up, for I was low in spirit. After the welcomed distractions of Stehekin and the excitement of exploring that little pocket in the woods the past few days, I had a three hour drive in which I felt miserable. My gut was restless and my body was fighting itself. I was pestered with the thoughts: *Why is this happening to me?;* and, *No, this can't be happening;* but then I repeatedly was confronted with the reality that, *Yes, this is happening.* My thoughts would at times be distracted, especially by sights along the way, but then I'd feel the abnormal churning of the gut, an urgency to pull over, and I'd have to repeatedly confront reality: *I'm ill.*

Eventually I arrived at Lake Roosevelt National Recreation Area. I had pulled over at one of the entrances to take my picture by the sign, something I try to do at every National Park unit. Feeling slightly better about my current state after seeing my photo, I pulled into Kettle Falls Campground. It was a very open arid campground. There were a few pine trees here and there, but mostly dry grass and dusty ground. I was atop a bluff beside the lake and on a rounded island, very close to the mainland. As much as I love the deep forest, there is always something very comforting to me about wide open spaces. I think it's the midwestern Illinois blood flowing through me. It's calming for me to see the big sky and gaze over long distances, and there I could see that sky and could look across the land over the lake.

## Conservationists vs. Preservationists

Lake Roosevelt really is a part of the Columbia River formed by the Grand Coulee Dam created by president Franklin D. Roosevelt in 1941. I love natural places, and there is something remarkable about a beautiful lake naturally occurring in the wild, but there is something mildly disappointing about a dammed lake. I am not against dams. I think dams are fascinating in how much renewable energy they can provide and all the outdoor recreation they can afford. However, I am well aware that there are people who are completely against dams altogether and any human influence upon the land. When I consider these people, I know I differ with them in the type of naturalist I am. I believe I am a conservationist, which I would define as one who calls for responsible use of the land to maintain its benefit for further generations. This is certainly different from exploiting the land, for I have great reverence for the land. If we were to exploit it, we would rid it of all its benefits, rendering it useless and defacing its natural beauty. Rather, I believe we conserve it, so we can have it for its benefits for generations.

In some instances the best step we should take as conservationists is leave some things alone, preserve them. However, my worldview is that the earth is designed for man's benefit, and therefore we should use the earth for its intended purposes, and sometimes that benefit is simply of its beauty. An example is the Yosemite Valley. Don't touch it. Let it be. It holds remarkable beauty. Other times the best purpose is for recreation or energy. Perhaps that's the assessment here for Lake Roosevelt. Sometimes the best purpose is agriculture, mining, cattle raising, farming, housing. Historically, the National Forest Service has been a conservationist department, their motto: "land of many uses." The National Park Service is different, in that its "to preserve and protect," a largely preservationist mentality.

The preservationist, as an individual, doesn't believe in any human involvement with the land. They believe in leaving it completely untouched. They want preservation as is. A conservationist believes in preservation as well, but the preservationist doesn't share the same view of land use as the conservationist. Historically speaking, I have great respect for both types of people. Theodore Roosevelt was a great conservationist, and John Muir was a great preservationist. Together they accomplished a lot. I think the input of both, the challenging view of one upon the other, is good to find a balance and approach situations reasonably. Unchecked, the conservationist could be corrupted into an exploiter of land, but the preservationist helps bring the conservationist back to his roots of mighty respect for the land. Also the unchecked preservationist can become an extremist, viewing the human as merely a hindrance to the planet, restricting his due duty to the earth. As a consequence the planet actually suffers. Unfortunately, I think many have arrived at this harmful viewpoint today, or at least those with loud voices and showy influence have.

Let's take the example of forestry. It was once common practice for those working in forestry to attend to the forest. Fallen trees would be cleared from the forest and used for timber. This would benefit the man, but also benefit the forest as a whole. When lightning would strike and forest fires began, there would not be all the dry dead wood on the forest floor as ripe kindling, and therefore forest fires wouldn't be as large and destructive. I know forest fires are natural and can be good things too, for the aftermath of a forest fire regenerates new growth and provides nutrients to the soil, but forest fires have grown bigger and more deadly, causing much damage, killing habitats, and disrupting air quality. People today want to blame out-of-control forest fires on "climate change," but really the main factor is that in many parts, because of preservationists' no intervention policies, forest floors are not cleared out of fallen timber. I see this as man not attending to his duty. Man, in my view, was created to attend to and take care of the land. He benefits from it, but he also takes care of it.

Many preservationists of today are treating humans like an invasive species. Not only do we have man not attending to his duty to care for the land, but we also prohibit and restrict him in so many instances, which may not be necessary or good. I am so glad the infrastructure of our National Park system and the creation of all our beautiful National and State Park lodges and roads occurred at a time of the healthy pull of both sound thinking conservationists and preservationists. Today the preservationist would prohibit humans from all of what we have and enjoy in terms of parks. We wouldn't have the richness of our access to these beautiful places. We have to be responsible, but we cannot throw out reason. After all, this is ours too!

# Each Animal Has a Job

Take a look around the animal kingdom. All animals manipulate the earth. I think the strongest example is the beaver. They gnaw down trees, create dams as well, creating whole ponds and waterways that otherwise would not exist. They use their creations for their homes, their habitats, and cultivating their food sources. We don't see huge movements and people taking to the streets to protest beaver dams now, do we?

What about bees? They build these hives, enormous in comparison to their size, then they go around stealing pollen from all these flowers. Should they just let these flowers be? Should we regulate bees and restrict them from tampering with all these flowers? Should we place zoning restrictions on their hives? What would happen then? Well, there would be no pollination of our flowers. They would cease to reproduce. We'd have no flowers and would lose many fruits to extinction. Also, bears feed off of beehives.

Let's talk bears. They have a responsibility to the forest too. They clean up dead carcasses and their waste serves as fertilizer and spreads berry seeds to propagate growth of many plant species. Should we regulate bears and not let them roam free and confine them, for they are tampering with the forest by moving all those carcasses and spreading all their waste?

# Man's Role in Nature

Just like the bear and the bee, God has given every creature its role. Birds build nests, bees build hives, beavers build dams, prairie dogs build entire underground towns. Can't the human build for himself a home or build his own dam? Every animal has a role with the environment. The human has a role too. The discussion should not be, how do we remove humanity from nature, but rather what is man's responsible role in nature? Ignoring his role, the earth suffers. As written in the book of Genesis, "The Lord God put man in the Garden to cultivate and tend to it," (Genesis 2:15), and not to ignore it. We should especially not ignore our forest and waterways in this great garden. We need to attend to them.

This is not to say I am careless, but man is not an invasive species. I believe the Earth is created for man. The bigger issue is that man doesn't know who he is. The further we get away from God as a society, the less we know who we are; and the less we know about who we are, the less we know about our role and responsibility to the Earth.

Here I stood at Lake Roosevelt. *What do I make of this dammed lake?* When it was constructed, at the time of the U.S. coming out of the Great Depression and into World War II, it provided much needed energy for the economy, and today it provides great recreation. I acknowledge and have an appreciation for these things, but I also was a bit saddened learning more about it. Kettle Falls, the waterfalls

which were a great and prominent gathering place for many Native American tribes of the Pacific Northwest, to trade and fish along the Columbia River, was now flooded over because of the dam. I was saddened that such beautiful things as waterfalls were eliminated by man, and I was sad considering tribes had lost such an important location for them. When the dam was built and the falls were being flooded over, a number of tribes got together for a "ceremony of tears."

This site was also so important to their salmon economy. At one time the Columbia River was home to the world's largest salmon runs with over thirty million salmon taking the route. The dam changed that. *Oh, what should I make of Roosevelt Dam?* Some things we just have to accept. There's no changing. Things won't go back. The Kettle

Falls are gone. The salmon run is not what it once was. Lake Roosevelt is here to stay, and so I have to approach it, not by the past, but in the present. Lake Roosevelt is unarguably beautiful. I chose to appreciate it and enjoy it.

## Mission Point

I drove just a few miles up the road to Mission Point, a little peninsula on the lake where the Jesuits had formed a mission in 1838, beginning with the visit of two Canadian-French Catholic missionaries, Francois Norbert Blanchet and Modeste Demer. They witnessed to the Colville Indians and the fur trappers and traders of the Hudson Bay Company visiting the nearby Fort Colville. The following year, they held the first recorded mass between the Rockies and the

Cascades and baptized nineteen Native Americans. This was my first time learning of Catholic missions in the U.S.. I would go on to learn of many more on my travels through Montana. There at Mission Point was the old mission meeting hall. It looked like nothing more than a cabin. I walked around and read the interpretive signs. There was a small path that led out to the tip of the peninsula. I walked out there and sat down for a moment. Everything was still, calm, and quiet. The sun was setting behind the hills in the distance, on the other side of the lake.

On my walk back down the path to my car, I spotted a deer. It was watching me through a window of pine trees in the forest. I paused and locked eyes with it, then I moved slowly and quietly towards it before it trampled off.

Back in my tent, I looked through the pictures I had taken on my phone and reviewed my itinerary. Tomorrow I'd arrive at perhaps the climax of the summer adventure, at what I was considering the National Park of all National Parks– Glacier National Park!

# My First Day Ever in Montana And Wrestling with God's Promise

*Something inside of me is dying,* and *I feel like death.* These were the exact thoughts, exact words running through my mind. I was restless in my tent at night, rolling around on my sleeping bag. I had never felt quite like this before. I wasn't in pain, for there wasn't any sharpness of feeling. But there was this subtle aching, and even more so than a feeling, it was a knowledge that stirred within me. I am not well. I couldn't get comfortable. My body was in utter forthright rebellion. Inflammation was raging on. The illness was winning in this battle despite my will. I wanted to be well. I wanted to relax. The body wasn't having it. Therefore my sleep was interrupted, shallow, brief, and, before I knew it, it was morning.

The day before I had traveled from Lake Roosevelt National Recreation Area in Washington here to West Glacier, Montana. I had traveled nearly six hours, around Spokane, through the panhandle of Idaho, past St. Regis, Montana, and up the west side of Flathead Lake. In St. Regis, I made one of my more notable stops of the day at the St. Regis Travel Center, right off Highway 90, just across the Idaho border in Montana. This gas station establishment boasts "restaurant, casino, Montana's largest gift shop, espresso" and "free live trout aquarium." I just pulled over to go to the bathroom. I didn't need all this, but I'll take it (minus the casino)! It was like the Montana version of Buccees.

I was greeted by a bag of free popcorn and a near endless supply of Montana t-shirts, huckleberry everything; and every Montana, grizzly bear, and Western knick-knack. Many items were boasting common Montana mottos and phrases: "The Treasure State," "Big-Sky Country," "The Montana way," "Grab life by the horns"… I browsed around and didn't purchase anything but was impressed by the inventory. In later summers, working in Montana, I'd be back here a couple of times.

Shortly after, I found myself traveling upside Flathead Lake. I didn't know that was its name. All the places I'd see in the next few days I'd have much more experience, knowledge, and memories of in the future, with my subsequent summers working in Montana, but now it was all new. When I write about my adventures, I like to talk about my experiences and observations at that time. As difficult as it is, I make a conscious effort to restrict myself from injecting later knowledge and experiences of these places. Although now I know it was Flathead Lake, then it was just some big lake I was traveling by. I was impressed by such an immense lake. Why hadn't I heard of this before? It is the largest lake west of the Mississippi. I stopped in the community of Lakeside. I was very hungry and found a little cafe right off the road. I went inside, but after seeing the prices, I decided to continue on. I wasn't used to the tourist prices in the Flathead Valley.

Atop the lake lies the biggest city in the valley, Kalispell. My hunger was so ravenous. I stopped at a Kentucky Fried Chicken. It genuinely sounded so good to me. I know it was not the best choice for my gut, but I was in need of some comfort food. This solo traveler from Kentucky, a little bit weary and beaten down by health issues, needed a bit of comfort from back home. Now it is pitiful, because I know of way better and nourishing choices in the valley for food.

Leaving Kalispell, more and more tall pines filled in the landscape, and the road just seemed to roll along these wooded hills, swooping up and down with the great Rocky Mountains of Glacier National Park standing in the distance. Although the woods were everywhere, I did not feel nestled in the woods, because the road was wide and beside it was a path for bikers and snowmobiles. Everything around me just seemed so big, with the land and forest just so immense. I passed by a few tourist traps: "The Huckleberry Patch" and "Huckleberry Haven" boasting their huckleberry pie, and a Western ranch style building called, "The Montana Fur Trading Company," with a tipi and Native American relics out front. Most prominent was this place called the "Ten Commandments Park," with a dozen or so billboards situated together in a half circle, each loudly displaying a religious or political message. This seemed like something I'd see in Texas. *Is Montana the Texas of the North?* This I certainly thought.

Some National Parks have no real build up, not much of a tourist economy around it. Others, such as the Great Smoky Mountains, have an extreme excess. Glacier seemed to have a moderate amount of tourist build-up. The place seemed touristy, but not in an obnoxious way. Its quantity and quality was of such a way that it served the park well in building up just the right level of excitement and anticipation without being obnoxious or tacky.

I wouldn't make it into the park this evening, but according to plan, I would stay at the West Glacier KOA. I had read this was the flagship KOA. I'd stayed at many Kampgrounds Of America and had become a big fan, so to stay at the allegedly best of all KOAs was an exciting thing for me. I had noticed, while booking my stay online, that this KOA was also the one featured on the front cover of the KOA directory. This was big stuff! Rolling along wide wooded Highway 2, suddenly to my right appeared the big bold beautiful KOA sign made of rich dark wood with black letter insignia, and it didn't say "Kampground," as most are identified; it read "KOA Resort." *Ooh, fancy!*

I checked in at the office, where I also was given a free KOA koozie. I don't drink, but I was still glad to have a KOA souvenir. The campground was enormous. I had a standard tent pad, which backed up to some woods, at the junction between where the cabin guests stayed and the RV

area. I quickly set up my tent, because I was on a mission: I
wanted to enjoy the hot tub, which I did. It was small and
busy, but I enjoyed a nice warm soak. I then finished setting
up my camp– blowing up my air mattress and throwing my
pillow and sleeping bags in the tent. I felt calm and relaxed
walking around the campground and getting familiar with
the place. There was a vibrant energy, a positive one of happy families on vacation and kids on their bicycles. I kept
having to make frequent trips to the bathroom. Although I
felt relaxed in many ways, my gut was not happy.

I noticed on the resort map there were some little
hiking trails in the woods just behind my site. I went on a
stroll through the woods, and there I decided to call my parents and let them know of my sickness. I had procrastinated
telling them. I guess I was hopeful it'd just go away as suddenly as it seemed to come upon me, and therefore be a non
issue. But I felt like now I was in for a long haul. I should let
them know. Just talking about it, and my experience with it
so far, was draining. I didn't want to really talk about it. I
wanted to ignore it, but I couldn't.

Soon after, I settled in my tent for the night, and this
was the night things took a major turn for the worse: *Something inside of me is dying,* and *I feel like death.* After tonight, the
illness would not just bother me but rage on.

In the morning I ate at the KOA resort. It had a restaurant with a nice outdoor patio. I ordered the Montana
Breakfast of eggs, potatoes, and thick sausage patties. I was
impressed by the quality here. In the subsequent days, I'd
learn this trio is the standard Montana breakfast almost eve-

rywhere. After breakfast, I was driving, for the first time ever, into Glacier National Park with great excitement. I was going to hike the famous Skyline Trail, which in my present state of health, would not be easy.

As I was driving, I thought back to what I would consider my greatest thoughts and reflections on this trip so far. I thought about Nurse Logs and the life-enriching ability one leaves behind after he or she has died. I considered my previous thoughts on the colors of my sunset and the qualities of one's life, that can be evident and seen, when a life comes to completion, or to put it more bluntly, one dies. There was so much thought about death, but not in any dark way, rather in an inspiring way, thinking more about the quality of a life truly lived before time naturally runs out. I was only twenty-eight, not an age one normally contemplates what they leave behind upon their passing, but these were my thoughts. It was curious to me that shortly after these thoughts came to me, unexpectedly my health had been taken from me to the point my mind spoke, "I feel like death."

Were my deepest thoughts and personal revelations preparing me for this, preparing for *the end?* It sounds very dramatic in retrospect, but in the moment it was quite sincere. The only other time my body was under this attack, with ulcerative colitis brutally flaring, was when I was in college, and it was severe. There were the restless nights of rolling around the floor in pain, the hospitalization, the intense pain, the blood loss, the anemia, my body not digesting food, the malabsorption, the withering away, the affected

eyes, the suffering teeth, the weakness, the fatigue, the faint-
ing, the crying. The option of surgically taking out my colon
wasn't on the table, because the doctor believed I was too
weak to survive the surgery. I look back and marvel how,
despite everything, I continued onward.

At that time of the first onset, I was a student in education, and I was due for student teaching the next semester.
With my current state of health, I felt I just couldn't do it. I
informed my parents I was coming home. I notified the education department at my school, telling them I had to post-
pone my student teaching because of my health. Then, this
decision sat horribly with me. I didn't feel at peace about it
at all. Although now officially unenrolled, I called a meeting
with the dean of education. I knew how rigid and firm to
policies and procedures the whole institution was. I felt embarrassed, but I was going to plead and beg them to let me
back in the program. I wanted to proceed with student
teaching despite my health and weakness. I told the dean, "I
am very sick, but I may not get better. I may be like this for
the rest of my life, so I don't want to let this sickness stop
me. I must learn to live with it."

I'll never forget what the dean told me. Somewhat
surprised, looking at me square in the eyes, she said, "Well,
that says an awful lot about your character." I was back
in! God gave me an inner strength and fierce resistance to
face my illness while moving forward in life.

In the struggle, I clung on with a tight grip to a harmony of Bible verses I felt God spoke directly to me, 1 Peter 5:10 and Phillipians 4:7 together: "After you have suf-

fered a while, the God of grace Himself, whose knowledge surpasses all understanding, will restore you and make you strong in Christ Jesus."

*It's just for, "a while,"* I thought. That helped me persevere. God will "restore" me and make me "strong." That gave me hope. However, I was struggling with this. I wanted to believe it. I held the word of God to be true. It had proved itself over and over again to be so, but this night was exceptionally long, and there was no improvement in my health whatsoever. I felt myself slowly dying. *What does this promise and these verses really mean?*

One evening in my quiet time, alone in a little study nook in my university, in my sickly state with increasing complexity of illness, I was journaling and thinking over this promise of God. Then it dawned on me: *I think I know what it means.* The first part about "suffering a while," well I was there, no doubt. I knew that to be true. The second part, "I will restore you and make you strong." I struggled with that because I was not seeing it as I expected it to be, in this life. *Maybe, that is the part God will accomplish when he calls me home. When I die. In his eternal presence I will be restored and He will make me strong. So maybe God is telling me, "After you have suffered a while, I will bring you home to restore you and make you strong."*

It was profound to me and haunting in some ways. I didn't want to die so young, but at the same time the notion was comforting in knowing, that whether it be in life or be in death, God restores me and makes me strong. I am victorious through Him, either way! I took a deep breath, as though accepting my fate, not sure I felt ready for the responsibility set before me, to proceed into death with faith, resting on His promise. I zipped up my backpack, tucked away my journal and Bible, and carried on with life's demand. *Live strong and fiercely to the end.* But oh what an ache it was still to my soul! This was a silent disease. Few would know. I'd be here, and then I wouldn't.

God's promise did hold entirely true, as it always does, and to my own heart's desire, for God is good! I was restored and made strong in this life shortly after.

When I look back at this period of sickness in my life, it doesn't seem so dark, and actually never felt dark in the moment either, though it may seem so from the casual observer. Actually, I am extremely grateful for that time of sickness and for the wrestling with faith. These were times of some of the greatest spiritual intimacy and dependency on God in my life. His promise held so much more, too, than what I even thought at the time. When God promised to restore me and make me strong, I considered that just in the physical sense. God did mean that, but He also meant it in a spiritual sense. God would strengthen me spiritually, beyond what I could see in the moment. To go through such an experience of facing a prospect of death so young, and doing so walking hand in hand with God, I think produces a level of wisdom and maturity that I am eternally grateful for and has become an integral part of my character and outlook on life and death. I would never want to go back and relive those days, but I'd also never wish they didn't happen. Dolly Parton captures the sentiment in her song *The Good Olde Days When Times Were Bad:* "No amount of money could buy from me, the memories that I have of then, No amount of money could pay me, To go back and live through it again."

But now, what was happening to my body here on this journey out West, here at Glacier, with the return of this great grave sickness? My thoughts went back to this previous era of life, to the promises, to the pain, to the prospects. I didn't want to have to face and reconsider everything, but here it was again, in my face (or in my gut rather). There was a bit of initial panic, and I felt overwhelmed. *What do I believe again?* I saw how God's promises applied back then, *but how do they apply now?* I thought I had closed that chapter and had moved on, but it was back. Was it the same chapter of life? No. This was chapter two. I was more prepared in the spiritual sense. Something was about to go down (or come down rather). That would soon become evident.

# Going-To-The-Sun and Grinnell Glacier

In my mind Glacier National Park was the National Parks of National Parks, like a next level experience, only conquered by the very bold and adventurous, or something like that. I made it! I had seen pictures of course, and I was astounded by the unbelievable views, and now I was here! I turned left off Highway 2, through a little tunnel under the railway, and into the little tourist village of West Glacier. I passed by a visitor center for Alberta, Canada. Although I was not in Canada, I was so close. I also passed by a few little tourist shops, Glacier Raft Company, and a little restaurant and ice cream shop called Friedas.

  The pines hugged in closer, after I crossed the bridge over the Middle Fork of the Flathead River, and there in the shade of the dark rich pines was the National Park sign. Bold and beautiful it read, "Glacier National

Park." I admit it's now commonplace for me, after having spent many summers in Glacier, but at the moment this was a big deal. It was my first time here. This was an accomplishment. This was one of the more out-of-the-way National Parks I'd visit. Its mountains were extreme, with moving glaciers, and its forests held grizzly bears and wolves! This was no ordinary place to be. I was swept with a sense of accomplishment, gratitude, and wonder, being here.

Nearby I parked at the Apgar Visitor Center. It was early and it was still closed, but there was a National Park bus stop on site. The plan was to take the bus up to Logan Pass, the highest point on the famous Going-To-The-Sun Road. From there I'd hike the Skyline Trail one way, about fourteen miles up to the Garden Wall, to catch a view of Grinnell Glacier, then I'd continue north to the Granite Park Chalet, where I'd take the Granite Park Trail down to "The Loop," another spot on the Going-To-The-Sun Road. There I'd catch the bus back down to my car. This would be a full day endeavor, hence the getting started so early.

As I stood there waiting for the bus, I was cold. I needed the sun to rise and warm things up. I had a few layers on, including my new Under Armour base layer I bought at the thrift store outside Seattle, yet I was still just wearing shorts. I knew the weather would warm up. I double checked all I had in my backpack: a map, snacks, water, flashlight… just in case. I was prepared. My boot laces were pulled tight. I was ready! Anxiously I walked around, reading all the signs, observing what other tourists were doing, and checking messages on my cell phone. I had caught a wifi signal from the visitor center.

I chose to take the bus, as opposed to driving, for a few reasons. I was nervous about driving the Going-To-The-Sun Road. It seemed intimidating. The road is known as the most scenic drive in America, but was also snug against dramatic cliff edges, gaining 2,560 feet in elevation. I knew I would have to drive it to carry through with my next few days' itinerary, but I wanted to size it up first and just observe it with someone else behind the wheel. I didn't have to drive it until the following day. I also read that parking can be difficult to find at Logan Pass, where my trailhead was, so I didn't want to risk not being able to park. Lastly, I like the energy in the air on a bus in a National Park with everyone geared up for adventure. It's a unique culture that I find to be part of the park experience.

The bus ride was terrifying! I sat on the right side near the front of the bus. I swear this bus was too big for the road. Around every bend I felt as if my side of the bus was jutting off the cliffside. The first few miles of the road were easy, relaxing, just through the mysterious, dark, wet, mossy forest, with light peaking through in the most intriguing and mystifying ways. The bus took us alongside Lake McDonald, the long-stretching wonder. Then we were along the beautiful McDonald Creek, where the water runs clear, if not in a surreal turquoise. But then the real ascension began and things got hairy. It wasn't so bad until rounding a place called "The Loop," where the road makes a dramatic turn and narrows. There's supposed to be two lanes, but it seems more like one by any other comparison.

The trees lessened and boulders became more prominent. I began to notice the forest below, no longer aside us. We were up in the mountains. The views were astounding, more magnificent and boisterous than anything I'd seen before, as if the mountains were calling for attention. However, I would appreciate them more the next day. Right now I was distracted by the thousands of feet expanse just beside me, to which I felt I'd be plummeting down at any moment if for some reason I didn't cling hard enough to my bus seat. The tension was real.

We proceeded through a few tunnels, for which we were too big, and a few bridges, built into the rock walls, better suited as foot paths in a Vanderbilt garden. I have never been more nervous on a ride in my life. Around each wind in the road, I felt I was just swinging out over valleys on my corner of the bus, dangling over great heights.

I could not understand how the bus driver was just so casual and relaxed, making friendly conversation with another passenger. She was loudly talking over the vehicle engine about how she was a school bus driver and this was just a summer job. I was carefully watching her in case I had to spring into emergency assistance, I suppose. At one point she grabbed her water bottle for a sip. *Two hands on the wheel!* I wished to telepathically impart.

I would be gripping that steering wheel so tight, head tilted forward, focused on the road. I wouldn't be talking to anyone. I would have to be totally focused on the road. In fact, I couldn't even drive a bus on this road. We would already be plummeting down to McDonald Creek. *Maybe if she is so relaxed I should be too.* I tried to, but I was so tense. I couldn't wait to get off this bus safely.

The bus stopped for some mountain goats crossing the road. We were getting close! We were now near the tundra. Water flowed around in many different directions and spread everywhere from the melting snow. Tight shrubs and alpine grasses hugged the rocks, and the tops of mountain peaks stood as monuments around us.

*I survived!* I got off at Logan Pass, on top of the world! Here is the Continental Divide. Water flows east to the Atlantic, west to the Pacific, and north to the Hudson Bay. There's a real feeling of being at the pinnacle of North America. There's also a big parking lot with a visitor center along with two big flags, one of the U.S. and the other of Canada. Glacier National Park shares a boundary with Waterton National Park in Canada. Together they form what is called an "International Peace Park."

A short distance from the parking lot at Logan Pass is the trailhead for the Highline Trail, often touted as the best hike in the park by many visitors. It begins at such an elevation that the mountain peaks around it are obviously bald, exposed to the wind and sun, reminding me of some of the rock formations of the Southwest in Arizona or Utah. The trail starts just off the Going-To-The-Sun road, and goes down a shallow decline with rich green grasses and a few pines. Then it snugs very close to a cliff-side. The trail is just a couple feet wide, right up against a rock wall. The other side is a sheer cliff, plummeting hundreds, maybe thousands, of feet down. This did not bother me at all. The difference: I was in control of my body, but I wasn't of the bus. This was an experience to marvel at. I loved it! The trail was already pretty busy this morning. There were other hikers right in front of me and others trailing up behind. "Be careful," they told one another as they carefully maneuvered the small path.

This trail lives up to its hype. It was extravagant. At times it opened up to just enormous views atop these mountainous meadows, spread with yellow blooming glacier lilies and patches of snow, stretching before dramatic mountain peaks carved by glaciers. Each mountain valley was framing another stunning view in the distance. There was forest too, a grand immensity of it, but I was mostly above it. The descending display of each little triangular pine tree top spoke of the grandeur of the landscape before me. The sky was rich blue, the snow bright white, the mountains gray with

skirts of dark green pines around their bases, and just before me was the vibrant green and yellow of the glacier lilies. I was right in calling this a next level National Park. These were the most immense, grandiose, dramatic, and beautiful views I had seen out of any National Park. This was the cream of the crop, or as they say, "the crown of the continent." Each dramatic mountain peak was like the palisades on a crown, the landscape adorned with the finest things of nature: glaciers, waterfalls, forested basins— the crown jewels of God's creation.

This morning the sun was also very bright and positioned at just the right angle to illuminate these jewels, reaching into every little crevice and wrinkle on the mountainside, adding to the depth and detail of everything.

After about an hour in, I stopped at one majestic meadow to shed a few layers and eat some electrolyte gummies. I was getting quite warm in the morning sun. The trail was still busy, and hikers continually passed me. I found a rock to first set my backpack on and then to sit down on for a moment and behold the landscape. Although warm from the sun, the air was cool, and I took in a deep refreshing breath of rich snow-chilled mountain air. Then I carried on.

About seven miles in, I came to the Grinnell Glacier Overlook spur trail. It was just a half mile and would lead up to the feature called the Garden Wall, which is a natural rock wall, that is a definitive line between the east side and west side of the park. It's like a great narrow spine of the park.

From here I could look down and see Grinnell Glacier. The spur trail was completely exposed above the treeline and very steep, gaining one thousand feet in a half mile distance. Sometimes when going uphill, I try to go fast and just get the exertion over with. I tried here, but the air was very thin on top of the world. My whole body felt so heavy and gravity felt extra strong. When I arrived, I was utterly amazed! I didn't know what to expect. I hadn't looked up any images prior. I was stunned. I hadn't seen anything like this.

This may be a strange comparison, but it kind of was like when someone reveals a bloody wound, and you're shocked by the look of it. You weren't expecting to see something so abnormal on the skin's surface which is usually smooth and predictable. It's a grand abnormality on the skin and in the flesh. This glacier view was that grand abnormality on the Earth's surface and in its crust. But replace the disgust with awe, and replace the red of blood with rich turquoise blue and a white so bright and so angelic it burns.

Grinnell Glacier

*Wow!* I had never felt so high up. I was way on top of the world. I thought I was on top of the world at Logan Pass. I was wrong. This was even next level! I sat on a spine's edge. Below me rocks crumbled down, slanting into a blanket of snow which then spread over Grinnell Glacier. Then hundreds of feet below, I could see the ice rippling with white and turquoise blue. It was the glacier descending and melting into a bright opaque turquoise glacial lake. The lake fed into another lake, and then into another lake, in a chain of glacial lakes spread out immensely into the forest below. I was on top of everything, looking across at the other gray mountains tops, up here above the treeline, rippled through the ages with rock layers. There were blankets of snow littered amidst these mountains, drooping in every which way. It was also clear, here, to see the carving power of a glacier. It's where a whole mountainous valley began. This was, and stands to be, one of the greatest sights I have ever beheld.

I sat to snack on a Clif Bar and enjoy the view for a spell. A little chipmunk came very close. I'm sure he was hoping for a bite or two. That wasn't going to happen, but I did take his photo, which he couldn't have cared less about. Then shortly after, a group of Chinese tourists arrived all wearing the same off-white sun hat. They were all oohing and aahing and talking in their sharp-sounding language.

This place was unbelievable. I had really arrived somewhere! I couldn't have conjured up such a view in my mind. Now it was resident in my mind. So satisfied, I began my descent to carry on, back on the Highline Trail.

# Victorious No Matter What

As I continued on my journey among amazing glacier peaks on the Highline Trail in Glacier National Park, I wanted to be fully present in the moment and take in the natural views around me, but my mind wasn't entirely present with the beauty at hand. It was occupied, troubled by my present health. I couldn't stop thinking about it, the merciless rampage of ulcerative colitis and the fiery inflammation in my body. I so desired, as anyone would, for it to go away. Here I was on a mountain top, and although I was still strong, because I did make it here after all, I was mourning that my strength was on decline with this illness. I knew what would happen with weakness taking over. Thus, with this prospect, I was faced with a major temptation to give into despair and let my spirit be crushed by this situation. I had tried so long to become physically strong. I was quite successful, so much so that my strength and physique had become part of my identity. It was now being taken from me so unjustly, I thought. It was all out of the blue. Suddenly I was sick. My heart so terribly ached to just be healthy again more than anything. As much as this was a physical problem, I believe it was also spiritual, for the body and spirit are connected, and the physical sickness was leading my spirit to despair.

As I was hiking here on the Highline Trail, I was thinking back to how I dealt with this illness back in college. There was one particular journal entry in 2010, that I read over many times. It always sort of lingered with me. When I was very sick back then, I wrote:

*"I do think it is so true that I am trying to be destroyed, and I am wanted to be taken out so badly, but that is because I have power. The Holy Spirit lives in me and works through me, and the devil wants to destroy this vessel from working. And even though the attack is hard and painful, because of God's mercy and love...I am still alive. And God is all powerful and can stop everything instantly, but here He chooses not to... Maybe He allows me to go through these hard times because He knows they will make me even stronger. I can't see the big picture. I can only see and experience what is here now. God knows better than I, and He has declared his plans to me – plans for my well-being, hope, and a future.*

*So in these times I should not give up. All I can do is take care of myself and live my life. I will feel sad, I will feel pain, and I will be discouraged, but those things will not consume me. I will find hope and encounter peace, as I rely on God every day. Every day He must give me strength."*

As I continued on hiking, I was thinking of when Jesus was led to the wilderness by the Spirit to be tempted by the devil. I too was in a wilderness being tempted. Here on the mountainside, among glaciers, blankets of forest, and majestic peaks, I was now alone with only the spiritual forces around me. There were no distractions. Following Jesus' example, I was going to stand up to temptation. The lies of despair said, "You are weak," "You will suffer," "I'm going to stop you." Despair tried to rob me of hope, rid me of peace, steal motivation. It tried to focus my life on the illness, take away my sense of identity, which I recognized I should have placed solely in Christ instead of in my own efforts. It also tried to take away my focus on truly living. The temptation to give into these thoughts and feelings were real, but I was not going to have it. I was going to take this head on. It was still early on in this episode of illness, but enough was enough!

First off, I will never speak to the devil to address any matter. It's not a door I ever want to open, even if my intentions are pure. When Jesus was tempted in the wilderness, He only responded to Satan through Scripture. There's one additional thing Jesus said which became Scripture. I saw myself employing it too. At the end of His defense and resistance, Jesus said, "Get behind me Satan!" I would be doing the same. First, I needed a clear precise declaration over my life rooted in the Word of God. I had never done anything quite like this before. It wasn't a journal entry. It wasn't a prayer. It would be a moment of both acceptance, accepting the situation at hand, but also resistance, not letting the situation have dominion over me. It would be a moment of resolution, and a definitive attitude, for the path before me. Quietly, yet with great force and passion, I verbalized and declared these words:

*I accept I am sick. I will face pain. I will face blood. This can be ugly. This will be hard, but in this circumstance I denounce the lie that I am weak and that this illness will get the best of me, for I know, "I can do all things through Christ who strengthens me," (Phillipians 4:13). God will give me the strength to get through this, for I know, as His Word says, "Even youth grow tired and weary. Young men stumble and fall, but those who trust in the Lord will renew their strength. They will soar on wings like eagles. They will run and not grow weary. They will walk and not be faint," (Isaiah 40:30-31).* I looked over the mountainous valley below me and imagined an eagle swooping high above the pines.

*The illness rages on. Physically I am not well, but spiritually I will be fierce through the power of Jesus Christ in my life. I ask, in the name of Jesus, for this cup to pass from me, and I condemn it in the name of Jesus. But if this illness is here to stay, I will bear this cross joyfully. As it is written, "Consider it pure joy when you face trials of many kinds, for you know the testing of your faith develops perseverance, and perseverance must finish its work so that you may be mature and complete not lacking anything," (James 1:2-4).*

*Despite the uncertainty I will feel, and the testing of my faith I'm likely to encounter, I will not fear and will not despair. For it is written, "God has given you a spirit not of fear but of power and love and self-control," (2 Timothy 1:7). With His Spirit I will choose in my sickness to glorify God.*

I remembered back to when I was in college, when I was gravely sick, someone anonymously put a note in my mailbox: "I see Jesus in your trust amidst hardship."

That note had a huge impact on me. With this in mind, I continued on:

*"Let it be known that in my sickness, the battle is already won. I win through the power of Christ Jesus. In Him I have complete and utter victory over whatever comes my way. In the meantime, in all my suffering, I will choose to praise God, thus this suffering gives me the amazing and humbling experience to put on display the strength and hope He provides. Then when God does heal me, I will share this story of healing and the strength He provided. He will get all the glory from this, and for however long this sickness stays before I am healed, I will use it to bring God glory as well. In sickness and in health, God gets the glory.*

I looked out at the mountains and thought how alone they bring so much glory to God as a display of His wondrous creation. I knew at this moment God was using me as he does the mountains, to bring Him glory. The beauty and testament of the glory of God, which I see in the mountains, He was going to bring about in my life as well. I couldn't contain this emotion and immense humility I felt. I knew from my prior episode of sickness how burdensome this illness can be, but the fact God was allowing it to happen again was so humbling, knowing He entrusted me with such suffering. In some ways it is an honor. I had this incredibly unique opportunity and the confidence He would see me through and give me support in every way, so the fact God let this heavy of a weight come upon me was a testament to the strength He provides me in my life. I had to accept this with obedience. It was less about me, and more about His strength and glory. After all, the purpose of all life is to bring God glory, justly so. The righteous desire of my heart and my identity should be in bringing Him glory.

Then I had to face and accept another prospect: *On the contrary, if this illness kills me, what then?…Well… then so be it! I became even more impassioned as the tears rolled down my face. Even in death there is victory, because I will rely on and praise God to my very end, discrediting this spirit of despair and all the hopelessness the devil stands for. Also when I "die," I will live again greater than ever in God's glorious presence, fully restored and healed. There would be no defeat! Whether it be in life or be in death I am victorious! There is no defeat! There is no despair! I win!*

I pulled from God's promise to me back in college: *"For after you have suffered a while, the God of grace Himself, whose knowledge surpasses all understanding will restore you and make you strong in Christ Jesus,"* (1 Peter 5:10 and Philippians 4:7). *Whether it be in life or in death, God restores me and makes me strong. God gets the glory in whatever outcome.* I remembered Jesus' crucifixion, something Satan thought for his profit, but what God used for salvation and ultimately His glory. *In my situation, despite the devil's intention, there will be no defeat either! "There is no weapon fashioned against me that will stand,"* (Isaiah 54:17). *Nothing in my life will hinder the glory of God. He wins!*

I felt the weight of responsibility for praising God in my illness, but then, instantly the burden was lifted from me, as if God said, "That's mine. I will handle this. I will hold you." His great peace filled me. Then everything was lifted. The weight upon my soul and consciousness of dealing with this illness began to rise. I could feel despair crippled with the sharp slashes of God's Word. With awesome wonder, I sort of paused to marvel at the spiritual sword I was holding and could feel the immensity of its power. At the same time, I was faced with the whole new perspective of the freedom found in Christ. I previously understood the freedom from sin and the power of salvation, but here I was understanding that there is nothing in this life, in this world that has dominion over my soul, what a freedom! *No sickness has power over me. No circumstance will hinder the hope I have in Jesus. Nothing can diminish His glory. Not even death. Nothing can take from me the victory I have in every circumstance through Him. Nothing will hinder the colors of my sunset. I am free! I am not hoping for victory, nor waiting for victory. I am living in victory. I am victorious already through Him. We win!*

I continued to verbalize my thoughts with Scripture: *"Even though I walk through the valley of the shadow of death I shall fear no evil," (Psalm 23:4). I will walk boldly through this valley no matter what happens, no matter how dark how painful it is, for the God of grace, mercy, power, greatness, awesomeness, strength, might, justice, love, patience, comfort, purpose, hope is with me. The victory is ours! This is a done deal sealed with the blood of Christ.*

Then I finished with a spiritually resounding, *"Get behind me Satan!"*

On that mountain, God drew me close to Him.

# Onward I'd Run

I was trying to catch my breath. I had run and sprinted, giving it all I got, putting all my strength and force into the end of this run. I was running alongside the creek on the road just outside of the St. Mary KOA, on the east side of Glacier National Park, with the towering Rocky Mountains in the distance. Behind all this was not just the motive of wanting to take a morning run. It was a physical manifestation of my frustration, an outpouring of my emotion. I was so fed up with my body and this illness. Sometimes I'd feel fine. Then I'd be plagued with the most uncomfortable feelings in my gut, reminding me I was unwell, and this grave feeling of desperation would take over.

So this early morning, I ran, faster, and faster, and gradually ran more and more onto the front of my feet. Soon I was sprinting. As I did so, my heart pounded forcefully in my chest, feeling as if it was about to burst out. My sides began to ache, naturally from the exertion, and I wasn't accustomed to running this fast. The exertion was painful as my lungs were desperate for more air than they could take in. Normally I'd slow down, or take a break, but I pushed onward, relentless to the pain. I was fueled by fierceness. I suppose maybe in some ways I felt, despite my will and desire, my body had control over me lately with this illness, and now, through forcing it through such extreme exertion, I was proving to myself I still had control over this vessel, or maybe I just wanted an outlet for all this build-up burning frustration.

The more I pushed myself, and the more I ached and desperately drew in breath, the more I realized it was pointless. I was sick. I could pour out all my efforts, all my strength, all my energy into this, and my desire could be so strong, my efforts relentless, yet this wasn't going away. I was still going to be sick. This wasn't all on the forefront of my mind, but it was buried in there somewhere, and it explained how suddenly my legs and arms became limp as I slowed down running. I hit a realization as tears of desperation and frustration ran down my face. I stopped running. The harsh reality fell upon me again. I could not not make this go away. Alone, I was helpless. I wanted to be in control. It was all out of my control.

Just a few days before, I had my great moment of declaration upon the Highline Trail, in which I resolved I would not give into despair, and, no matter my circumstance, I'd bring glory to God through my illness. Often, when we make ground spiritually and draw close to the heart of God, the devil has a counter attack. He did here, I believe. Just moments after my heartfelt declaration of resolve, I experienced great cramping, desperation and urgency. Sparing you from unpleasant details, I was above the treeline, on tundra, exposed. There was nowhere to run away to, no privacy, and tourists were around me. With great anxiety I made do. But it happened over and over again, a persistent physical attack, leaving me exhausted.

Exercising, especially running, I thought would be an outlet for this stress and inflammation in the body. After good exercise the body calms down and relaxes. I needed that. Ulcerative colitis also sometimes feels like there is a misplaced energy or fire within the body. The energy or fire was focused on attacking and burning my intestines. If I could, through physical exercise, displace the fire from the intestines and channel that energy into a more productive means, I'd be okay. It's an abstract feeling, that I know is not exactly medically accurate, but it's how it felt. There was also the feeling that I could force this all to go away, just as it came on so quickly, so too it could leave, like there was a switch in my body that needed to be flipped and it'd all be over. I felt I could flip this switch through exertion. I was trying so hard to displace this energy and flip the switch. After all, I felt there had to be something I could do to fix this problem.

"Forgive me God, for putting my body before you..." I prayed "...for setting it up as an idol, for being so caught up in my health and physical strength and appearance that I failed to put my deepest value in you. I let myself become distracted from that which is most important." I knew this illness would be painful in any circumstance, but the fact I had idolized my body so much, made it all hit harder, emotionally, now that I lost my health. I realized I needed this moment of repentance. "Help me focus on you and put you first."

I continued onward, calm and quiet, in the presence of God on the Highline Trail, among the majestic mountains and alpine meadows. For a while I escaped the turmoil of my condition. I had distractions.

"Look there are two bears," another hiker called out. Sure enough, pretty far in the distance, but still visible with the naked eye, two big grizzlies grazed on the mountainside. This was my first grizzly bear sighting! I was approaching the Granite Park Chalet. Here hikers, lucky enough to score a spot, can stay in the rock chalet overnight. I was only there

briefly, observing the bears and then descending four miles
to The Loop.

Just in time, I caught the last bus back down to the
Apgar Village. I was the only one there at the bus stop. I
didn't realize it was the last bus until the bus driver told me
how lucky I was. I was exhausted. I had hiked around fifteen
miles in total, and my legs were very heavy. Although I had
completed it, I went through such physical desperation and
anxiety with my colitis, that in many ways I felt defeated by
this hike. I enjoyed it in some short spurts, but mostly I was
in survival mode. I didn't conquer this trail. It got the best
of me.

The rest of the evening was relatively relaxing. There
were other great distractions from my illness, and my body
was, for the most part, at peace. One such distraction was
my visit to the Lake McDonald Lodge built in 1913. It's a
National Historic Landmark and built in the beautiful Swiss
chalet-style. Inside it was composed of rustic National Park
Service architecture, in which design elements mirror the
natural surroundings. It featured exposed rough wooden
logs as beams, and railings and fixtures carved of rough
planks and tree branches. It had a coarse stone floor and
taxidermied animals of all kinds all over, including elk,
moose, and goat, to name a few. Great big murals of mountain landscapes and Native Americans adorned the walls,
and an enormous chandelier of Native American lanterns,
painted on in a petroglyph manner, glowed warm in the otherwise dimly lit space.

The focal point of the lodge was an enormous stone

fireplace and chimney, so big there were benches within the mantle, like a foyer to the fire. The precise term I learned is called an "inglenook." I'm a big fan. There is nothing that says, "Northwest North America," greater than this lodge. I poked around its three different levels and balconies, observing the art and taking in the extraordinary ambiance. Around some chairs and leather couches, animal furs hung and coffee tables stood on Native American rugs. Theodore Roosevelt would have absolutely loved this place. It was just his style, and although gentle and calm, it seemed to boastfully proclaim such words as "hunter," "taxidermist," "naturalist," "America," and "the great outdoors." I thought about how I'd love to sit here and work on my writing. It would be the perfect cozy and inspiring place to write.

After snooping around the lodge a bit, I returned to the West Glacier Village and had my first elk burger at

Lake McDonald Lodge

Frieda's. I decided to go full-on tourist and pay a pretty penny for the burger. Its lean and gamey meat was delicious. It was also relaxing to be waited on and enjoy a full meal after such a rigorous day. Having multiple cups of water, brimming with cold refreshing ice, was also just what I needed. This evening I felt normal and at peace. The next few days I'd have other moments like this, in that for a while I escaped the reality of my illness, but then at other times something would shift within my body and the feelings of being unwell would kick in, with the anxiety and desperation that accompanied it. Over and over again I'd shift from feeling well and carefree to slapped with reality that inside I wasn't well. I had to come to terms with this reality, not just once, but over and over again. In more ways than one, it was exhausting and frustrating, leading me to my fierce early morn-

ing run ending in a tearful mess and the feelings of defeat…
*but I'm not defeated,* I'd remind myself. *It's only an emotion. I
must live and lead a life above these emotions. Onward!*

# My First Grizzly Bear Encounter

"Let's all get together and look like one giant creature. Maybe we can scare it off." We were face to face with a grizzly bear and its two cubs. We had a line of defense in front with the bear spray canisters positioned and ready for deployment. The rest of us were huddling behind. How did we get here? Well…

First, I had conquered the famed Going-To-The-Sun Road in Glacier National Park by myself. It was stressful and nerve wracking yet beautiful and epic. Although not exactly relaxed, I felt much better being in control of my vehicle as opposed to being a passenger on the bus the day before. On my way up to Logan Pass I stopped when I could, at little pull-offs, to take in the amazing views. Clouds were rising up out of the mountain valleys, and ones already hanging around me would occasionally part ways to deliver majestic mountain peaks. Upon beginning the drive, I was hoping for a blue-sky day, but this was far better. The clouds swirling around added a special mystique, and there was constant surprise, as the clouds would part ways revealing what I didn't know I was amidst. This was, is, and will forever be a drive like none other.

Proceeding past Logan Pass, I began the descent over the Continental Divide. St. Mary Lake, long and beautiful, soon came into view, although I didn't take time to stop and enjoy it. I'd learn in the future that it provides some of the most amazing views, especially when looking back westward, but I didn't know to look backward nor where the best viewpoints were. I was focused on making it through to the end of this harrowing road. Looking eastward, I began to see a rounded plateau— the start of the Great Plains. So drastically the landscape changed.

Just past the eastern boundary of the park, I stopped at the visitor center to watch the park film, and just ahead was the town of St. Mary, where I stopped at the local grocery store for a few overpriced grocery items. The place was unusual. It didn't seem well put together. In our more modern terms we would say the vibe was really off. Northward I continued, until I turned back into another pocket of the park: Many Glacier, my favorite section of Glacier National Park. The National Park has a number of pockets accessible through different entry points. There's the most known and famous Going-To-The-Sun corridor, then there's Many Glacier, Two Medicine, the North Fork, and sights along Highway 2 (a.k.a. Theodore Roosevelt International Highway).

Soon I was traveling on a dirt road. Rocks were ping-
ing under my car, and my car was creating little dust storms
as it traveled along the gravel road by Swiftcurrent Creek.
Then there was a bit of ascending and the revealing of Lake
Sherburne. I got out of my car to savor the beauty. Waves
were crashing and the wind was whipping. This part of the
valley seemed to be a wind tunnel. I noticed, further up the
valley, a mountainous peak stood way up in the sky, standing like a ginormous wall and displaying lots of snow on its
side. I didn't know at the time, but I was looking up at Grinnell Glacier and the Garden Wall I had climbed to the top of
the day before.

I then proceeded to drive by some meadows ladened
with glacier lilies and other wild flowers alongside the lake.
This pocket of the park was gorgeous, and the fact I was

driving on a dirt road made it seem even more remote and more adventurous of an endeavor. My destination was the Swiftcurrent Motor Lodge from where I'd take the trailhead to Iceberg Lake, but first I stopped at The Many Glacier Lodge. This lodge, perhaps, has the best setting of any National Park lodge I've been to. From the parking lot one ascends a walkway with stairs over a hill, and from atop the hill one looks over and down upon this Swiss Alpine themed lodge. It's huge, like a series of connected chalets. Behind it is picturesque Swiftcurrent Lake. To the right of the lodge an enormous mountainside of Altyn Peak slopes right down into the lake, and straight ahead, most prominent and immediate, is in tall standing, perfectly triangular, Grinnell Peak, a majestic centerpiece for the vista. Everything about this place emits a Swiss Alps wintery. Although I've

Many Glacier Lodge

never been to the Swiss Alps, it's what I'd imagine them to be like.

Inside, the lodge lobby was enormous. It had a beautiful exposed dark wood timber frame rising four stories. Though large, it was cozy with lots of plush seats, carpeted floor, and dozens of warm lanterns of cylindrical and circular shapes, hanging down from the ceiling individually at various heights. To one side of the lobby was a free-standing circular fireplace with a copper roof on it. Around it was a stone island or hearth where one could sit and warm up. There was a charming dated aspect of this lodge. You could most prominently sense the rustic, yet classy, and historic 1915 aspect of the lodge, and then also see that maybe it was updated a bit in the 1960s or 70s, and since then it's just been locked in time. This gave it a unique charm.

On the opposite side of the lobby were two staircases spiraling downward in the floor to the lower level, creating an artistic visual display. Back over by the fireplace side, was a desk with tourist information. I stopped there to inquire about Iceberg Lake. I pretty much had my mind made up, but I wanted to see what information the host could provide.

"What can you tell me about Iceberg Lake?" I inquired.

She immediately started suggesting another hike. I wasn't even really listening. I wanted to hear about Iceberg Lake. Then she concluded "...but if you want to go to Iceberg Lake, it's nice too, but it's just a lake with chunks of ice floating in it. Interesting, I suppose, if that's your thing." Her tone and delivery was as if she was trying to downplay Iceberg Lake. But for me, that sounded like something really neat! I was excited to see icebergs. She gave me a map and I was off.

The Swiftcurrent Motor Lodge was about a mile up the road from the Many Glacier Lodge and was a part of this Many Glacier village, which consisted of the lodge, campground, restaurant, and gift shop. The "Motor Lodge" was a series of rustic cabins for park guests behind the restaurant and gift shop. The parking lot here was full. I drove around twice. Then I found a spot! I was ready to go!

The trail began right from the parking lot with a little brown sign posted, "Iceberg Lake." There was a junction of a few different trails, so I was studying my map to make sure I was going in the right direction. The beginning of this trail ribboned through the motor lodge cabin area, then it began to ascend on what I wouldn't call stairs exactly but rather little platforms, I suppose. These embankments held up by logs, created a milder means of ascension for the guest. After a while, the ground leveled off, the trees gave way, and I felt as if I was high up, as if a grand view should be to my left side, but the view, in this case, was of clouds. There was no telling what was there behind the veil of white.

Much of the hike was cloudy, but nevertheless beautiful, for that which was right before me itself was so notable: wild flowers sprinkled among shards of rocks, and wet pines adorning these misty meadows. The fact that it was cloudy and cold added to this novel feeling of being somewhere so far north, so much so in fact, that I was going to see icebergs!

A few miles in I came to Ptarmigan Falls. All that was really visible was a small underwhelming cascade, a white ribbon which flowed into a crystal clear pool from where a creek traveled and a small wooden bridge crossed over. A lot of people were congregating, taking breaks and photos, and perhaps deciding if they would continue on to the lake.

Onward I went back into the forest, hiking between these wet resilient northern pines on a forest floor of damp pine needles. If not being held snug in the storybook forest, I was a hearty mountaineer on the exposed mountainside, trampling on rocks among large white blooms of beargrass.

Eventually the clouds lifted higher into the mountains, revealing enormous valleys and meadows. Most of the hike had been a gradual ascension, but after about five miles, the path began to descend a bit, the valley did not continue, I was coming to a basin– to Iceberg Lake! A path led perfectly straight up to the lake. Pine trees stood along the path like guards of a great castle. I approached feeling either as royalty or a peasant that doesn't belong here. I couldn't quite

figure out which, but I had arrived!

Wow! I marveled at the mighty fortress of a rock wall surrounding the lake, diminishing all the tall standing pines to just mere little toys. It was so bold and so tall that it was quite humbling. *Who am I that I should be here?* Even some clouds hadn't risen high enough to escape this basin, adding even more glorious mystic and grandeur to its display. Along the dark rock wall were rivulets and ledges of snow leading down into the lake. The lake was perfectly clear, and I could see all the flat tiles of rock layered on top one another, on the lake bed, so perfectly defined. In the lake's further reaches, up against the rock wall and against the icebergs, the water gave off a chilling, bright, almost neon turquoise color.

I stood there marveling at the basin wall, and observing the icebergs. There were only a few, but they were a

sight to behold. There was one large and very prominent one, not far off at all in the lake. Its bright white peak reached up a few feet to the sunbeams just perfectly illuminating it, setting ice ablaze, sweating in burning white. The other half dipped chillingly down into the cold turquoise water, subtle and frozen. I had never beheld a vista like this before. I was completely captivated. I wished to capture it the best I could in photos.

I would be rewarded on this hike, not just with the sights along the way, and the beautiful view of the lake with its floating icebergs and basin wall, but the encounter on the way back.

Here's how it went down: The sun had lifted the clouds higher, and the vistas were gradually becoming larger and more colorful. There was sky blue, forest green, wildflower purple and yellow. The sunlight was starting to illuminate everything. The trail was also getting more congested with people. I kept passing people, trying to get ahead and to some peace and quiet. I also wanted to save daylight, so I thought I'd do some trail running. I had passed everyone up to a point in the trail, where it was just me, the forest, the path, and…

A grizzly bear!

I ran around a bend on the forest path and it was right there, a mere ten feet or so from me– a great big brown bear. I knew it was a grizzly by its wide face, hunched back, and enormous size. I didn't have bear spray because I thought it was a gimmick. I did know I didn't want to startle a grizzly bear, although I nearly ran into the thing. Despite my entry to the scene, it seemed unphased. Its head hung low as it was munching on some underbrush on the side of the trail.

"Hey bear," I said calmly. I repeated it a few times "Hey bear. Hey bear." It did not acknowledge me at all. It ignored my presence. Surely it has to know I'm here. *It just doesn't care?* I began to clap lightly.

Behind me approached another hiker. I calmly informed him of the situation. I stated the obvious: "There's a bear," and I followed it immediately with, "do you have bear spray?"

"Yes." He unzipped his backpack and nervously pulled it out. I was very relieved. He held the bear spray pointed forward. I got behind him. Then a few more people approached with muffled gasps and whispered exclamations.

The bear, still seemingly unphased, began to approach us on the trail, but not aggressively so, just munching on the side brush. She was going to walk right into us, if we didn't all step off the trail into the woods to get out of its way. As we stepped off the trail into the woods, the bear decided to follow us, not once lifting its head to acknowledge us. We slowly walked backward, deeper into the woods, as the bear kept moving in our direction. This is when one of the ladies suggested, "Let's all get together and look like one giant creature. Maybe we can scare it off." Bunched together, all nine of us now, we raised our hands and made strange animals-like hoots and hollers, trying to defer this beast from our direction.

"Look over there!" I pointed and exclaimed. Trampling up behind momma grizzly were her two cubs. They were adorable, but this was far from ideal. You never want to be found amidst a bear and her cubs. With a huff, momma bear moved her head to the left and trailed around us. It was good that momma bear wasn't approaching us any longer, but it was not good that we were all standing between momma bear and her cubs. *What are we going to do?*

We all paused our crazy-looking antics and just observed, perhaps privately each one of us assessing the situation. *This is not something that happens everyday.* I reached for my camera. At least I could provide some photo evidence of our demise. As momma bear kept slowly munching her way deeper into the forest, the two little cubs got on the trail and ran off ahead in the direction we all needed to go. They rounded a bend, and we couldn't see them anymore.

"Hopefully they go off into the woods and still aren't on the path ahead," I told someone.

We all got back on the trail, and cautiously proceeded. Gradually, as time passed, we became more and more comfortable, and we all had something to talk about. Suddenly these nine strangers on the trail had this incredibly unique shared experience. We became a hiking pack together, best of friends for the remainder of the hike. An observer would have thought we had all known each other before. "Can you believe that?" "What did you think?" "Have you ever been in a situation like that?" "I wonder where the cubs went." We were all talking lively and high off having the experience. We came from a moment of great tension and fear, down to relief and the dawning of what an incredible experience it was. We were quick to inform everyone we encountered on the trail of what we experienced.

As we approached the trail head by the Swiftcurrent Motor Lodge, we saw a park ranger. One man from our group began to inform the ranger, and we all chimed in, as though hoping to impress with our story. What an experience!

After dropping off my backpack in my car, I walked over to the restaurant at the Swiftcurrent Motor Lodge. It was the perfect chill ambience after the eventful hike. I sat up at the bar and enjoyed a bison burger with huckleberry jam, as I looked over my photos on my camera. If only I would have taken one of that grizzly. I had attempted, but I got distracted by the approaching cubs. Taking photos was not the priority in the moment.

My second full day in Glacier National Park was coming to a close. Seeing a grizzly bear up close, as well as icebergs, was so rewarding. Leaving the Many Glacier area of the park, I'd go check into the St. Mary/East Glacier KOA and enjoy a relaxing moonlight soak in the hot tub before going to sleep. Tomorrow I'd explore the Two Medicine section of the park.

# In Hot Water

As my feet entered the steaming water and I plunged downward, the water reaching up to my neck, my sore legs and muscles gave the most wonderful sighs of comfort and relief. The water was bubbling all around me, as if alive, and the temperature was the greatest welcoming contrast to the cold nighttime glacial air. After a long day of hiking, this was perfect.

I was camping at the St. Mary/East Glacier KOA, just outside Glacier National Park. The campground was beautiful. It was a wide open space, within a valley of sorts, with glorious views unobstructed. To one side was a panorama of the Rocky Mountains within Glacier National Park and the start of the St. Mary Lake valley, with layers of giant mountains standing next to each other. Most prominent was Flattop Mountain, right there crescendoing up into the air like a giant wave. Pine trees spread across its side down to the edges of the campground in a glorious display of divine artistry. On the other side, just beyond the back of the campground, was a giant bluff that plateaued at the start of the Great Plains.

After today's grizzly bear encounter, there was something comforting to no longer be immersed in the thick of it, amidst the mountains in the park, but rather out here in this open area, with space to breathe and take in the majestic beauty of the mountains at a distance. It was also such a novelty to be in between two worlds, to see where the Rocky Mountains and the Great Plains meet. Nothing, however, was more perfect than this hot tub. From here I could take it all in.

This was probably the best KOA I've stayed in. It has all the offerings of KOAs, with the various types of sites: tent, RV, and cabin. To add to modern comforts, this KOA also had a pool, food options, and a general store with ice cream and coffee. The staff were so welcoming, but what made it truly the best were the mountain views and this glorious twenty person hot tub. However, taking those two things and putting them together... even better!

I rested my back against the concrete side of the hot tub, facing the mountains. The moon illuminated and cast shadows upon the mountains, stars dotted the sky, and subtle underwater lights on the sides of the hot tub made the water glow a turquoise blue. Whatever aches I had from being on my feet, hiking all day, were soothed in these waters.

There were quite a few people here in the hot tub, maybe a dozen, yet it wasn't crowded. Everyone seemed to be in good spirits talking to one another. Overhearing quite a bit, I noticed everyone was talking about their day's adventures and experiences in the National Park. There was a definite culture within this hot tub. It was a gathering place for the adventurer– a place to share stories and debrief from a day in the park. I loved it. It is so pleasing to me to see strangers, and people from distant lands, all connecting together over something wholesome. There were people of all ages and surely of different backgrounds here, but there was a commonality. We all loved the mountains. We loved to be immersed in them. We saw their beauty. For as different as we may have been, beauty is not subjective. The beauty of our Creator is objective and universal. Everyone can recognize it.

An older man, sitting next to me, began to engage with me in conversation. He was on vacation from Washington state. I told him I was from Kentucky. He had been on a big road trip with his wife. They had traveled so far as Alaska. "Alaska is amazing. But I'll tell you something, the views you get here in Glacier are very much like Alaska. If you've seen Glacier, you've seen Alaska." I'm not sure if that statement holds true, but it's what he said and something that stuck with me. He went on to praise the beauty of Glacier National Park and Montana. I agreed with him.

"So what do you do for a living in Kentucky?" he asked.

"I am a teacher. I teach Spanish in elementary school," I replied.

"Oh, I was in education too. I am a retired superintendent." At the time, it was a little intimidating for me to know I was sitting next to someone of such status. I view things differently now, but then I was a young enough teacher that I felt my job hung on the superintendent. After all, I was hired by a superintendent, and the term superintendent meant someone with great authority over me. However, hearing him speak in such a down-to-earth manner, the superiority complex I had in my mind deteriorated. In this hot tub everyone was equal. We were all travelers. We were all adventures. What we did for a living, our labels, didn't matter. What mattered here were the mountains, the beauty of the setting, the spirit of adventure. I listened to him talk about his drive along the Going-To-The-Sun Road. I acknowledged that the road alone is an adventure, but I was thinking the thrill of that road had been so diminished by my experience today with the grizzly bear encounter. For some reason I didn't bring it up. I'm not sure why. I suppose part of me found it to be unbelievable, and I didn't want to put forth the effort in trying to convince anyone. I just wanted to rest and take it easy. Also, it was such a unique, terrifying, yet amazing experience, that it was almost too special to bring up yet, especially since it was so recent. First I needed to fully process it and revel in it solo before sharing it with others.

I just enjoyed listening to him. I love engaging in conversation with strangers and new people when I travel. It's easier on vacation. Back in the rush of ordinary life, people are too focused in their tunnel vision and too busy to engage. Plus there is an uncertainty of where to begin. What common ground is there to begin a conversation? Where is the open door? Is there even an open door, or must one force it open? It feels like breaking and entering. Among travelers, however, there is such an accessible door, a clear pathway to conversation: "Where are you visiting from?" "What have you seen in the park today?" From there, conversation can abound, and people are more relaxed, carefree, and ready to engage. I've met so many great people on my travels, some I still keep up with.

When this man bid me goodnight, I stayed a bit longer. I moved to the other side of the hot tub and faced the Great Plains. From this side, I could recline a bit and rest my feet on this giant boulder that stood in the middle of the hot tub. The coarseness of the rock massaged my feet which had been trapped in hiking boots all day. The natural element of the rock in the pool helped give the whole setting an earthy feel and less sterile of an environment. People were starting to leave, but among the few who remained was a family. The little brother and sister were tossing some pool rings around and fetching them, but doing so in a quiet and respectful way. They tossed one at me. I caught it with my foot. There were some laughs exchanged. This soon became a tub-wide activity. Eventually the mother called it a night. "Alright kids. It's time for bed. Let's dry off." I decided my day was about over too. I dried off and walked back to my campsite, where I bundled up for the cold northern night in sweatpants and sweatshirts. I lay in my tent upon my air mattress and under layers of sleeping bags. My body was at ease and refreshed from the long warm soak. Breathing the cold mountain air heavier and heavier, soon I fell asleep.

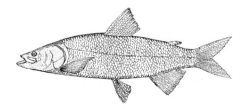

# BAREFOOT AT TWO MEDICINE

*I'm leaving my shoes behind,* I decided. I was at the Two Medicine area on the east side of Glacier National Park, bright and early after my morning run at the KOA. The place was already bustling this morning. I was lucky to secure a parking spot. My plan was to hike alongside Upper Two Medicine Lake to Twin Falls. I had studied this on the map, but arriving here, something caught my eye. An employee was unroping and positioning kayaks along the lake shore, and I noticed the sign, "boat rentals," affixed to a little rental shack. I wasted no time. *I may be here just early enough,* I thought.

There was a nice sleek orange kayak, all mine for the next four hours. I went back to the car to gear up. I fetched snacks, a water bottle, my map, and my waterproof camera. Then I considered footwear. *They are going to get wet, so what's best suited for this?* Then I realized, *nothing. I'll spend the day bare-*

*foot. Once I get to the other side of the lake, I can hike the mile to the*
*falls barefoot. It'll be fun and add to the experience.*

I stood there before Two Medicine Lake. It was
beautiful and very reminiscent of Swiftcurrent Lake I had
seen the day before. This seemed like another interpretation
of the same artistic idea or concept. God didn't leave us with
just one. He gifted us both versions. This lake had a giant
prominent triangular peak at its far end, as well, called
Sinpah Mountain, but it wasn't as close as Grinnell Point in
Many Glacier. A bit further in the distance were other very
sharp triangular peaks, and this lake was narrower and longer, with a peninsula called Paradise Point, jutting out in its
middle and pine trees just seeming to drape across mountains right up to the lake waters.

I sat down in the kayak and scooted my vessel into
the water. It was a cloudless blue-sky day, and so one might

expect the water to reflect that, but in the shallow stretches just before me the water was actually red, for in its bed lay red rock, and the water was so clear and pure, I could see right through to the rock below. Further out, as the water deepened and met distant shorelines of pine trees, the water was a deep dark blue.

The air was a little brisk, as all Montana summer mornings start off, but the sun was very powerful, warming my skin. The two contrasts at once upon the body was refreshing. There was a bit of breeze too, causing a number of little waves to lap against the front of the kayak and occasionally splash up into my face. *Oh what a beautiful lake!* Drawing nearer to majestic peaks, and being surrounded on all sides by pine trees, was so perfect to me. I paused, breathing in the rich cool mountain air, closing my eyes while facing the sun and feeling it's warm rays on my face.

This was blissful.

Returning to paddle, I did notice the wind was not in my favor, making it a little strenuous, but I was embracing it as a workout. After a little more than halfway down the lake, I decided to pull off to the shoreline in a little cove. I found a beach of rocks to pull in the kayak. After securing my boat on my little private rock beach, I found a large flat rock embedded in the ground which I could lay down on. It was nice to have this private little cove with no one else around. Everywhere in front of me were mountainous views and lapping water. I set my backpack down as a pillow and lay there on the shore, basking in the sunlight. I sat up occasionally, and, through squinted eyes, admired the crystal clear water shining atop these red rocks and enjoyed the purity of this environment.

Back in my boat, I finished the three miles to the end of the lake. There was a little dock, but I parked my vessel a little bit more inland and out of the way. I stepped out, my bare feet landing on the wet stones of the lake bed and then up onto the mud packed earth. I walked in wonder, grounded on the earth, flinching every once in a while from stepping on a sharp rock on the path. The forest here was all pine and thick with underbrush and an occasional bear grass bloom. I felt so wild being barefoot, like an animal at home in this place. No one else was around. I was on this trail at the end of the lake all by myself, barefoot, wild and free. Walking barefoot makes me walk slower, and therefore I take things in more carefully.

After about a mile, I arrived at Twin Falls. I got into the natural pools beneath them and walked up and over rocks and log jams to get close to the base of the falls. The two falls cascaded down eighty feet and were not immediately next to each other. Rocks protruded and a few trees grew in between the falls. They were distinct falls individually and distinct together, being just a stone's throw away from each other. It was all a water wonderland with the sounds of water crashing, cascading, rushing, trickling; and water swirling in clear pools beneath the falls, free falling, colliding against rocks in bright white, and sending tiny sparkling beads of water into the air to capture the sunlight. This was a place for the senses– nature's waterpark.

Crouched down, I balanced myself on a slick fallen log beneath the falls. I had an idea. I had pulled out my water-proof camera. I hit the record button and then dipped the camera into the water beneath the falls. After about thirty seconds I pulled it up out of the water and hit the play button. To my surprise I observed four cutthroat trout

swimming stationary at the bottom of the falls. I was not expecting this. Amazed, I submerged the camera again, catching a few more fish but not as clear and as impressive as the first reel.

This became my activity, climbing from one log and one rock to the next, like Tarzan or Mowgli, and then submerging my camera in the water at all sides of the waterfall and in all parts of the stream. This was my playground.

I eventually took this sport back to Two Medicine Lake. A few more people had arrived at the dock, and a man was out in the water fly fishing. The water was very shallow, for quite a great distance by this side of the lake, so I walked out and around a bit, submerging my camera. More than fish, I had many shots of the pinkish rocks and the water fading into an aquatic teal in the underwater distances. It was all very fun and something new I had never done. After it all, I was still most impressed by my first capture.

The paddle back to the other side of Two Medicine lake seemed to go by faster. Although there was still a mountain view ahead, it was less scenic facing this direction, and the wind was in my favor, propelling me onward. Back in the village it was very windy. I turned in my kayak. I had used just about my full four hours, and it cost me sixty dollars.

I then went back to my car to get my shoes. I wanted to check out the Two Medicine General Store right here by the lake. It was a rather substantial sized Swiss chalet style building, fitting in nicely with the theme. Inside were various souvenirs, supplies, and food, but most notable was a big stone fireplace. When I was at the cashier purchasing a small Glacier National Park sticker for my water bottle, the cashier informed me this was where president Franklin D. Roosevelt delivered one of his famous fireside chats. In that particular fireside chat he was addressing the value of our National Park Service. The cashier handed me a laminated copy of his speech. Standing there by the fireplace where it was delivered, I read:

*"...Today, for the first time in my life, I have seen Glacier Park. Perhaps I can best express to you my thrill and delight by saying that I wish every American, old and young, could have been with me today. The great mountains, the glaciers, the lakes and the trees make me long to stay here for all the rest of the summer.*

*Comparisons are generally objectionable and yet it is not unkind to say, from the standpoint of scenery alone, that if many, and*

*indeed most, of our American national parks were to be set down any-
where on the continent of Europe thousands of Americans would journey all the way across the ocean in order to see their beauties.*

*There is nothing so American as our national parks. The
scenery and wild life are native. The fundamental idea behind the parks
is native. It is, in brief, that the country belongs to the people, that it is
in the process of making for the enrichment of the lives of all of us. The
parks stand as the outward symbol of this great human principle.*

*…The Secretary of the Interior in 1933 announced that this
year of 1934 was to be emphasized as 'National Parks Year.' I am
glad to say that there has been a magnificent response and that the
number visiting our national parks has shown a splendid increase. But
I decided today that every year ought to be 'National Parks Year.'
That is why, with all the earnestness at my command, I express to you
the hope that each and every one of you who can possibly find the means*

*and opportunity for so doing will visit our national parks and use them as they are intended to be used. They are not for the rich alone. Camping is free, the sanitation is excellent. You will find them in every part of the Union. You will find glorious scenery of every character; you will find every climate; you will perform the double function of enjoying much and learning much.*

*We are definitely in an era of building, the best kind of building— the building of great public projects for the benefit of the public and with the definite objective of building human happiness.*

*I believe, too, that we are building a better comprehension of our national needs. People understand, as never before, the splendid public purpose that underlies the development of great power sites, the improving of navigation, the prevention of floods and of the erosion of our agricultural fields, the prevention of forest fires, the diversification of farming and the distribution of industry. We know, more and more, that the East has a stake in the West and the West has a stake in the East, that the Nation must and shall be considered as a whole and not as an aggregation of disjointed groups.*

*May we come better to know every part of our great heritage in the days to come."*

# A FEATHER IN THE CHICKEN

There was a feather in my roasted chicken. I was dumbfounded. I poked it around with my fork. *Yes,* I confirmed, *I can believe my eyes.* I was quickly losing my appetite. It wasn't just this feather in my chicken. I could perhaps forgive this, after all I was in the wilds of Montana, but there was an array of other things stealing my appetite.

I was in East Glacier, Montana, and food options here in this unincorporated community of the Blackfeet reservation were few. There was this one stand alone establishment, just down the street from the main row of businesses or had-been businesses. Many now were empty, and their authentic Western facades were weathering away. This restaurant I found, too, was in a weathered building but looked like it could hold potential to be a "mom and pops" establishment of delicious home cooking. Either that, or it could be a real dive. It proved to be the latter. When I entered, everything seemed normal. I saw some pies on display in a case. *I might even get dessert,* I thought. A waitress grabbed a laminated paper menu and guided me out to the front patio. The cement slab had a canopy and a fence around it. I sat in a white plastic flimsy lawn chair that was turning grey and chalky with age. It twisted a little bit as I sat in it. I was looking over the menu, fiddling with its frayed corners, where the plastic was peeling from the paper, until I was interrupted with, "What do you want?"

That's when I ordered the quarter roasted chicken and a side salad. It sounded delicious and healthy, but it was a mistake. I think ordering anything here would be a mistake.

The waitress came back with a cup of water. It was in what I believed to be an original 1980s Tupperware Sippy Cup, just minus the lid, but appearing as if a toddler had been teething around the rim of the cup. Hesitantly I took a sip. It tasted like Tupperware too. I set it down to notice a hound of some sort sniffing my feet. It wandered over to another table where it stopped and begged for food. My thought was, *there is no way this is up to health code.* As I sat there with my Sippy Cup, observing the dog, a few flies pesteringly buzzed around. The dog gave up begging and curled up in the middle of the patio with a begrudging sigh.

When my chicken came out, the dog perked up and came over to my table. I tried to push him away with my feet. This had to be obvious to the staff or the owners. They didn't seem to care. I guess this was a normal part of the dining experience. I took my first bite. The chicken was exceedingly moist, unsettling so. *Why is roasted chicken so wet, so greasy?* Then I noticed the feather sticking up in the chicken skin. With a full bite of chicken in my mouth, looking at the oven seared feather,  I grabbed my Sippy Cup to wash down this slimy chicken with my plastic water. The dog was barking, while one fly landed on my arm and the other on my chicken. I shooed them away. *What have I gotten myself into?*

This was quite the contrast to where I had just been. Just around the corner, in walking distance, was the Glacier Park Lodge, a massive lodge of elegant stature. It was once the signature lodge of the Great Northern Railway, and it was the first built at Glacier National Park to rival the accommodations at Yellowstone National Park.

Entering the lodge, the large central rectangular atrium had enormous log poles, standing as pillars, holding the place up. They were coastal douglas fir, harvested from Oregon with bark still intact. The Lodge rose three stories, each balcony participating in the theme with log-pole railings. On the far end of the second story stood a large Indian tee-pee, visible from the ground level. A large central part of the ceiling was glass, letting a lot of natural light inside, perfect to accent it's already natural look.

Walking curiously around this atrium, the floor was soft and carpeted in red and green. Chairs and tables were thoughtfully sprinkled about. On one far end was a dining room. I peeked in. It looked cozy and elaborate with its fireplace blazing. Here also stood a fully dressed Christmas tree. I looked it up and down. I soon noticed garland adorning the fireplace mantel in the restaurant, and a vintage Santa Claus figurine sitting upon the reception desk. A simple sign, printed on a 8.5 by 11 inch piece of white paper attached to a free standing pole, headed the words, "Christmas in July." I approached to read that Glacier National Park claims to have invented the term. Seasonal employees, working the park and lodge, wished to be able to celebrate Christmas together in each other's company, but because the park was only seasonal and open in the summer, this would never be a reality. The employees thus invented an annual tradition of celebrating Christmas in July. I found that to be a fun bit of information.

On the opposite side of the grand hall from the Christmas tree, dining room, and tipi, was another large stone fireplace and some boards and displays on the history of the lodge. These were telling the story of its construction by the Great Northern Railway in 1913 and how it was a part of the "See America First," and "Visit the American Alps," campaigns. Mark R. Daniels, superintendent of the National Park at the time, noted the amount of money Americans were spending on vacations abroad. He said that Americans "are taking this money out of the United States to spend it in foreign lands upon a commodity that is inferior to the home product." A vision was thus born to recreate a Switzerland experience here in the American wilderness.

As I continued to snoop around the place, I made my way to the second and third floors, observing the large framed paintings on the walls depicting the beautiful mountains, lakes, and glacial scenery of the park.

Leaving the lodge out front, I looked across the long pathway adorned with flowers and intricate landscaping swooping across the front lawn directly to the Amtrak station, where the Empire Builder would make its stops. How exciting that would be after a long train ride, to disembark and walk across, with a suitcase, to stay in this magnificent lodge. When I was looking at the historical displays within, I learned how back in the early days the lodge employed Native Americans in their traditional garb, head dresses and all, to welcome passengers coming off the train.

I also read up on the Red-Jammers, the elongated motor coaches with roll-back convertible canvas roofs, classy in style and appearance, which tourists would ride in tours of the park. These still existed. Some were parked out in front of the lodge, and I had seen them traversing the Going-To-The-Sun Road, but they weren't the staple that they had once been.

There was for a long while, this great era of really showcasing the park. One could step off the train, and the hosts of the various services of the park were there to really ensure a memorable stay and show you around. There is something to admire about that. Now, everything is very much self-serve. Find a way to get here. Find your way around. You're on your own. There is a great deal of freedom to enjoy from this new style, but there's a sort of classy hospitable pride that is lost, which can now only be imagined, and I do like to imagine it. It is very captivating to my thoughts, trying to put my mind there in the past...

# A Night at Glacier Park Lodge

Imagine it's the early twentieth century. You're a city dweller from New York, accustomed to the rush and flow of city life, trapped in the constant noise and often city filth neighboring high class society. You and your spouse board a train and travel a few days all across the East, reaching Chicago, the beating heart of the nation. There you step out into another grand metropolis. You transfer onto the Western Star. From your little enclosed cozy sleeper car you gaze out the window. Eventually watching the city fade into the endless expanse of the Great Plains. You see field after field, enormous prairies, the legendary home of the great buffalo. You've seen their hides in the city, on Fifth Avenue, but now you are seeing the animal alive.

A day later, you begin to wonder if the Great Plains will indeed ever end. You are filled with a sense of wonder though, traveling into the West, the great frontier land, the land of the homesteader, the legendary cowboys and Indians of dime-store novels, the Wild West of often told stories and fables. Another day later, you find yourself approaching a range of mountains, unlike anything you've seen before, absolutely enormous. The train quickly moves past the Great Plains and is enveloped into a thick pine forest. You were up upon the land on the prairie, now you seem to be in the land, hidden in this pocketed wonderland at the foot of these beastly giants capped with snow and glaciers still evident from the Ice Age.

As the train slows down, pulling into the East Glacier station, you are filled with a sense of awesome wonder. Where are you but in a world so far removed from anywhere you know, so isolated from any other city, a place only a few Americans have been privileged to see. The train stops at the station, you and your spouse anxiously grab your bags and descend. There, a group of natives with their dark sun-leathered skin, stern faces, elaborate garb of color and beads, and wild feathered headdresses, welcome you both with traditional song and dance. You're not sure how to respond. You've never seen anyone like this in the city except for in Buffalo Bill's Wild West Show. You have only heard and read about these Indians otherwise. They were the men of tales, but here they are real, reminding you that you are so far from home. They offer to grab your bags, and walk you across the lawn to the lodge. It feels so invigorating to be out in the wild, out of the city, out of the enclosed train. You have arrived!

As you walk, you notice the overwhelming silence of

the land. There's no noise of hustle and bustle, no traffic, no car horns, just the faint sound of the train chugging away. All that's left is the fresh cool mountain air, the warm sun so close you feel it on your face, and you can hear nearby birds tweeting and a rushing river out there somewhere.

There, beautifully positioned, is the mighty Glacier Park Lodge. You saw sketches of it in a magazine, but now here it is in real life. It's been a number of days since you've seen a building of any grand stature, or a building at all rather, after the long journey across the Great Plains, also known as "the Great American Desert." Here the lodge stands as a mighty fortress. Its lodge pillars out front announce you have really arrived somewhere. A door man opens the door and ushers you in. You are stunned that something so grandiose exists in a place so remote and so wild. It has the feel of a Swiss chalet combined with a mighty northern hunting lodge. It has a rustic charm yet it's new. The wood smells fresh, the carpets just installed. At the desk, a woman in a traditional dirndl dress politely checks you in, giving you the schedule for tomorrow's tour in the park via a Red Jammer on the newly opened Going-To-The-Sun Road.

You walk with a sense of wonder in the main atrium, looking up at the tall ceiling and the many levels and landings of this place. You haven't been to the Redwood Forest or seen a mighty Sequoia, so the girth of the log poles holding up this place astounds. You feel small and diminished. Already you have a new perspective of the forests of the West.

Glacier Park Lodge

You find your way to your room. Although it's very nice and luxurious, especially after days and nights on a train, its design, of exposed wood logs and freshly hewn furnishing adorned with Western finishings, makes you feel already an outdoorsman, and you feel yourself falling in love with the American West. Setting your bags down, you go to the far end of your room to open the doors and step foot out on the balcony. Immediately you encounter the thick rich, moist, pine forests of Glacier National Park. You're high enough up that you can see this endless forest crawl up the mountainside. It evokes mystique. You know great beasts live in these woods, and much of it hasn't even been explored. It is a mystical, daunting frontier.

You hear, overhead, the screech of an eagle and look up to see the stark white head on this swooping king of the sky– the nation's symbol, the bald eagle! A great sentiment of patriotism sweeps over you. You never imagined your own country was this expansive, this rich in beauty, and this diverse in land.

Again you look into those deep sprawling woods, and you note the silence. It is almost foreboding. You aren't used to this. For a moment an anxiety sharply sweeps over you. You are so far from home and from the city. These woods are so daunting and mysterious, and there is no city for hundreds of miles. There is no connection with the outside world. You feel a great loneliness and vulnerability set in, here in the wild, but then you turn around back to your lodge room. The warm glow of electricity illuminates the room. It's uncommon to find such a luxury outside of the

The Colors of My Sunset

city. The big lodge is your fortress, a hideaway, a safe oasis in this wild rugged forested wilderness. You close and latch the balcony doors. Through the glass, the pines stand dark blue in the evening light, contrasted with the warmth of the glow inside.

It feels so good to stretch out on a large comfortable bed, upon a Native American woven blanket of exotic and colorful designs. It's such a comfort after nights cramped in a train's sleeper car. You are here with your lover, your spouse. Shortly after you change to get ready for dinner, arm in arm you walk down to the lobby. This time you notice the great animal skins hanging from the balconies of grizzly bears, wolves, and giant cats, so big they strike a bit of fear in you, considering they roam the forests surrounding this place. Then it excites you. As a hunter, what incredible sport it could be to hunt such creatures!

As you walk across the lobby, you notice the lanterns hung above on circular rustic chandeliers, reminiscent of a castle, and you hear the relaxing tunes of a pianist on a grand piano. The melodies seem to blend in and get lost amidst the ambience of the place. You feel as if you are in an American castle. It rivals those of Europe and here you are the royalty!

There at the end of the grand hall is the restaurant, "The Northern." Next to it is a taxidermied mountain goat positioned just in the same way as the iconic logo of the rail line. It is that logo of the Great Northern Railroad in physical form.

Inside the restaurant, the ceiling is lower, the lodge

poles shorter, inviting you into a more intimate environment. You are escorted to a candlelit table, not far from the crackling stone fireplace. The table is set, napkins folded, silverware shining, crystal stemware sparking fixed upside down. Such luxury in the wild is nearly unfathomable. It's a great accomplishment of the railroad, seeing what it can bring to such a remote place.

You are served an appetizer of red wine poutine: roasted potatoes, cheese curds, red wine gravy and herb garnishes. It's a dish from nearby Canada, which seems but a stone's throw away. The main dish is wild caught Pacific salmon upon wild rice, with roasted vegetables and a side of huckleberry puree.

You set the menu down, after you place your order, and smile over at your spouse looking so elegant for the evening. The fireplace is glowing upon the face, the flicking light of the candles dancing upon the tablecloth. You are swept over with so much gratitude, it gives you goose bumps. You were engrossed in the menu, but the reality set in again of where you are, so far away. "We made it. We are in Montana! The wild America!" You know none of your friends have had this experience. Few people have. Along with just the other tourists here, you are collectively exploring new lands, on the precipice of something new for the entire nation. You will write home about this. Others will be eager to know the wonders of such a myth-filled place.

After the lovely dinner, you walk back on the wooden terrace behind the lodge. It's dark, very dark— a dark you have never experienced before. Billions of stars create an infinite depth above you, and the milky way splashes across the sky so illustrious. Everything is still and quiet. The moon casts light upon the snowy peaks in the distance. You revel in the beauty but are still the slightest bit spooked by its mystique, considering the darkness within the woods and the beasts that lurk within the chilling cold that creeps beneath forest branches. Then, from the silence, pierces the haunting howl of a distant wolf. It sends chills up your spine. This certainly isn't New York anymore.

You turn back inside to the warm fire, the glowing lanterns, the gentle piano music, the clatter of the bus boy collecting dishes. You walk on the soft carpet past the giant log pillars, reminding you of the fortress in which you reside, here pocketed in the beautiful American wilderness.

Note: In this past chapter I wanted to be true to my imagination at the time, but I also want to be true to historical fact. What we view as American Western style today is not the same as it was in the early twentieth century. Oriental influence, due in part to the large flux of immigrant miners, was great upon the interior design styles of the American West. Thus, Glacier Park Lodge reflected this with many hanging Chinese lanterns and clean cut designs. It was also quite a busy place. There were but few furniture pieces in the lobby. It's look and feel was more like that of a bustling train station. The Blackfeet Indians did not escort travelers from the train station to the Lodge, but rather stayed by the railway performing traditional Blackfeet ceremonial dances. Lastly, the cuisine in the Lodge dining room was presented in buffet style and often consisted of Western staples such a pork roast and cowboy beans.

# The Story of God in My Life

It was my last day in Montana. It had been an easy-going morning. I was supposed to travel about six hours to Farragut State Park, Idaho, in between Glacier and Seattle, but I was in no rush to leave Montana. It was too beautiful. I wanted to stay, and I would end up staying an extra day.

Here at the KOA, I ate breakfast provided from a shed converted into a kitchen. From the picnic table I enjoyed some potatoes, eggs, and sausage. After packing up camp, I drove into downtown Kalispell. I had not yet taken the time to figure out how to pronounce it, but I knew I drove here on my way to Glacier National Park days earlier. I recognized the old courthouse with its elaborate design and its steeple reaching above the trees. There isn't a roundabout, but the road does curve in two directions around the courthouse.

Downtown Kalispell has a typical Western main street with small stores, gift shops, cafes, and various other services. Main streets are very much still alive in Montana. It was very quiet this Monday morning, not much of anyone about and few cars on the road. I stopped at a coffee shop and bought a cup of tea. The tea was called "Montana Gold." What stood out to me in the description was cinnamon and orange, but I failed to notice rooibos, not my favorite, but I'd drink it on this cool Montana morning.

Back in my car, with my hot tea in hand, on my GPS I tapped the button on the touch screen that read, "parks/recreation," and I found a state park only about five miles away. I left town, crossed over the highway, and Lone Pine Road slithered its way up to the top of a forested hill. At the entrance to Lone Pine State Park was a sign and collection box. I had to pay $8 to enter the park. I filled out the collection envelope and detached my little permit to display in the car window. As I dropped my money into the collection box, I verbalized, "I guess I'll put a little bit of treasure back into the state," humoring myself with the connection to Montana's state motto as, "The Treasure State."

By observing the maps, I learned there were a lot of small trails, but nothing would seem too scenic after what I had just seen in Glacier. I did find interest in the one prominent overlook that gave an unobstructed view of the Flathead Valley. It was just a short walk from the parking lot. There I could look down and across the valley and see the town of Kalispell, even the downtown where I had just been. I could also see the towering Rocky Mountains of

Glacier National Park across the valley. Here was such an unobstructed view of a grand spread of mountains and a complete view of the valley. The valley was so flat, then boom, the mountains arose. The perspective of them, contrasted with the roads and buildings of the small city, was astounding. This main overlook had its own stone and cement platform with a barrier wall, but off to the side, I saw a small path going just slightly lower to a more natural overlook atop a rock face. I carefully walked down.

I thought I was alone but was soon surprised to find out I wasn't. There was another young man sitting down there. I kept to myself and stood on the other side of the rock face. For a few minutes I just stood there, figuring out where I had driven down in the valley today and the day I arrived at Glacier. I also observed the beauty and immensity of the whole view. Then I heard, "It's pretty amazing, isn't it?" The young man spoke.

"It is," I confirmed

"It's God's beauty."

I agreed.

"Do you believe in God?" he asked. I looked over at him to get a better assessment of whom I was dealing with. He looked to be about my age. He was a redhead with a funny looking face. Funny in that part of it seemed welcoming, but in the eyes and brow it was somewhat villainous in appearance.

"Yes, I do."

"My name is Luke," he introduced himself.

"I'm Josh."

"Where are you from, Josh?"

"I'm from Kentucky," I replied," but I've been traveling for a month all over, going from National Park to National Park. I started in Death Valley and drove all the way up California, into Oregon and Washington, and I've been in Glacier the past few days."

"Right on."

"Where are you from?" I asked. He told me he was from here in Kalispell. We continued with basic pleasantries and questions of introduction…

"I'd love to hear your story," he asked, in regard to my faith.

*Oh boy,* I thought, *I don't know if I'm ready for this.* I love my story of faith, and I do like to share it, but I knew telling it could take a long time, and I had no time to prepare. My mind had been in a state of rest. Now I needed to really engage it, to remember, to synthesize, to try and do my story justice in this telling. My story is something so sacred to me, that there is a reverence I have about it, that makes me approach my own story with a sacred fear. *How many details should I share? I want to avoid pity for myself and any means to glorify me. I need to keep it focused on what God has done.* I felt like I hadn't fine-tuned my story to really make the main points poignant. It deserved time and space, but I realize there can always be excuses, so whenever the opportunity presents itself to share my story, I must seize it. I should not worry about my delivery and what I will say and what I won't say. I just need to trust God's Spirit. It is Him who wills and acts in me according to His good purpose,

(Philippians 2:13). What I need to do is simply be obedient when the opportunity arises. Soon I was very excited to share my story.

"You have time?" I asked Luke. "It's going to take a while."

I sat down and began…

I explained it in pretty full detail. I explained how I grew up in a family of loving parents, and how my father was a pastor. I shared how I had a good upbringing as a child. Then, in high school, I had acquaintances in my life and the mere mirage of friendships, but I was very alone. At school I did not connect with anyone on a deeper level. At the church youth group, many of my peers were purely nasty to me. The local church was a major contributing factor to everything in my life at the time, and there was so much division and so much sickness in this church. It was the church my father pastored, but its troubles were not his fault. It had a long broken history and chronic sickness. Through a series of events, I became very depressed, and to top it off I had become sick with chronic juvenile pancreatitis. Many nights I cried myself to sleep between feeling loneliness, physical pain, and despair. Nobody knew this. I kept it all inside. It came to the point that I didn't want to live. One night I cried out to God, "Why did you make me if I'm just going to suffer?" I was angry at God. Despite me and my behavior, looking back, I believe God blanketed me with peace that dark and lonely night.

I carried on and it eventually came time to graduate high school. I left Massachusetts to go to school in Kentucky amidst one of the largest episodes of drama in the church. With my dad being pastor it was inevitable that church life would be unavoidably integrated and profoundly impactful on our family life. What happened? I was an inquisitive and keen observer in my youth, and I had some suspicions that held true. I caught the youth pastor embezzling money, something he had been doing for a long time with the help and assistance of other church members. Another youth leader was glorifying sexually promiscuous behavior online and flippancy towards God's word. I felt I needed to bring these areas of darkness and expose them to light. In doing so, I felt I nearly put the nail in the coffin of the church. The fighting, backstabbing and polarization within the church reached new levels.

When I left to go to school in Kentucky, these culminating events at the church would propel me into a faith crisis. I moved into Asbury College, far from home. Here immersed in a Christian culture, contemplating my faith and the church was inevitable. I was struggling. *If the people at my church were "Christ followers" and "the people of God," is God even real?* I considered this because their behavior was antithetical to the teachings of Christ and no different than the rest of the world. From what I had experienced, their behavior was perhaps even worse. These people were mean towards one another, lying, stealing, and giving into the lusts of this world. Not everyone at the church was this way, but it was perhaps the most influential ones to me, whom I had been most focused on, who behaved this way.

During my first week of college, one night I needed

some alone time. I had thoughts and things to sort out. I walked to the soccer fields. I lay down in the middle of one field and gazed up at the stars. My faith was deeply scarred. So looking up at the stars I said, "God, if you are real, I need a sign, because I feel as though I don't have faith anymore." I figured the all-powerful God of the universe, if that's who He was, could prove himself to me in this moment. But I found myself walking back to my dorm thinking, *well, if God can't even prove himself to me, why should I believe?*

I used to be a staunch rule follower, and I wanted to do things the way they are to be done, and so I wanted to be the best Asbury College student I could be. Many chapel speakers and professors kept driving in their point that we all should have a life of "devotion," meaning we needed to be reading the Bible and praying daily. If that was expected of me, I wanted to do it, even if I didn't see the value in it, not sure I believed any of it anymore. However, the first evening I sat down for my devotion time, I found myself in the first chapter of James. It reads, "Consider it pure joy, my brothers, whenever you face trials of many kinds, for you know the testing of your faith develops perseverance, and perseverance must finish its work so that you may be mature and complete, not lacking anything. And if any of you lacks wisdom, he should ask God who gives it freely to all without finding fault…"

I was blown away, completely captivated, spoken to by this Scripture. I was to consider it "pure joy" to face trials of many kinds and the testing of my faith? My faith had surely been tested. The testing of it had been a stress on me for a while. The first directive was clear: be joyful. The second directive: to persevere. *Okay, I'm going to persevere in this so-called devotion time, despite my lack of faith.* Then I focused on the third directive: ask God for wisdom, and so I did just that. It was one of those prayers that started out like, "God, if you are real…" then concluded with, "…I ask you for wisdom."

Then in the upcoming days, weeks, and months, things started to shake! I was still dealing with my depression, but in moments of mental anguish I always seemed to come across the right Scripture, or someone would speak a word of encouragement into my life, or I'd read something by a true believer that inspired and spoke directly to my situation. I prayed for strength. God gave it to me. I prayed for perseverance, God gifted it. I prayed for friends, and they came, and they were so very different from the so-called "Christians" from youth group. These people would engage with me in conversation, care about what I was going through. There was a light they carried I hadn't seen before this close-up. I was starting to see there really are "people of God." Their lives were evidence. I was starting to feel incredibly blessed. Day by day my faith in God was growing stronger and stronger. Eventually phrases and words would come to mind, as if out of thin air. They would provide me strength, perspective, and propel me forward– *gifts from God perhaps?* I'd rush back to my Bible to confirm they were in accordance with the Word. *They were!* God was ministering directly to my soul! He was pursuing me!

I was still feeling hurt by my past church, I was still trying to adjust to college so far from home, and I had a lot of insecurity from past hurt that caused me anxiety in making friends. A lot was going on. So in my devotion time, I had many prayers, and many prayers were answered.

One day in our college chapel service, everyone was given an index card upon entry. The chapel speaker delivered his message and we were all instructed to write a note to God. I wrote three specific things: 1. I thanked God for all the good things he was doing in my life and for all the answered prayers; 2. I asked that God would show me how to worship Him. My only view of worship was through praise songs. There had to be more. *What was a "life of worship"?*; and 3. I felt God's presence so near to me. I prayed that I would always feel his presence close to me. I was sitting up on the balcony. I walked down to the front of the chapel where we were instructed to place our cards on the kneeling altar in front of the podium. We were told to grab a Bible verse card out of a basket. I did so. I got back up to my seat on the balcony. I read it and burst forth silently in tears. This was the ultimate sign. God responded directly to my three requests. The card read: "'I will make an everlasting covenant with you, promising not to stop doing good for you. I will put a desire in your heart to worship me, and you will never leave me. I will rejoice in doing good to you," (Jeremiah 32:40-41).

My faith had been growing over the past few months, but this was the final push– the final verification. God was real! He was with me! He was here! And he had been here all along! I also realized, in the moment, this was the sign I prayed for months ago when I was lying out in the soccer field at night. I realized, during the past few months, God was teaching me patience and perseverance. Now I was a complete mess of gratitude. I had a class I was supposed to go to after chapel, but I stayed. I skipped my class and wept and thanked God. This was momentous in my life. My faith became real and became my own.

Then it was time to get to work spiritually. God had pursued me. He caught me, and now He wanted to restore me. We had to bring my own darkness captive to the light. I thought my faith alone, my belief in God, would resolve my depression. It didn't. Some days I didn't want to deal with life, with my own thoughts, my own problems and insecurities, so I developed a habit of just sleeping them away. I was aware of this. It had to stop. It was a big step for me to seek counseling. I thought only truly crazy people did that. I was wrong. I had to set my pride aside. My counselor, I believe, was ordained by God. She was able to reach into my life and rework the wiring. I had developed some horrible snowballing thought processes that led to anxiety and depression. She taught me how to stop my thoughts in motion, hold them captive, and expose them to truth. I also had trouble opening up to others in any capacity. I was an extremely private person, because of my own insecurities. The counselor said, after hearing all my stories and learning who I was, "I believe the world is really missing out on Josh Hodge." That was profoundly impactful for me to hear.

Also, at this time, a part of God's plan for my restoration was introducing a specific friend into my life. This was the most overtly influential friend I have ever had. His name was Danny. I had seen him around campus. He was a student athlete, and I thought he was way too cool to be my friend. One morning, walking across campus, he approached me for the first time. "I know I don't know you, but I want you to know I've been praying for you… I've seen you around campus and God told me to pray for you. So, I have been," Danny said. I opened up to Danny and he did the same with me, telling me he was once a drug addict and given completely to the lusts of the world, but then he surrendered to God and his life was completely changed. He soon became my best friend.

Every night we'd meet together to pray or read the Bible. He'd leave voice messages of encouragement I needed to hear, on my phone, at just the right moments. I still hold those very special to this day. He seemed to know my heart more than myself, in an unexplainable way. He also prompted me, or told me to go on a mission trip to Mexico City through one of the student missionary organizations on campus. I went. Danny told me, "God is going to use you on that mission trip. Watch and see." I went and I shared my story of faith thus far at two churches. It was very fresh and raw to me at the time. Surprisingly it had brought some to tears, and two members of my mission team sought me out privately to say my story really spoke to them. My story of brokenness was now being used for something beautiful, for encouragement and inspiration to others. *Wow!* I marveled at it. My past hurts were not scars, not a dark spot on my life. Now these experiences were being redeemed. I was being redeemed! This was a new concept to me. Twice on that trip, journaling at night, sitting by a window in Mexico City, God spoke to me saying I was to come back to Mexico City. I was taken off guard, not expecting this. I wanted to know when. That detail I was not provided. God told me just to trust Him, and so I did.

Back at Asbury College, Danny continued to bless me richly with his friendship. The theme and Bible verse of our friendship was Proverbs 27:17, "As iron sharpens Iron, so one man sharpens another." We sharpened each other greatly. I tutored him in math and helped him academically. He encouraged and mentored me spiritually. He often reminded me of Romans 8:28, "We know that all things work together for good for those who love God and have been called according to His purpose."

One night in the midst of a terrible nightmare, Danny barged into my dorm room, woke me up, and prayed for me. Many things like this happened with Danny that I simply cannot explain apart from God's Spirit at work. How else would Danny know? It was like he was sent.

I was very sad when I learned Danny would not be returning to Asbury the next school year, but instead, would pursue seminary studies at a school in Florida. I was losing him, and for a while I was deeply saddened. Then I realized I can't be selfish. Danny had been so powerful and influential in my life that I needed to let him go and do the same he did for me for others. The next semester, we lost contact. His phone number ceased to work, His email, invalid. I tried to reach out to him in as many ways possible. Others who knew him at Asbury experienced the same results. I do not know what happened to Danny. I have some magnificent speculations, but all I truly know is that his friendship continues to be a model for me today, and his influence lasts with me. It has been woven into the fabric of my character.

Between the counselor at school and Danny, God had worked a number on restoring me. I often wondered why God didn't perform the miracles I'd read about in Scripture anymore, but I realized God had performed a miracle on me. His hands were at work through Danny and my counselor. I also came to see that He performs many miracles all around everyday. He channels His healing power and his wisdom through His people and through medicine. Who brings wisdom and knowledge to man? Who gives power for enzymes and for chemicals to react?

Despite all my progress, I came to realize I'll never be fully restored until I am with God in His Heavenly Kingdom, but here in this life, we are able to and should, bring darkness to light. I can say with confidence, by God's working in my life, and his hand through the people he placed in my life, I have fully conquered and overcome depression. Glory to God!

When I returned for my sophomore year at Asbury, I came early, for despite my rocky first year, I was chosen to become a T.A.G. leader. The acronym stands for Transition and Guidance. I was assigned a group of about twenty freshmen. Another sophomore and I would be their leaders

and guides throughout freshmen orientation and throughout their first semester. We'd check up on them regularly,
hold weekly meals together, and plan monthly events.

The night before all the freshmen arrived, I was
starting to feel anxious. I had some social anxiety, and the
thought of twenty freshmen looking at me at the same time
felt overwhelming. I didn't have the social confidence for
this. Despite all the training I went through, I didn't feel
prepared. So I went for a walk that night, to the same soccer
field I had prayed at during my first week of college. The
first time I went there I was in my faith crisis. Now, I had
faith. I was just dealing with my own insecurity. Lying there,
I talked to God. I wasn't praying necessarily as one might
think. I was just sharing my feelings. It went something like
this, "God I feel like this is all a mistake. I don't think I
should be a T.A.G. leader. I don't have the skills for this. I
feel so anxious about talking to all these students…" I went
on and on. Woe is me.

Then God spoke, and boy did He speak! It's interesting how the first time I came to this field I had no faith,
yet I sought something miraculous. Now, I had faith, and
wasn't expecting anything, but from my line of vision all the
stars in the sky disappeared except for one. There was one
single focal point, and God said directly to my soul, "Don't
be distracted by all the fears around you. Focus on me and
everything will be fine." I was amazed. I ran back to the
heart of campus to share the news. God's directive was exactly what I followed. I resolved to set my fear aside and be
courageous in what I do, and I truly focused on caring and

loving these freshmen. I did it all sincerely and as an act of worship, focusing on God. He was teaching me, as promised, how to worship Him through loving others. I would say the semester was a success. After all, three of my freshmen went on to become T.A.G. leaders the next year. I felt truly blessed.

After my mission trip to Mexico, I had felt convicted to study more Spanish, knowing God was taking me back to Mexico City at some point, but I found it hard to learn Spanish in Kentucky. I wanted to study abroad so badly, and of course I was dead set on studying in Mexico City and nowhere else. However, Asbury would not approve of a study abroad semester in Mexico City. If I wanted to study there, I'd have to drop out, apply as an international student, and reapply to Asbury as a transfer student with no guarantee I'd be accepted or they'd accept my credits from Mexico. It was a big risk. I was contemplating this risk, and I also was considering how I could follow the natural progression of leadership opportunities at Asbury and become a paid Resident Assistant, having the potential opportunity to influence a whole hall of students. *Oh what to do?*

I went for a walk to pray. *Lord, should I study in Mexico or should I stay and be an R.A.?* I wanted a clear answer. I got one, but it wasn't what I was expecting. God said, "I have given you the wisdom to make this decision. Make the decision and it will be the right one." I was incredibly humbled. I couldn't have come up with this answer. I had incredible peace. Okay, I'm going to Mexico…and so I did. I got accepted into La Universidad Iberoamericana as an international student.

I could write a whole book about that experience. I shared my faith a number of times in Mexico City, and went through a time of great spiritual and personal growth. I was also able to witness to a family with a son going through grave sickness. He was expected to die in a week. That's what the doctors said. In the hospital, I prayed for the young man. He was unresponsive and on life support. A week later he was completely healed. The mother wanted to credit me, saying I was sent by God to heal her son, but I could not take any of the credit. It was all God's power at work. Because of the miraculous healing of her son, and realizing it was God who healed him, the mother of the family developed a renewed faith and started a Bible study in her home. It's quite amazing how God works!

I wanted to stay in Mexico. It didn't work out. I came down with severe ulcerative colitis. I truly did have a dream of living in Mexico City. It was everything I was working for, but when I realized I could only get therapy for ulcerative colitis in the United States, my dream came crashing to the floor. It was hard being sick and dealing with a shattered dream at the same time, but I had to eventually surrender my plans, for God had other plans for me. I just couldn't see them at the time.

Through my sickness God also witnessed to me immensely, speaking to me a number of times, promising to restore me and make me strong, and doing just that. The day I passed out in the shower because I was so ill, when I woke up and went back to my dorm room, I laid my head upon my desk and said, "I just can't do this anymore."

God responded to me in the moment, "Thank you for being faithful," he said. "I will now heal you." A week later I was on the path towards remission.

I spent my first year out of college teaching in inner-city Houston, Texas. The big takeaway from that experience was the influence of the church I was a part of there. It was extraordinarily healthy. I needed to experience this after my rocky church experience as a teenager. I was a part of a study group and we went over the basics of our faith, but in an in-depth way. We studied topics of forgiveness, mercy, grace, glory…These were all words I'd heard, but came to understand at a much deeper and more meaningful level. There too, in that group, I shared my faith story. I was so excited about it!

Through all the sharing of my story, this and every time, I notice in retrospect, I never had addressed repentance. That is to say, talking about asking God for forgiveness of sins through Christ Jesus. This is essential for salvation and a relationship with God. Without repentance, the relationship is damaged. There is separation from God. Jesus' sacrifice makes it possible for the forgiveness of sins. He paid the price. If we repent and accept this forgiveness, it leads to the repairing of the relationship. It makes us right with God. Recently I've been pondering this as it pertains to my story. I've asked for forgiveness of sins countless times. It's a continual thing. Growing up in a Christian family, I always had a solid understanding of sin and my need for forgiveness.

When I share my story of faith, I have made it sound as if I first came to know God that day in chapel at Asbury. However, recently I've come to realize I did have a real and alive relationship with God as a child. I confessed my sin and prayed for forgiveness sometime as a small child, and it was real. I knew God to be real and He provided me immense comfort as a child. I had this burning desire, especially as an adolescent and young teenager, to study God's word and know Him better, and I can recall a number of times the Spirit at work in me, speaking to me and prompting me. But during all this time, I had the faith of a child. Some might call it ignorance. I don't think so. Rather, I say, pure faith. But then the world came in and corrupted it with all its confusion and all its doubt. My faith was tested, and it was tested severely. It went through the refiner's fire for sure. I had to transition from my childhood faith to a mature faith. By mature faith, I mean a faith put up to the test of the world. During the end of high school in my broken church, and in the early days of college, my faith faced that test of the world, and God carried me through.

Now when I think back to when I was a child, I am so incredibly humbled and so full of praise and gratitude that God was pursuing me back then. How incredible that even with all the powerful figures of the world, the Lord and master of the universe, pursued a mere helpless child for His Kingdom. I am so blessed, and I am so nothing, yet He pursued me and continues to pursue me. Some think it's crazy to believe in God, but after all I've experienced from my childhood to now, it would be simply crazy for me not to believe in God.

I finished my story by telling Luke I was sick again, and I didn't know what this meant. "I don't know what God is teaching me, but it's heavy and it weighs on me. Looking back I've seen God has carried me through a lot, and I believe he will carry me through again. I also need to remind myself of his promise to me to 'not stop doing good for me.' So all I can do is press onward in faith."

Upon finishing my story, Luke was eager to tell me his faith story too. In brief, and it was brief, according to him, he was tripping on acid and mushrooms in the woods and almost walked off a cliff, the very one we were sitting on. He then slipped into the spiritual realm and saw creatures with lots of eyes and the plants talking to him, and he felt God. That was it….The end. What can I say? Only God is the judge. I sincerely hope Luke has since found the richness of a true relationship with God, for God is not just an experience to have, but someone to know.

Dearest one,

I will make an everlasting covenant
with you, promising not to stop
doing good for you. I will put a desire
in your heart to worship me, and you
will never leave me. I will rejoice in
doing good to you.

Jesus
Jeremiah 32:40-41

I see JESUS in your
trust amidst
hardship.

[Ephesians 2:10]

485

Dear Joshua,

Thanks for all your help in life. Math wouldn't be the same without all your help. Keep growing in the LORD and serve Jesus!

YOUR GOING TO BE A GREAT TEACHER!

God Bless you!

Proverbs 3:5     -Danny

# The Last Chapter

I was nearing the end of my summer's journey, although I still had an eleven hour drive, leaving Montana and driving across the panhandle of Idaho, then traversing Washington to Seattle where I'd fly out. Despite all the wondrous things I'd seen and experienced, I was feeling in some ways a bit defeated. Today my sickness was constantly making itself known, and despite all I knew to be true, I was filled with a lot of uncertainty about the future, still mourning the loss of my health.

Because I stayed in Montana an extra day than what my original itinerary called for, I had this extra long drive ahead of me. I wouldn't have time to stop and sight-see. I just needed to make it from point A to point B. It was very sunny and hot outside for all of my drive. I had the air conditioning on full force and the tunes of Dolly Parton's 1971 gospel album, *The Golden Streets of Glory*, lifting my spirit.

I had a lot of time to think on this drive. I was about to return to normal life. *How would I navigate it so sickly? How could I return to work as a teacher? How could I work in such a state of health? How would I carry on day to day?* I considered the doctor's appointments and dealing with the insidious corruption of my health insurance company. All of my focus and energy would need to be reworked into different channels to survive and get well. I had already made a change in my diet. The past few days I had cut out refined sugars, but then in an act of rebellion I stopped somewhere in Washington for a McFlurry, something I never do, but I think I did it almost in anger, as if giving the middle finger to my illness, something I also never do.

At one point there was some rain in the distance. With the sun still glaring down, it created a rainbow, and it reminded me of something very encouraging. A few years prior, while I was at work, I received a call from my doctor's office. I was told there were some abnormalities in my blood work and I needed to come in to see the doctor as soon as possible. This concerned me. I wondered what was wrong. When I was driving from work to the doctor's office this weighed very heavily on me. I had already been through so much with my health. *Now what was wrong?* Then, while all this churned in my mind, I noticed to my left a magnificent double rainbow, and God spoke to me. "Never again," he said. "Never again will you have to endure the pain you've endured." I was incredibly comforted. Everything was going to be ok.

Shortly after, I had to give up my drug therapy for

ulcerative colitis, the last resort therapy that quite literally saved me. It was so effective for so long, but now my body was perhaps reacting adversely to it. Not only was it showing up in the blood work, but I was very ill as a result. We didn't know it at the time, but I was developing drug-induced lupus. One evening, while this was all weighing on my mind, I went for a hike on my trail in the Big South Fork. I stayed and watched the sunset over the Cumberlands from the overlook at the end of my trail, and I walked the two mile trail back to my car in the dark, singing Christmas carols to make my presence known to any bears trampling about the forest. The end of the trail traversed an old coal-mine tipple bridge over the Big South Fork of the Cumberland River. As I exited the forest at the top of that bridge, I saw the bright white moon so prominent in the sky. I already had a special connection with the moon. To me it symbolized the always present anchor, which is God in my life. Sometimes we don't see the moon, but it's always there. Tonight the moon was so visible, so bright, and around it stretched a moon bow. I was reminded, "never again." God was with me. I could face everything ahead of me with peace.

I was a heap of emotion. I should be grateful for the experiences I had this summer— for the monoliths and wonders of the Mojave Desert; for camping out in my favorite park, Death Valley; for what I learned in Bodie about arrested decay; for what I learned from nurse logs, volcanic mountains, caves, and sunsets. I should have been reflecting on all this, but instead I was focused on my survival for the unknown period of time ahead.

This was the longest drive I have ever done. Usually my maximum has been eight hours, so driving for eleven expanded my knowledge of what I am capable of doing. I rolled into the KOA just outside of Seattle still with a little bit of sunlight to spare. The campground was fenced in, and it was essentially a parking lot with little islands of grassy and dusty tent pads without trees nor privacy. I decided I wouldn't even bother setting up my tent. It would be a noisy place with everyone so close and probably beaming with lights at night, since we were in an urban environment. I'd just sleep in the back seat of the car and have less to deal with in the morning. Now I'd get packed up for the airport tomorrow, consolidating everything into my suitcase and backpack. I had packed so many layers and types of clothing, from the shorts and cuts offs for the hot scorching desert, swimsuit and flips flops for the Pacific shores, soft checkered flannel shirts to assimilate into the woodsy culture of Northern California, and hearty layers for the chilling Montana nights and mornings.

I brushed out sand from the desert and pine needles from the forest. I secured all my National Park brochure maps and pins I had collected. I packed away my bandana I got at Mount Rainier and a t-shirt I bought at Glacier with an elk and a grizzly bear on it. My suitcase wasn't much heavier than when I arrived, for I hadn't accumulated much. I also was carrying, around in the car, a bundle of firewood, a lighter, and some metal campfire sticks. I wouldn't be needing these. I noticed, at the campsite just next to me, another young man poking around his camp. I'll go offer him these things.

He gladly accepted, and we got to talking. His name was Lenard and he was from Germany. He was here in the United States, just by himself, doing a very similar thing as me. He had been coming up from Southern California and a big highlight of his trip so far was Yosemite National Park. I know it takes a special kind of person to travel solo, someone who is not afraid of being alone with their own thoughts and has a great deal of confidence in their abilities. I commended him for this and especially for doing such a trip as a foreigner. I learned he'd be heading on to where I had most previously been, to North Cascades and Glacier National Park. I gave him tips and we talked about those parks. He had that adventurous road tripping spirit as myself, and we hit it off quite well.

Soon the sun was setting somewhere behind the city, and I was growing tired. I informed Lenard that I had a flight in the morning. I bid him goodnight and went into my car to sleep. Per usual, while trying to sleep in the car, I didn't sleep the best, waking up a few times sore in certain parts, trying to readjust, but finding no remedy, as the back seat of the car was just not big enough for me. After tossing and turning a bit, I had some of the deepest sleep in the early morning, until suddenly it was interrupted and I was startled by a knocking on my car door window.

I quickly sat up. I couldn't see. I was frantically searching for my glasses. I found them and put them on, but I still couldn't see who was outside, for the window was covered with condensation, distorting everything. I was concerned that I was in trouble. *Was I not allowed to sleep in a car in this campsite? What has gone wrong?* I was expecting to see a KOA host, but when I opened the door I saw it was Lenard.

"Good morning. I just want to say goodbye before your flight, and it was nice to meet you." I suppose one might feel bothered by such an abrupt morning interruption but not me. I found it to be very thoughtful and an act of boldness. That takes some guts to wake up someone you barely know, no matter what friendly motive. I suppose I felt the gesture needed to be reciprocated. Without much thinking, only having been awake for mere seconds, I asked, "Do you want to go get some breakfast." He got in his rental car and followed me just up the road.

Today was the day, returning back to my normal life, the real world for me. That weighed on me with a bit of anxiety. I am not an anxious person, but ulcerative colitis messes with the nervous system. Though much of it is located in the brain, also a large part of the nervous system is associated with the gut. When my gut is under attack, also my nervous system is a wreck. Sitting across from me in a booth in McDonalds, I unloaded on Lenard. Holding a cup of warm coffee in hand, I told him all about my sickness and all the uncertainty I felt about the future. He was a good listener, but I'm sure this is not what he signed up for, when waking me up this morning. Maybe because he was a stranger, I felt I had nothing to lose with such a strange and personal conversation. I had also spent hours on end in the car the day prior. I needed someone to hear my thoughts. After explaining the past and the present, I addressed the future: "...so I don't know what's going to happen. I guess I just have to trust God has a plan in all this."

That morning I boarded a plane in Seattle, starting my journey back to ordinary life in Kentucky. What a summer!

The following months were hard. The sickness caused me a lot of trouble. I tested out different medicines that made me even more sick. I continued to question, "God, why are you letting this happen to me?" It's a mystery I'll never know, but perhaps it's more of putting me through the refiner's fire and an honor to be entrusted with something this heavy for His glory.

Work was very difficult and a daily struggle. Everyday leaving the school building, I was hit with enormous relief. "I survived!"

Through all the struggle, God was faithful. His promises held true. I never was in pain. Things were uncomfortable, and things were troublesome, but the pain that had accompanied this illness in the past was absent.

There were many doctor appointments, and I disagreed with my specialist doctor. There was a new medication to treat the illness, but my doctor wouldn't prescribe it. He shared no explanation for his resistance. Thus I made a seven hour journey to the Cleveland Clinic in Ohio to see a renowned specialist, determined to make ground with my health. That winter, after much navigating through the complexities of the healthcare system, eventually I was put on a new infusion therapy. It put me into remission! My health was found again.

Then with time, looking back upon all this, I realized I have a story to tell. When it was all said and done, I decided it was time to write this book. I cracked open the laptop and began to type.

As we come to a close of our adventure together, it is my sincere desire that you take something away from all this to help you in your own journey of life and faith. Maybe it's realizing who's in your life, whose book you can write into. Perhaps it's considering what's in your spiritual storeroom and what is in arrested decay. Maybe it's considering who you will be as a nurse log or what kind of mountain you are. Maybe it's considering the colors of your sunset. What will it look like? Perhaps it's simply in my story of pushing forward in times of trial, times of sickness, the times when faith is tested.

Someone recently told me, "You say 'onward' a lot. It's like *your* word." She was referring to when we were hiking. We'd stop to take in a view, have a drink of water or for a trail snack, and then I'd nudge us forward, "onward!" I'd proclaim. I wasn't aware of this habit before, but she was right. *Yes, I say onward!* We often don't know what awaits us. We never know what kind of beauty or beast we may encounter around the bend of the trail of life, but onward I say! God is with us to equip us and see us through. Onward we go with security and confidence. Whether it be in life or be in death, we press onward, boldly living for and abiding in God's eternal glory.

"...Thou art giving and forgiving,
Ever blessing, ever blest,
Wellspring of the joy of living,
Ocean depth of happy rest!...

Ever singing, march we **onward**,
Victors in the midst of strife,
Joyful music leads us Sunward
In the triumph song of life."

*"Joyful, Joyful, We Adore Thee"* - Henry van Dyke

# Afterword

9 months later…

My GPS was programmed. I was not sure my car could make it to where I was headed. This time I was in my very own car, not a rental. I traveled all across the enormous Great Plains and into the mountains. I was about an hour up a dirt road with no house in sight, just the company of a mighty rushing river, sharp rich pines, and majestic mountain peaks. I was at the outskirts of the park which, in many ways, had left me feeling defeated. I had fought so hard for my health, and it was about back. Determined to make it, I was almost there. I signed up for a summer job at Glacier National Park, at a little old historic mercantile and bakery off the grid in the wildest river valley of the lower forty-eight states.

"Turn left," the GPS sounded. *No way!* I thought. There was barely a road there. It looked to be nothing more than a little old wagon trail, overgrown in the woods. This has to be a mistake. I'll continue on this dirt road. The little rocks flung up under the car. As the road climbed, the views of the mountain valley were just astounding. The river wandering was picturesque, and the mountain peaks were so beautiful, laden with snow in their loftiest reaches. I was so far out in the valley and in the wild, and I couldn't believe this was going to be my summer home. I passed by some meadows and over a rushing creek. Then I saw a sign. I knew I was getting close. I made a right turn, and there a half-mile away, at the end of the road, peeking out from the pines, welcoming me onward, I saw a humble little red building with big white western letters affixed.

This would be the start of a new chapter, or rather a new book. This would be the next great part of my story. I felt as if I was closing a book, putting it on the shelf, and taking down a new one. The new book was empty. What an opportunity! What an adventure to be had!

# ACKNOWLEDGEMENTS

First and foremost, my deepest gratitude and appreciation go to my mother, Amy Hodge, for her countless hours of editing and revision, and for her unwavering enthusiasm for my series on the National Parks and the beautiful wild. Her inquiries about when I would finish this book were motivating for me to see it through to completion.

I would also like to extend heartfelt thanks to the following outstanding individuals: A special thank you to Cynthia Goulet, whom I had the pleasure of meeting and working with in Medora, North Dakota. Her support in promoting my books at the annual Gathering of the Teddy Roosevelts, along with her encouraging words, has affirmed all I hope my writing to be. ▲▲ Great appreciation goes to Shar Reed, my former manager in Montana, and an irreplaceable part of my cherished summer family. Her investment in my writing, on a personal and business level, helped make it possible for me to sell my books at the Polebridge Mercantile at Glacier National Park and bring my adventures to a wider audience. ▲▲ I thank Michael Hodge for all his always consistent support as my father and for his great example in the journey of life. ▲▲ I also want to acknowledge Susan Melcher, a kindred spirit who has taken a deep interest in my words and travels. Her resilience, faith, and adventurous heart continue to inspire me. ▲▲ Special credit is due to the East Multnomah Soil and Water Conservation District and the talented artist Jon Wagner for allowing me to feature his beautiful illustration of a nurse log in this book. I am honored to have his artwork as part of my story. ▲▲ Thanks to Luna Lu, Lenard, and "Zeke" for the memories shared and the unique new characters they added to this book. ▲▲ I want to thank Dolly Parton, whose efforts afforded me the opportunity to write for her theme park. It was so uplifting for me as a writer, and her HeartSong Lodge and Resort proved to be an invaluable place for me to write. ▲▲ My sincere thanks as well to Amber Davis, who believed in me and brought me onto the Dollywood Insider team, teaching me some of the art of PR and effective blogging, which in return has made me a better writer. ▲▲ I wish to acknowledge Matthew Parker. His lyrics and melodies became the soundtrack of my summer, harmonizing with my writing and propelling my thoughts into deeper philosophical reflections.

I want thank all the following Kampgrounds of America for hosting me this summer.: Longview North/Mount St Helens KOA, Concrete/ Grandy Creek KOA, Winthrop/N. Cascades National Park KOA, West Glacier KOA, St. Mary/East Glacier KOA and Seattle/Tacoma KOA. I am a big fan of KOA, and my critiques will always be sincere.

As a writer, I deeply value the public spaces that have served as my creative workshops or offices. I extend my gratitude to the following coffee shops, which provided not only great coffee but also the perfect environments for writing: The Hub Coffee House and Cafe (Danville, KY), School Grounds Coffee (Lebanon, KY), Vibe Coffee (Elizabethtown, KY), Unify Coffee Co. (Nicholasville, KY), The Burg Coffeehouse (Lawrenceburg, KY), and Stehekin Pastry Company… That cinnamon role was delicious.

Finally, and most importantly, I give thanks to God. To Him "be the glory, great things He has done." He is the source of all inspiration, healing, and the "joy of living." He places the stars in the sky, moves the waves in the ocean, and paints the colors of the sunset.

With Him, we move onward!

More adventures by Joshua Hodge :

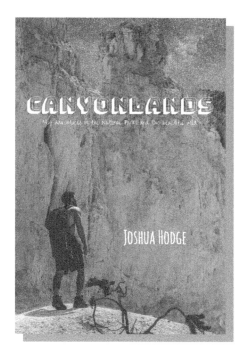

**Canyonlands: My adventures in the National Parks and the beautiful wild**

*It was the summer of the National Park Service's centennial. With just a compact car, a pop-up tent, and spirited ambition, I set out on a month long camping road trip through the American Southwest to visit as many National Parks as possible and soak up the rich beauty and wonder only found in the wild. — The journey created a story of its own with episodes of whim and sheer adventure from falling into Bryce Canyon, getting lost in the Rocky Mountains, summiting Nevada's highest peak, exploring rural ghost towns, to watching seals swim onto California's Golden Coast. — As I retell my adventure I also journal my musings from out on the trails of how the beauty of nature inspires me and causes me to look inward. I explore the concept of being unwavering and what it means to traverse my own spiritual canyons.*

**Still, Calm, and Quiet:**
**More adventures in the National Parks and beautiful wild**

On the eve of adventure and the verge of new wonders, the young man dusts off his boots and turns to the West where endless canyons sprawl and towering mountains beckon. "Come..." they say, "get lost and find yourself." Memory ignites recollection of sliding down rocks, trudging through snow, listening to aspen rattle, hearing coyotes howl in the distance, the moon looking down overhead, the campfire blazing, the pines sheltering, the river rushing, the sun beating, laying awake in the night under the star filled sky, embracing existence. It's now. The story continues... In this second installment of his National Park adventures, Joshua Hodge takes us on a descriptive journey over land, and in his thoughts, through the marvels of West Texas and New Mexico, to the wonders of Yellowstone, and over the volcanic peaks of California. This thoughtfully crafted account shares the inspiration gleaned from nature, contemplates one's approach to beauty, and explores the significance found in being still, calm, and quiet.

Made in the USA
Monee, IL
18 April 2025

15922098R00275